COLLECTED WORKS OF
MARY WOLLSTONECRAFT SHELLEY

CONTENTS

NOTES TO THE COMPLETE POETICAL WORKS OF
    PERCY BYSSHE SHELLEY 9

MATHILDA 97

PROSERPINE & MIDAS 237

NOTES TO
THE COMPLETE POETICAL WORKS OF
PERCY BYSSHE SHELLEY

PREFACE BY MRS. SHELLEY TO FIRST COLLECTED EDITION, 1839.

Obstacles have long existed to my presenting the public with a perfect edition of Shelley's Poems. These being at last happily removed, I hasten to fulfil an important duty,—that of giving the productions of a sublime genius to the world, with all the correctness possible, and of, at the same time, detailing the history of those productions, as they sprang, living and warm, from his heart and brain. I abstain from any remark on the occurrences of his private life, except inasmuch as the passions which they engendered inspired his poetry. This is not the time to relate the truth; and I should reject any colouring of the truth. No account of these events has ever been given at all approaching reality in their details, either as regards himself or others; nor shall I further allude to them than to remark that the errors of action committed by a man as noble and generous as Shelley, may, as far as he only is concerned, be fearlessly avowed by those who loved him, in the firm conviction that, were they judged impartially, his character would stand in fairer and brighter light than that of any contemporary. Whatever faults he had ought to find extenuation among his fellows, since they prove him to be human; without them, the exalted nature of his soul would have raised him into something divine.

The qualities that struck any one newly introduced to Shelley were,— First, a gentle and cordial goodness that animated his intercourse with warm affection and helpful sympathy. The other, the eagerness and ardour with which he was attached to the cause of human happiness and improvement; and the fervent eloquence with which he discussed such subjects. His conversation was marked by its happy abundance, and the beautiful language in which he clothed his poetic ideas and philosophical notions. To defecate life of its misery and its evil was the ruling passion of his soul; he dedicated to it every power of his mind, every pulsation of his heart. He looked on political freedom as the direct agent to effect the happiness of mankind; and thus any new-sprung hope of liberty inspired a joy and an exultation more intense and wild than he could have felt for any personal advantage. Those who have never experienced the workings of passion on general and unselfish subjects cannot understand this; and it must be difficult of comprehension to the younger generation rising around, since they cannot remember the scorn and hatred with which the partisans of reform were regarded some few years ago, nor the persecutions to which they were exposed. He had been from youth the victim of the state of feeling inspired by the reaction of the French Revolution; and believing firmly in the justice and excellence of his views, it cannot be wondered that a nature as sensitive, as impetuous, and as generous as his, should put its whole force into the attempt to alleviate for others the evils of those systems from which he had himself suffered. Many advantages attended his birth; he spurned them all when balanced with what he considered his duties. He was generous to imprudence, devoted to heroism.

These characteristics breathe throughout his poetry. The struggle for human weal; the resolution firm to martyrdom; the impetuous pursuit, the glad triumph in good; the determination not to despair;—such were the features that marked those of his works which he regarded with most complacency, as sustained by a lofty subject and useful aim.

In addition to these, his poems may be divided into two classes,—the purely imaginative, and those which sprang from the emotions of his heart. Among the former may be classed the "Witch of Atlas", "Adonais", and his latest composition, left imperfect, the "Triumph of Life". In the first of these particularly he gave the reins to his fancy, and luxuriated in every idea as it rose; in all there is that sense of mystery which formed an essential portion of his perception of life—a clinging to the subtler inner spirit, rather than to the outward form—a curious and metaphysical anatomy of human passion and perception.

The second class is, of course, the more popular, as appealing at once to emotions common to us all; some of these rest on the passion of love; others on grief and despondency; others on the sentiments inspired by natural objects. Shelley's conception of love was exalted, absorbing, allied to all that is purest and noblest in our nature, and warmed by earnest passion; such it appears when he gave it a voice in verse. Yet he was usually averse to expressing these feelings, except when highly idealized; and many of his more beautiful effusions he had cast aside unfinished, and they were never seen by me till after I had lost him. Others, as for instance "Rosalind and Helen" and "Lines written among the Euganean Hills", I found among his papers by chance; and with some difficulty urged him to complete them. There are others, such as the "Ode to the Skylark and The Cloud", which, in the opinion of many critics, bear a purer poetical stamp than any other of his productions. They were written as his mind prompted: listening to the carolling of the bird, aloft in the azure sky of Italy; or marking the cloud as it sped across the heavens, while he floated in his boat on the Thames.

No poet was ever warmed by a more genuine and unforced inspiration. His extreme sensibility gave the intensity of passion to his intellectual pursuits; and rendered his mind keenly alive to every perception of outward objects, as well as to his internal sensations. Such a gift is, among the sad vicissitudes of human life, the disappointments we meet, and the galling sense of our own mistakes and errors, fraught with pain; to escape from such, he delivered up his soul to poetry, and felt happy when he sheltered himself, from the influence of human sympathies, in the wildest regions of fancy. His imagination has been termed too brilliant, his thoughts too subtle. He loved to idealize reality; and this is a taste shared by few. We are willing to have our passing whims exalted into passions, for this gratifies our vanity; but few of us understand or sympathize with the endeavour to ally the love of abstract beauty, and adoration of abstract good, the to agathon kai to kalon of the Socratic philosophers, with our sympathies with our kind. In this, Shelley resembled Plato; both taking more delight in the abstract and the ideal than in the special and tangible. This did not result from imitation; for it was not till Shelley resided in Italy that he made Plato his study. He then translated his "Symposium" and his "Ion"; and the English language boasts of no more brilliant composition than Plato's Praise of Love translated by Shelley. To return to his own poetry. The luxury of imagination, which sought nothing beyond itself (as a child burdens itself with spring flowers, thinking of no use beyond the enjoyment of gathering them), often showed itself in his verses: they will be only appreciated by minds which have resemblance to his own; and the mystic subtlety of many of his thoughts will share the same fate. The metaphysical strain that characterizes much of what he has written was, indeed, the portion of his works to which, apart from those whose scope was to awaken mankind to aspirations for what he considered the true and good, he was himself particularly attached. There is much, however, that speaks to the many. When he would consent to dismiss these huntings after the obscure (which, entwined with his nature as they were, he did with difficulty), no poet ever expressed in sweeter, more heart-reaching, or more passionate verse, the gentler or more forcible emotions of the soul.

A wise friend once wrote to Shelley: 'You are still very young, and in certain essential respects you do not yet sufficiently perceive that you are so.' It is seldom that the young know what youth is, till they have got beyond its period; and time was not given him to attain this knowledge. It must be remembered that there is the stamp of such inexperience on all he wrote; he had not completed his nine-and-twentieth year when he died. The calm of middle life did not add the seal of the virtues which adorn maturity to those generated by the vehement spirit of youth. Through life also he was a martyr to ill-health, and constant pain wound up his nerves to a pitch of susceptibility that rendered his views of life different from those of a man in the enjoyment of healthy sensations. Perfectly gentle and forbearing in manner, he suffered a good deal of internal irritability, or rather excitement, and his fortitude to bear was almost always on the stretch; and thus, during a short life, he had gone through more experience of sensation than many whose existence is protracted. 'If I die to-morrow,' he said, on the eve of his unanticipated death, 'I have lived to be older than my father.' The weight of thought and feeling burdened him heavily; you read his sufferings in his attenuated frame, while you perceived the mastery he held over them in his animated countenance and brilliant eyes.

He died, and the world showed no outward sign. But his influence over mankind, though slow in growth, is fast augmenting; and, in the ameliorations that have taken place in the political state of his country, we may trace in part the operation of his arduous struggles. His spirit gathers peace in its new state from the sense that, though late, his exertions were not made in vain, and in the progress of the liberty he so fondly loved.

He died, and his place, among those who knew him intimately, has never been filled up. He walked beside them like a spirit of good to comfort and benefit—to enlighten the darkness of life with irradiations of genius, to cheer it with his sympathy and love. Any one, once attached to Shelley, must feel all other affections, however true and fond, as wasted on barren soil in comparison. It is our best consolation to know that such a pure-minded and exalted being was once among us, and now exists where we hope one day to join him;—although the intolerant, in their blindness, poured down anathemas, the Spirit of Good, who can judge the heart, never rejected him.

In the notes appended to the poems I have endeavoured to narrate the origin and history of each. The loss of nearly all letters and papers which refer to his early life renders the execution more imperfect than it would otherwise have been. I have, however, the liveliest recollection of all that was done and said during the period of my knowing him. Every impression is as clear as if stamped yesterday, and I have no apprehension of any mistake in my statements as far as they go. In other respects I am indeed incompetent: but I feel the importance of the task, and regard it as my most sacred duty. I endeavour to fulfil it in a manner he would himself approve; and hope, in this publication, to lay the first stone of a monument due to Shelley's genius, his sufferings, and his virtues:—

> Se al seguir son tarda,
> Forse avverra che 'l bel nome gentile
> Consacrero con questa stanca penna.

POSTSCRIPT IN SECOND EDITION OF 1839.

In revising this new edition, and carefully consulting Shelley's scattered and confused papers, I found a few fragments which had hitherto escaped me, and was enabled to complete a few poems hitherto left unfinished. What at one time escapes the searching eye, dimmed by its own earnestness, becomes clear at a future period. By the aid of a friend, I also present some poems complete and correct which hitherto have been defaced by various mistakes and omissions. It was suggested that the poem "To the Queen of my Heart" was falsely attributed to Shelley. I certainly find no trace of it among his papers; and, as those of his intimate friends whom I have consulted never heard of it, I omit it.

Two poems are added of some length, "Swellfoot the Tyrant" and "Peter Bell the Third". I have mentioned the circumstances under which they were written in the notes; and need only add that they are conceived in a very different spirit from Shelley's usual compositions. They are specimens of the burlesque and fanciful; but, although they adopt a familiar style and homely imagery, there shine through the radiance of the poet's imagination the earnest views and opinions of the politician and the moralist.

At my request the publisher has restored the omitted passages of "Queen Mab". I now present this edition as a complete collection of my husband's poetical works, and I do not foresee that I can hereafter add to or take away a word or line.

Putney, November 6, 1839.

PREFACE BY MRS. SHELLEY TO THE VOLUME OF POSTHUMOUS POEMS PUBLISHED IN 1824.

In nobil sangue vita umile e queta,
Ed in alto intelletto un puro core
Frutto senile in sul giovenil fibre,
E in aspetto pensoso anima lieta.—PETRARCA.

It had been my wish, on presenting the public with the Posthumous Poems of Mr. Shelley, to have accompanied them by a biographical notice; as it appeared to me that at this moment a narration of the events of my husband's life would come more gracefully from other hands than mine, I applied to Mr. Leigh Hunt. The distinguished friendship that Mr. Shelley felt for him, and the enthusiastic affection with which Mr. Leigh Hunt clings to his friend's memory, seemed to point him out as the person best calculated for such an undertaking. His absence from this country, which prevented our mutual explanation, has unfortunately rendered my scheme abortive. I do not doubt but that on some other occasion he will pay this tribute to his lost friend, and sincerely regret that the volume which I edit has not been honoured by its insertion.

The comparative solitude in which Mr. Shelley lived was the occasion that he was personally known to few; and his fearless enthusiasm in the cause which he considered the most sacred upon earth, the improvement of the moral and physical state of mankind, was the chief reason why he, like other illustrious reformers, was pursued by hatred and calumny. No man was ever more devoted than he to the endeavour of making those around him happy; no man ever possessed friends more unfeignedly attached to him. The ungrateful world did not feel his loss, and the gap it made seemed to close as quickly over his memory as the murderous sea above his living frame. Hereafter men will lament that his transcendent powers of intellect were extinguished before they had bestowed on them their choicest treasures. To his friends his loss is irremediable: the wise, the brave, the gentle, is gone for ever! He is to them as a bright vision, whose radiant track, left behind in the memory, is worth all the realities that society can afford. Before the critics contradict me, let them appeal to any one who had ever known him. To see him was to love him: and his presence, like Ithuriel's spear, was alone sufficient to disclose the falsehood of the tale which his enemies whispered in the ear of the ignorant world.

His life was spent in the contemplation of Nature, in arduous study, or in acts of kindness and affection. He was an elegant scholar and a profound metaphysician; without possessing much scientific knowledge, he was unrivalled in the justness and extent of his observations on natural objects; he knew every plant by its name, and was familiar with the history and habits of every production of the earth; he could interpret without a fault each appearance in the sky; and the varied phenomena of heaven and earth filled him with deep emotion. He made his study and reading-room of the shadowed copse, the stream, the lake, and the waterfall. Ill health and continual pain preyed upon his powers; and the solitude in which we lived, particularly on our first arrival in Italy, although congenial to his feelings, must frequently have weighed upon his spirits; those beautiful and affecting "Lines written in Dejection near Naples" were composed at such an interval; but, when in health, his spirits were buoyant and youthful to an extraordinary degree.

Such was his love for Nature that every page of his poetry is associated, in the minds of his friends, with the loveliest scenes of the countries which he inhabited. In early life he visited the most beautiful parts of this country and Ireland. Afterwards the Alps of Switzerland became his inspirers. "Prometheus Unbound" was written among the deserted and flower-grown ruins of Rome; and, when he made his home under the Pisan hills, their roofless recesses harboured him as he composed the "Witch of Atlas", "Adonais", and "Hellas". In the wild but beautiful Bay of Spezzia, the winds and waves which he loved became his playmates. His days were chiefly spent on the water; the management of his boat, its alterations and improvements, were his principal occupation. At night, when the unclouded moon shone on the calm sea, he often went alone in his little shallop to the rocky caves that bordered it, and, sitting beneath their shelter, wrote the "Triumph of Life", the last of his productions. The beauty but strangeness of this lonely place, the refined pleasure which he felt in the companionship of a few selected friends, our entire sequestration from the rest of the world, all contributed to render this period of his life one of continued enjoyment. I am convinced that the two months we passed there were the happiest which he had ever known: his health even rapidly improved, and he was never better than when I last saw him, full of spirits and joy, embark for Leghorn, that he might there welcome Leigh Hunt to Italy. I was to have accompanied him; but illness confined me to my room, and thus put the seal on my misfortune. His vessel bore out of sight with a favourable wind, and I remained awaiting his return by the breakers of that sea which was about to engulf him.

He spent a week at Pisa, employed in kind offices toward his friend, and enjoying with keen delight the renewal of their intercourse. He then embarked with Mr. Williams, the chosen and beloved sharer of his pleasures and of his fate, to return to us. We waited for them in vain; the sea by its restless moaning seemed to desire to inform us of what we would not learn:—but a veil may well be drawn over such misery. The real anguish of those moments transcended all the fictions that the most glowing imagination ever portrayed; our seclusion, the savage nature of the inhabitants of the surrounding villages, and our immediate vicinity to the troubled sea, combined to imbue with strange horror our days of uncertainty. The truth was at last known,—a truth that made our loved and lovely Italy appear a tomb, its sky a pall. Every heart echoed the deep lament, and my only consolation was in the praise and earnest love that each voice bestowed and each countenance demonstrated for him we had lost,—not, I fondly hope, for ever; his unearthly and elevated nature is a pledge of the continuation of his being, although in an altered form. Rome received his ashes; they are deposited beneath its weed-grown wall, and 'the world's sole monument' is enriched by his remains.

I must add a few words concerning the contents of this volume. "Julian and Maddalo", the "Witch of Atlas", and most of the "Translations", were written some years ago; and, with the exception of the "Cyclops", and the Scenes from the "Magico Prodigioso", may be considered as having received the author's ultimate corrections. The "Triumph of Life" was his last work, and was left in so unfinished a state that I arranged it in its present form with great difficulty. All his poems which were scattered in periodical works are collected in this volume, and I have added a reprint of "Alastor, or the Spirit of Solitude": the difficulty with which a copy can be obtained is the cause of its republication. Many of the Miscellaneous Poems, written on the spur of the occasion, and never retouched, I found among his manuscript books, and have carefully copied. I have subjoined, whenever I have been able, the date of their composition.

I do not know whether the critics will reprehend the insertion of some of the most imperfect among them; but I frankly own that I have been more actuated by the fear lest any monument of his genius should escape me than the wish of presenting nothing but what was complete to the fastidious reader. I feel secure that the lovers of Shelley's poetry (who know how, more than any poet of the present day, every line and word he wrote is instinct with peculiar beauty) will pardon and thank me: I consecrate this volume to them.

The size of this collection has prevented the insertion of any prose pieces. They will hereafter appear in a separate publication.

MARY W. SHELLEY.
London, June 1, 1824.

NOTE ON QUEEN MAB, BY MRS. SHELLEY.

Shelley was eighteen when he wrote "Queen Mab"; he never published it. When it was written, he had come to the decision that he was too young to be a 'judge of controversies'; and he was desirous of acquiring 'that sobriety of spirit which is the characteristic of true heroism.' But he never doubted the truth or utility of his opinions; and, in printing and privately distributing "Queen Mab", he believed that he should further their dissemination, without occasioning the mischief either to others or himself that might arise from publication. It is doubtful whether he would himself have admitted it into a collection of his works. His severe classical taste, refined by the constant study of the Greek poets, might have discovered defects that escape the ordinary reader; and the change his opinions underwent in many points would have prevented him from putting forth the speculations of his boyish days. But the poem is too beautiful in itself, and far too remarkable as the production of a boy of eighteen, to allow of its being passed over: besides that, having been frequently reprinted, the omission would be vain. In the former edition certain portions were left out, as shocking the general reader from the violence of their attack on religion. I myself had a painful feeling that such erasures might be looked upon as a mark of disrespect towards the author, and am glad to have the opportunity of restoring them. The notes also are reprinted entire—not because they are models of reasoning or lessons of truth, but because Shelley wrote them, and that all that a man at once so distinguished and so excellent ever did deserves to be preserved. The alterations his opinions underwent ought to be recorded, for they form his history.

A series of articles was published in the "New Monthly Magazine" during the autumn of the year 1832, written by a man of great talent, a fellow-collegian and warm friend of Shelley: they describe admirably the state of his mind during his collegiate life. Inspired with ardour for the acquisition of knowledge, endowed with the keenest sensibility and with the fortitude of a martyr, Shelley came among his fellow-creatures, congregated for the purposes of education, like a spirit from another sphere; too delicately organized for the rough treatment man uses towards man, especially in the season of youth, and too resolute in carrying out his own sense of good and justice, not to become a victim. To a devoted attachment to those he loved he added a determined resistance to oppression. Refusing to fag at Eton, he was treated with revolting cruelty by masters and boys: this roused instead of taming his spirit, and he rejected the duty of obedience when it was enforced by menaces and punishment. To aversion to the society of his fellow-creatures, such as he found them when collected together in societies, where one egged on the other to acts of tyranny, was joined the deepest sympathy and compassion; while the attachment he felt for individuals, and the admiration with which he regarded their powers and their virtues, led him to entertain a high opinion of the perfectibility of human nature; and he believed that all could reach the highest grade of moral improvement, did not the customs and prejudices of society foster evil passions and excuse evil actions.

The oppression which, trembling at every nerve yet resolute to heroism, it was his ill-fortune to encounter at school and at college, led him to dissent in all things from those whose arguments were blows, whose faith appeared to engender blame and hatred. 'During my existence,' he wrote to a friend in 1812, 'I have incessantly speculated, thought, and read.' His readings were not always well chosen; among them were the works of the French philosophers: as far as metaphysical argument went, he temporarily became a convert. At the same time, it was the cardinal article of his faith that, if men were but taught and induced to treat their fellows with love, charity, and equal rights, this earth would realize paradise. He looked upon religion, as it is professed, and above all practised, as hostile instead of friendly to the cultivation of those virtues which would make men brothers.

Can this be wondered at? At the age of seventeen, fragile in health and frame, of the purest habits in morals, full of devoted generosity and universal kindness, glowing with ardour to attain wisdom, resolved at every personal sacrifice to do right, burning with a desire for affection and sympathy,—he was treated as a reprobate, cast forth as a criminal.

The cause was that he was sincere; that he believed the opinions which he entertained to be true. And he loved truth with a martyr's love; he was ready to sacrifice station and fortune, and his dearest affections, at its shrine. The sacrifice was demanded from, and made by, a youth of seventeen. It is a singular fact in the history of society in the civilized nations of modern times that no false step is so irretrievable as one made in early youth. Older men, it is true, when they oppose their fellows and transgress ordinary rules, carry a certain prudence or hypocrisy as a shield along with them. But youth is rash; nor can it imagine, while asserting what it believes to be true, and doing what it believes to be right, that it should be denounced as vicious, and pursued as a criminal.

Shelley possessed a quality of mind which experience has shown me to be of the rarest occurrence among human beings: this was his UNWORLDLINESS. The usual motives that rule men, prospects of present or future advantage, the rank and fortune of those around, the taunts and censures, or the praise, of those who were hostile to him, had no influence whatever over his actions, and apparently none over his thoughts. It is difficult even to express the simplicity and directness of purpose that adorned him. Some few might be found in the history of mankind, and some one at least among his own friends, equally disinterested and scornful, even to severe personal sacrifices, of every baser motive. But no one, I believe, ever joined this noble but passive virtue to equal active endeavours for the benefit of his friends and mankind in general, and to equal power to produce the advantages he desired. The world's brightest gauds and its most solid advantages were of no worth in his eyes, when compared to the cause of what he considered truth, and the good of his fellow-creatures. Born in a position which, to his inexperienced mind, afforded the greatest facilities to practise the tenets he espoused, he boldly declared the use he would make of fortune and station, and enjoyed the belief that he should materially benefit his fellow-creatures by his actions; while, conscious of surpassing powers of reason and imagination, it is not strange that he should, even while so young, have believed that his written thoughts would tend to disseminate opinions which he believed conducive to the happiness of the human race.

If man were a creature devoid of passion, he might have said and done all this with quietness. But he was too enthusiastic, and too full of hatred of all the ills he witnessed, not to scorn danger. Various disappointments tortured, but could not tame, his soul. The more enmity he met, the more earnestly he became attached to his peculiar views, and hostile to those of the men who persecuted him.

He was animated to greater zeal by compassion for his fellow-creatures. His sympathy was excited by the misery with which the world is burning. He witnessed the sufferings of the poor, and was aware of the evils of ignorance. He desired to induce every rich man to despoil himself of superfluity, and to create a brotherhood of property and service, and was ready to be the first to lay down the advantages of his birth. He was of too uncompromising a disposition to join any party. He did not in his youth look forward to gradual improvement: nay, in those days of intolerance, now almost forgotten, it seemed as easy to look forward to the sort of millennium of freedom and brotherhood which he thought the proper state of mankind as to the present reign of moderation and improvement. Ill-health made him believe that his race would soon be run; that a year or two was all he had of life. He desired that these years should be useful and illustrious. He saw, in a fervent call on his fellow-creatures to share alike the blessings of the creation, to love and serve each other, the noblest work that life and time permitted him. In this spirit he composed "Queen Mab".

He was a lover of the wonderful and wild in literature, but had not fostered these tastes at their genuine sources—the romances and chivalry of the middle ages—but in the perusal of such German works as were current in those days. Under the influence of these he, at the age of fifteen, wrote two short prose romances of slender merit. The sentiments and language were exaggerated, the composition imitative and poor. He wrote also a poem on the subject of Ahasuerus—being led to it by a German fragment he picked up, dirty and torn, in Lincoln's Inn Fields. This fell afterwards into other hands, and was considerably altered before it was printed. Our earlier English poetry was almost unknown to him. The love and knowledge of Nature developed by Wordsworth—the lofty melody and mysterious beauty of Coleridge's poetry—and the wild fantastic machinery and gorgeous scenery adopted by Southey—composed his favourite reading; the rhythm of "Queen Mab" was founded on that of "Thalaba", and the first few lines bear a striking resemblance in spirit, though not in idea, to the opening of that poem. His fertile imagination, and ear tuned to the finest sense of harmony, preserved him from imitation. Another of his favourite books was the poem of "Gebir" by Walter Savage Landor. From his boyhood he had a wonderful facility of versification, which he carried into another language; and his Latin school-verses were composed with an ease and correctness that procured for him prizes, and caused him to be resorted to by all his friends for help. He was, at the period of writing "Queen Mab", a great traveller within the limits of England, Scotland, and Ireland. His time was spent among the loveliest scenes of these countries. Mountain and lake and forest were his home; the phenomena of Nature were his favourite study. He loved to inquire into their causes, and was addicted to pursuits of natural philosophy and chemistry, as far as they could be carried on as an amusement. These tastes gave truth and vivacity to his descriptions, and warmed his soul with that deep admiration for the wonders of Nature which constant association with her inspired.

He never intended to publish "Queen Mab" as it stands; but a few years after, when printing "Alastor", he extracted a small portion which he entitled "The Daemon of the World". In this he changed somewhat the versification, and made other alterations scarcely to be called improvements.

Some years after, when in Italy, a bookseller published an edition of "Queen Mab" as it originally stood. Shelley was hastily written to by his friends, under the idea that, deeply injurious as the mere distribution of the poem had proved, the publication might awaken fresh persecutions. At the suggestion of these friends he wrote a letter on the subject, printed in the "Examiner" newspaper—with which I close this history of his earliest work.

TO THE EDITOR OF THE 'EXAMINER.'

'Sir,

'Having heard that a poem entitled "Queen Mab" has been surreptitiously published in London, and that legal proceedings have been instituted against the publisher, I request the favour of your insertion of the following explanation of the affair, as it relates to me.

'A poem entitled "Queen Mab" was written by me at the age of eighteen, I daresay in a sufficiently intemperate spirit—but even then was not intended for publication, and a few copies only were struck off, to be distributed among my personal friends. I have not seen this production for several years. I doubt not but that it is perfectly worthless in point of literary composition; and that, in all that concerns moral and political speculation, as well as in the subtler discriminations of metaphysical and religious doctrine, it is still more crude and immature. I am a devoted enemy to religious, political, and domestic oppression; and I regret this publication, not so much from literary vanity, as because I fear it is better fitted to injure than to serve the sacred cause of freedom. I have directed my solicitor to apply to Chancery for an injunction to restrain the sale; but, after the precedent of Mr. Southey's "Wat Tyler" (a poem written, I believe, at the same age, and with the same unreflecting enthusiasm), with little hope of success.

'Whilst I exonerate myself from all share in having divulged opinions hostile to existing sanctions, under the form, whatever it may be, which they assume in this poem, it is scarcely necessary for me to protest against the system of inculcating the truth of Christianity or the excellence of Monarchy, however true or however excellent they may be, by such equivocal arguments as confiscation and imprisonment, and invective and slander, and the insolent violation of the most sacred ties of Nature and society.

'SIR,
'I am your obliged and obedient servant,
'PERCY B. SHELLEY.
'Pisa, June 22, 1821.'

NOTE ON "ALASTOR", BY MRS. SHELLEY.

"Alastor" is written in a very different tone from "Queen Mab". In the latter, Shelley poured out all the cherished speculations of his youth—all the irrepressible emotions of sympathy, censure, and hope, to which the present suffering, and what he considers the proper destiny of his fellow-creatures, gave birth. "Alastor", on the contrary, contains an individual interest only. A very few years, with their attendant events, had checked the ardour of Shelley's hopes, though he still thought them well-grounded, and that to advance their fulfilment was the noblest task man could achieve.

This is neither the time nor place to speak of the misfortunes that chequered his life. It will be sufficient to say that, in all he did, he at the time of doing it believed himself justified to his own conscience; while the various ills of poverty and loss of friends brought home to him the sad realities of life. Physical suffering had also considerable influence in causing him to turn his eyes inward; inclining him rather to brood over the thoughts and emotions of his own soul than to glance abroad, and to make, as in "Queen Mab", the whole universe the object and subject of his song. In the Spring of 1815, an eminent physician pronounced that he was dying rapidly of a consumption; abscesses were formed on his lungs, and he suffered acute spasms. Suddenly a complete change took place; and though through life he was a martyr to pain and debility, every symptom of pulmonary disease vanished. His nerves, which nature had formed sensitive to an unexampled degree, were rendered still more susceptible by the state of his health.

As soon as the peace of 1814 had opened the Continent, he went abroad. He visited some of the more magnificent scenes of Switzerland, and returned to England from Lucerne, by the Reuss and the Rhine. The river-navigation enchanted him. In his favourite poem of "Thalaba", his imagination had been excited by a description of such a voyage. In the summer of 1815, after a tour along the southern coast of Devonshire and a visit to Clifton, he rented a house on Bishopsgate Heath, on the borders of Windsor Forest, where he enjoyed several months of comparative health and tranquil happiness. The later summer months were warm and dry. Accompanied by a few friends, he visited the source of the Thames, making a voyage in a wherry from Windsor to Crichlade. His beautiful stanzas in the churchyard of Lechlade were written on that occasion. "Alastor" was composed on his return. He spent his days under the oak-shades of Windsor Great Park; and the magnificent woodland was a fitting study to inspire the various descriptions of forest scenery we find in the poem.

None of Shelley's poems is more characteristic than this. The solemn spirit that reigns throughout, the worship of the majesty of nature, the broodings of a poet's heart in solitude—the mingling of the exulting joy which the various aspects of the visible universe inspires with the sad and struggling pangs which human passion imparts—give a touching interest to the whole. The death which he had often contemplated during the last months as certain and near he here represented in such colours as had, in his lonely musings, soothed his soul to peace. The versification sustains the solemn spirit which breathes throughout: it is peculiarly melodious. The poem ought rather to be considered didactic than narrative: it was the outpouring of his own emotions, embodied in the purest form he could conceive, painted in the ideal hues which his brilliant imagination inspired, and softened by the recent anticipation of death.

NOTE ON THE "REVOLT OF ISLAM", BY MRS. SHELLEY.

Shelley possessed two remarkable qualities of intellect—a brilliant imagination, and a logical exactness of reason. His inclinations led him (he fancied) almost alike to poetry and metaphysical discussions. I say 'he fancied,' because I believe the former to have been paramount, and that it would have gained the mastery even had he struggled against it. However, he said that he deliberated at one time whether he should dedicate himself to poetry or metaphysics; and, resolving on the former, he educated himself for it, discarding in a great measure his philosophical pursuits, and engaging himself in the study of the poets of Greece, Italy, and England. To these may be added a constant perusal of portions of the old Testament—the Psalms, the Book of Job, the Prophet Isaiah, and others, the sublime poetry of which filled him with delight.

As a poet, his intellect and compositions were powerfully influenced by exterior circumstances, and especially by his place of abode. He was very fond of travelling, and ill-health increased this restlessness. The sufferings occasioned by a cold English winter made him pine, especially when our colder spring arrived, for a more genial climate. In 1816 he again visited Switzerland, and rented a house on the banks of the Lake of Geneva; and many a day, in cloud or sunshine, was passed alone in his boat—sailing as the wind listed, or weltering on the calm waters. The majestic aspect of Nature ministered such thoughts as he afterwards enwove in verse. His lines on the Bridge of the Arve, and his "Hymn to Intellectual Beauty", were written at this time. Perhaps during this summer his genius was checked by association with another poet whose nature was utterly dissimilar to his own, yet who, in the poem he wrote at that time, gave tokens that he shared for a period the more abstract and etherealised inspiration of Shelley. The saddest events awaited his return to England; but such was his fear to wound the feelings of others that he never expressed the anguish he felt, and seldom gave vent to the indignation roused by the persecutions he underwent; while the course of deep unexpressed passion, and the sense of injury, engendered the desire to embody themselves in forms defecated of all the weakness and evil which cling to real life.

He chose therefore for his hero a youth nourished in dreams of liberty, some of whose actions are in direct opposition to the opinions of the world; but who is animated throughout by an ardent love of virtue, and a resolution to confer the boons of political and intellectual freedom on his fellow-creatures. He created for this youth a woman such as he delighted to imagine—full of enthusiasm for the same objects; and they both, with will unvanquished, and the deepest sense of the justice of their cause, met adversity and death. There exists in this poem a memorial of a friend of his youth. The character of the old man who liberates Laon from his tower prison, and tends on him in sickness, is founded on that of Doctor Lind, who, when Shelley was at Eton, had often stood by to befriend and support him, and whose name he never mentioned without love and veneration.

During the year 1817 we were established at Marlow in Buckinghamshire. Shelley's choice of abode was fixed chiefly by this town being at no great distance from London, and its neighbourhood to the Thames. The poem was written in his boat, as it floated under the beech groves of Bisham, or during wanderings in the neighbouring country, which is distinguished for peculiar beauty. The chalk hills break into cliffs that overhang the Thames, or form valleys clothed with beech; the wilder portion of the country is rendered beautiful by exuberant vegetation; and the cultivated part is peculiarly fertile. With all this wealth of Nature which, either in the form of gentlemen's parks or soil dedicated to agriculture, flourishes around, Marlow was inhabited (I hope it is altered now) by a very poor population. The women are lacemakers, and lose their health by sedentary labour, for which they were very ill paid. The Poor-laws ground to the dust not only the paupers, but those who had risen just above that state, and were obliged to pay poor-rates. The changes produced by peace following a long war, and a bad harvest, brought with them the most heart-rending evils to the poor. Shelley afforded what alleviation he could. In the winter, while bringing out his poem, he had a severe attack of ophthalmia, caught while visiting the poor cottages. I mention these things,—for this minute and active sympathy with his fellow-creatures gives a thousandfold interest to his speculations, and stamps with reality his pleadings for the human race.

The poem, bold in its opinions and uncompromising in their expression, met with many censurers, not only among those who allow of no virtue but such as supports the cause they espouse, but even among those whose opinions were similar to his own. I extract a portion of a letter written in answer to one of these friends. It best details the impulses of Shelley's mind, and his motives: it was written with entire unreserve; and is therefore a precious monument of his own opinion of his powers, of the purity of his designs, and the ardour with which he clung, in adversity and through the valley of the shadow of death, to views from which he believed the permanent happiness of mankind must eventually spring.

'Marlowe, December 11, 1817.

'I have read and considered all that you say about my general powers, and the particular instance of the poem in which I have attempted to develop them. Nothing can be more satisfactory to me than the interest which your admonitions express. But I think you are mistaken in some points with regard to the peculiar nature of my powers, whatever be their amount. I listened with deference and self-suspicion to your censures of "The Revolt of Islam"; but the productions of mine which you commend hold a very low place in my own esteem; and this reassures me, in some degree at least. The poem was produced by a series of thoughts which filled my mind with unbounded and sustained enthusiasm. I felt the precariousness of my life, and I engaged in this task, resolved to leave some record of myself. Much of what the volume contains was written with the same feeling—as real, though not so prophetic—as the communications of a dying man. I never presumed indeed to consider it anything approaching to faultless; but, when I consider contemporary productions of the same apparent pretensions, I own I was filled with confidence. I felt that it was in many respects a genuine picture of my own mind. I felt that the sentiments were true, not assumed. And in this have I long believed that my power consists; in sympathy, and that part of the imagination which relates to sentiment and contemplation. I am formed, if for anything not in common with the herd of mankind, to apprehend minute and remote distinctions of feeling, whether relative to external nature or the living beings which surround us, and to communicate the conceptions which result from considering either the moral or the material universe as a whole. Of course, I believe these faculties, which perhaps comprehend all that is sublime in man, to exist very imperfectly in my own mind. But, when you advert to my Chancery-paper, a cold, forced, unimpassioned, insignificant piece of cramped and cautious argument, and to the little scrap about "Mandeville", which expressed my feelings indeed, but cost scarcely two minutes' thought to express, as specimens of my powers more favourable than that which grew as it were from "the agony and bloody sweat" of intellectual travail; surely I must feel that, in some manner, either I am mistaken in believing that I have any talent at all, or you in the selection of the specimens of it. Yet, after all, I cannot but be conscious, in much of what I write, of an absence of that tranquillity which is the attribute and accompaniment of power. This feeling alone would make your most kind and wise admonitions, on the subject of the economy of intellectual force, valuable to me. And, if I live, or if I see any trust in coming years, doubt not but that I shall do something, whatever it may be, which a serious and earnest estimate of my powers will suggest to me, and which will be in every respect accommodated to their utmost limits.

[Shelley to Godwin.]

NOTE ON ROSALIND AND HELEN BY MRS. SHELLEY.

"Rosalind and Helen" was begun at Marlow, and thrown aside—till I found it; and, at my request, it was completed. Shelley had no care for any of his poems that did not emanate from the depths of his mind, and develop some high or abstruse truth. When he does touch on human life and the human heart, no pictures can be more faithful, more delicate, more subtle, or more pathetic. He never mentioned Love but he shed a grace borrowed from his own nature, that scarcely any other poet has bestowed on that passion. When he spoke of it as the law of life, which inasmuch as we rebel against we err and injure ourselves and others, he promulgated that which he considered an irrefragable truth. In his eyes it was the essence of our being, and all woe and pain arose from the war made against it by selfishness, or insensibility, or mistake. By reverting in his mind to this first principle, he discovered the source of many emotions, and could disclose the secrets of all hearts, and his delineations of passion and emotion touch the finest chords of our nature.

"Rosalind and Helen" was finished during the summer of 1818, while we were at the Baths of Lucca.

NOTE BY MRS. SHELLEY.

From the Baths of Lucca, in 1818, Shelley visited Venice; and, circumstances rendering it eligible that we should remain a few weeks in the neighbourhood of that city, he accepted the offer of Lord Byron, who lent him the use of a villa he rented near Este; and he sent for his family from Lucca to join him.

I Capuccini was a villa built on the site of a Capuchin convent, demolished when the French suppressed religious houses; it was situated on the very overhanging brow of a low hill at the foot of a range of higher ones. The house was cheerful and pleasant; a vine-trellised walk, a pergola, as it is called in Italian, led from the hall-door to a summer-house at the end of the garden, which Shelley made his study, and in which he began the "Prometheus"; and here also, as he mentions in a letter, he wrote "Julian and Maddalo". A slight ravine, with a road in its depth, divided the garden from the hill, on which stood the ruins of the ancient castle of Este, whose dark massive wall gave forth an echo, and from whose ruined crevices owls and bats flitted forth at night, as the crescent moon sunk behind the black and heavy battlements. We looked from the garden over the wide plain of Lombardy, bounded to the west by the far Apennines, while to the east the horizon was lost in misty distance. After the picturesque but limited view of mountain, ravine, and chestnut-wood, at the Baths of Lucca, there was something infinitely gratifying to the eye in the wide range of prospect commanded by our new abode.

Our first misfortune, of the kind from which we soon suffered even more severely, happened here. Our little girl, an infant in whose small features I fancied that I traced great resemblance to her father, showed symptoms of suffering from the heat of the climate. Teething increased her illness and danger. We were at Este, and when we became alarmed, hastened to Venice for the best advice. When we arrived at Fusina, we found that we had forgotten our passport, and the soldiers on duty attempted to prevent our crossing the laguna; but they could not resist Shelley's impetuosity at such a moment. We had scarcely arrived at Venice before life fled from the little sufferer, and we returned to Este to weep her loss.

After a few weeks spent in this retreat, which was interspersed by visits to Venice, we proceeded southward.

NOTE ON "PROMETHEUS UNBOUND", BY MRS. SHELLEY.

On the 12th of March, 1818, Shelley quitted England, never to return. His principal motive was the hope that his health would be improved by a milder climate; he suffered very much during the winter previous to his emigration, and this decided his vacillating purpose. In December, 1817, he had written from Marlow to a friend, saying:

'My health has been materially worse. My feelings at intervals are of a deadly and torpid kind, or awakened to such a state of unnatural and keen excitement that, only to instance the organ of sight, I find the very blades of grass and the boughs of distant trees present themselves to me with microscopic distinctness. Towards evening I sink into a state of lethargy and inanimation, and often remain for hours on the sofa between sleep and waking, a prey to the most painful irritability of thought. Such, with little intermission, is my condition. The hours devoted to study are selected with vigilant caution from among these periods of endurance. It is not for this that I think of travelling to Italy, even if I knew that Italy would relieve me. But I have experienced a decisive pulmonary attack; and although at present it has passed away without any considerable vestige of its existence, yet this symptom sufficiently shows the true nature of my disease to be consumptive. It is to my advantage that this malady is in its nature slow, and, if one is sufficiently alive to its advances, is susceptible of cure from a warm climate. In the event of its assuming any decided shape, IT WOULD BE MY DUTY to go to Italy without delay. It is not mere health, but life, that I should seek, and that not for my own sake—I feel I am capable of trampling on all such weakness; but for the sake of those to whom my life may be a source of happiness, utility, security, and honour, and to some of whom my death might be all that is the reverse.'

In almost every respect his journey to Italy was advantageous. He left behind friends to whom he was attached; but cares of a thousand kinds, many springing from his lavish generosity, crowded round him in his native country, and, except the society of one or two friends, he had no compensation. The climate caused him to consume half his existence in helpless suffering. His dearest pleasure, the free enjoyment of the scenes of Nature, was marred by the same circumstance.

He went direct to Italy, avoiding even Paris, and did not make any pause till he arrived at Milan. The first aspect of Italy enchanted Shelley; it seemed a garden of delight placed beneath a clearer and brighter heaven than any he had lived under before. He wrote long descriptive letters during the first year of his residence in Italy, which, as compositions, are the most beautiful in the world, and show how truly he appreciated and studied the wonders of Nature and Art in that divine land.

The poetical spirit within him speedily revived with all the power and with more than all the beauty of his first attempts. He meditated three subjects as the groundwork for lyrical dramas. One was the story of Tasso; of this a slight fragment of a song of Tasso remains. The other was one founded on the Book of Job, which he never abandoned in idea, but of which no trace remains among his papers. The third was the "Prometheus Unbound". The Greek tragedians were now his most familiar companions in his wanderings, and the sublime majesty of Aeschylus filled him with wonder and delight. The father of Greek tragedy does not possess the pathos of Sophocles, nor the variety and tenderness of Euripides; the interest on which he founds his dramas is often elevated above human vicissitudes into the mighty passions and throes of gods and demi-gods: such fascinated the abstract imagination of Shelley.

We spent a month at Milan, visiting the Lake of Como during that interval. Thence we passed in succession to Pisa, Leghorn, the Baths of Lucca, Venice, Este, Rome, Naples, and back again to Rome, whither we returned early in March, 1819. During all this time Shelley meditated the subject of his drama, and wrote portions of it. Other poems were composed during this interval, and while at the Bagni di Lucca he translated Plato's "Symposium". But, though he diversified his studies, his thoughts centred in the Prometheus. At last, when at Rome, during a bright and beautiful Spring, he gave up his whole time to the composition. The spot selected for his study was, as he mentions in his preface, the mountainous ruins of the Baths of Caracalla. These are little known to the ordinary visitor at Rome. He describes them in a letter, with that poetry and delicacy and truth of description which render his narrated impressions of scenery of unequalled beauty and interest.

At first he completed the drama in three acts. It was not till several months after, when at Florence, that he conceived that a fourth act, a sort of hymn of rejoicing in the fulfilment of the prophecies with regard to Prometheus, ought to be added to complete the composition.

The prominent feature of Shelley's theory of the destiny of the human species was that evil is not inherent in the system of the creation, but an accident that might be expelled. This also forms a portion of Christianity: God made earth and man perfect, till he, by his fall,

'Brought death into the world and all our woe.'

Shelley believed that mankind had only to will that there should be no evil, and there would be none. It is not my part in these Notes to notice the arguments that have been urged against this opinion, but to mention the fact that he entertained it, and was indeed attached to it with fervent enthusiasm. That man could be so perfectionized as to be able to expel evil from his own nature, and from the greater part of the creation, was the cardinal point of his system. And the subject he loved best to dwell on was the image of One warring with the Evil Principle, oppressed not only by it, but by all—even the good, who were deluded into considering evil a necessary portion of humanity; a victim full of fortitude and hope and the spirit of triumph emanating from a reliance in the ultimate omnipotence of Good. Such he had depicted in his last poem, when he made Laon the enemy and the victim of tyrants. He now took a more idealized image of the same subject. He followed certain classical authorities in figuring Saturn as the good principle, Jupiter the usurping evil one, and Prometheus as the regenerator, who, unable to bring mankind back to primitive innocence, used knowledge as a weapon to defeat evil, by leading mankind, beyond the state wherein they are sinless through ignorance, to that in which they are virtuous through wisdom. Jupiter punished the temerity of the Titan by chaining him to a rock of Caucasus, and causing a vulture to devour his still-renewed heart. There was a prophecy afloat in heaven portending the fall of Jove, the secret of averting which was known only to Prometheus; and the god offered freedom from torture on condition of its being communicated to him. According to the mythological story, this referred to the offspring of Thetis, who was destined to be greater than his father. Prometheus at last bought pardon for his crime of enriching mankind with his gifts, by revealing the prophecy. Hercules killed the vulture, and set him free; and Thetis was married to Peleus, the father of Achilles.

Shelley adapted the catastrophe of this story to his peculiar views. The son greater than his father, born of the nuptials of Jupiter and Thetis, was to dethrone Evil, and bring back a happier reign than that of Saturn. Prometheus defies the power of his enemy, and endures centuries of torture; till the hour arrives when Jove, blind to the real event, but darkly guessing that some great good to himself will flow, espouses Thetis. At the moment, the Primal Power of the world drives him from his usurped throne, and Strength, in the person of Hercules, liberates Humanity, typified in Prometheus, from the tortures generated by evil done or suffered. Asia, one of the Oceanides, is the wife of Prometheus—she was, according to other mythological interpretations, the same as Venus and Nature. When the benefactor of mankind is liberated, Nature resumes the beauty of her prime, and is united to her husband, the emblem of the human race, in perfect and happy union. In the Fourth Act, the Poet gives further scope to his imagination, and idealizes the forms of creation—such as we know them, instead of such as they appeared to the Greeks. Maternal Earth, the mighty parent, is superseded by the Spirit of the Earth, the guide of our planet through the realms of sky; while his fair and weaker companion and attendant, the Spirit of the Moon, receives bliss from the annihilation of Evil in the superior sphere.

Shelley develops, more particularly in the lyrics of this drama, his abstruse and imaginative theories with regard to the Creation. It requires a mind as subtle and penetrating as his own to understand the mystic meanings scattered throughout the poem. They elude the ordinary reader by their abstraction and delicacy of distinction, but they are far from vague. It was his design to write prose metaphysical essays on the nature of Man, which would have served to explain much of what is obscure in his poetry; a few scattered fragments of observations and remarks alone remain. He considered these philosophical views of Mind and Nature to be instinct with the intensest spirit of poetry.

More popular poets clothe the ideal with familiar and sensible imagery. Shelley loved to idealize the real—to gift the mechanism of the material universe with a soul and a voice, and to bestow such also on the most delicate and abstract emotions and thoughts of the mind. Sophocles was his great master in this species of imagery.

I find in one of his manuscript books some remarks on a line in the "Oedipus Tyrannus", which show at once the critical subtlety of Shelley's mind, and explain his apprehension of those 'minute and remote distinctions of feeling, whether relative to external nature or the living beings which surround us,' which he pronounces, in the letter quoted in the note to the "Revolt of Islam", to comprehend all that is sublime in man.

'In the Greek Shakespeare, Sophocles, we find the image,

> Pollas d' odous elthonta phrontidos planois:

a line of almost unfathomable depth of poetry; yet how simple are the images in which it is arrayed!

> "Coming to many ways in the wanderings of careful thought."

If the words odous and planois had not been used, the line might have been explained in a metaphorical instead of an absolute sense, as we say "WAYS and means," and "wanderings" for error and confusion. But they meant literally paths or roads, such as we tread with our feet; and wanderings, such as a man makes when he loses himself in a desert, or roams from city to city—as Oedipus, the speaker of this verse, was destined to wander, blind and asking charity. What a picture does this line suggest of the mind as a wilderness of intricate paths, wide as the universe, which is here made its symbol; a world within a world which he who seeks some knowledge with respect to what he ought to do searches throughout, as he would search the external universe for some valued thing which was hidden from him upon its surface.'

In reading Shelley's poetry, we often find similar verses, resembling, but not imitating the Greek in this species of imagery; for, though he adopted the style, he gifted it with that originality of form and colouring which sprung from his own genius.

In the "Prometheus Unbound", Shelley fulfils the promise quoted from a letter in the Note on the "Revolt of Islam". (While correcting the proof-sheets of that poem, it struck me that the poet had indulged in an exaggerated view of the evils of restored despotism; which, however injurious and degrading, were less openly sanguinary than the triumph of anarchy, such as it appeared in France at the close of the last century. But at this time a book, "Scenes of Spanish Life", translated by Lieutenant Crawford from the German of Dr. Huber, of Rostock, fell into my hands. The account of the triumph of the priests and the serviles, after the French invasion of Spain in 1823, bears a strong and frightful resemblance to some of the descriptions of the massacre of the patriots in the "Revolt of Islam".) The tone of the composition is calmer and more majestic, the poetry more perfect as a whole, and the imagination displayed at once more pleasingly beautiful and more varied and daring. The description of the Hours, as they are seen in the cave of Demogorgon, is an instance of this—it fills the mind as the most charming picture—we long to see an artist at work to bring to our view the

> 'cars drawn by rainbow-winged steeds
> Which trample the dim winds: in each there stands
> A wild-eyed charioteer urging their flight.
> Some look behind, as fiends pursued them there,
> And yet I see no shapes but the keen stars:
> Others, with burning eyes, lean forth, and drink
> With eager lips the wind of their own speed,
> As if the thing they loved fled on before,
> And now, even now, they clasped it. Their bright locks
> Stream like a comet's flashing hair: they all
> Sweep onward.'

Through the whole poem there reigns a sort of calm and holy spirit of love; it soothes the tortured, and is hope to the expectant, till the prophecy is fulfilled, and Love, untainted by any evil, becomes the law of the world.

England had been rendered a painful residence to Shelley, as much by the sort of persecution with which in those days all men of liberal opinions were visited, and by the injustice he had lately endured in the Court of Chancery, as by the symptoms of disease which made him regard a visit to Italy as necessary to prolong his life. An exile, and strongly impressed with the feeling that the majority of his countrymen regarded him with sentiments of aversion such as his own heart could experience towards none, he sheltered himself from such disgusting and painful thoughts in the calm retreats of poetry, and built up a world of his own—with the more pleasure, since he hoped to induce some one or two to believe that the earth might become such, did mankind themselves consent. The charm of the Roman climate helped to clothe his thoughts in greater beauty than they had ever worn before. And, as he wandered among the ruins made one with Nature in their decay, or gazed on the Praxitelean shapes that throng the Vatican, the Capitol, and the palaces of Rome, his soul imbibed forms of loveliness which became a portion of itself. There are many passages in the "Prometheus" which show the intense delight he received from such studies, and give back the impression with a beauty of poetical description peculiarly his own. He felt this, as a poet must feel when he satisfies himself by the result of his labours; and he wrote from Rome, 'My "Prometheus Unbound" is just finished, and in a month or two I shall send it. It is a drama, with characters and mechanism of a kind yet unattempted; and I think the execution is better than any of my former attempts.'

I may mention, for the information of the more critical reader, that the verbal alterations in this edition of "Prometheus" are made from a list of errata written by Shelley himself.

NOTE ON THE CENCI, BY MRS. SHELLEY.

The sort of mistake that Shelley made as to the extent of his own genius and powers, which led him deviously at first, but lastly into the direct track that enabled him fully to develop them, is a curious instance of his modesty of feeling, and of the methods which the human mind uses at once to deceive itself, and yet, in its very delusion, to make its way out of error into the path which Nature has marked out as its right one. He often incited me to attempt the writing a tragedy: he conceived that I possessed some dramatic talent, and he was always most earnest and energetic in his exhortations that I should cultivate any talent I possessed, to the utmost. I entertained a truer estimate of my powers; and above all (though at that time not exactly aware of the fact) I was far too young to have any chance of succeeding, even moderately, in a species of composition that requires a greater scope of experience in, and sympathy with, human passion than could then have fallen to my lot,—or than any perhaps, except Shelley, ever possessed, even at the age of twenty-six, at which he wrote The Cenci.

On the other hand, Shelley most erroneously conceived himself to be destitute of this talent. He believed that one of the first requisites was the capacity of forming and following-up a story or plot. He fancied himself to he defective in this portion of imagination: it was that which gave him least pleasure in the writings of others, though he laid great store by it as the proper framework to support the sublimest efforts of poetry. He asserted that he was too metaphysical and abstract, too fond of the theoretical and the ideal, to succeed as a tragedian. It perhaps is not strange that I shared this opinion with himself; for he had hitherto shown no inclination for, nor given any specimen of his powers in framing and supporting the interest of a story, either in prose or verse. Once or twice, when he attempted such, he had speedily thrown it aside, as being even disagreeable to him as an occupation.

The subject he had suggested for a tragedy was Charles I: and he had written to me: 'Remember, remember Charles I. I have been already imagining how you would conduct some scenes. The second volume of "St. Leon" begins with this proud and true sentiment: "There is nothing which the human mind can conceive which it may not execute." Shakespeare was only a human being.' These words were written in 1818, while we were in Lombardy, when he little thought how soon a work of his own would prove a proud comment on the passage he quoted. When in Rome, in 1819, a friend put into our hands the old manuscript account of the story of the Cenci. We visited the Colonna and Doria palaces, where the portraits of Beatrice were to be found; and her beauty cast the reflection of its own grace over her appalling story. Shelley's imagination became strongly excited, and he urged the subject to me as one fitted for a tragedy. More than ever I felt my incompetence; but I entreated him to write it instead; and he began, and proceeded swiftly, urged on by intense sympathy with the sufferings of the human beings whose passions, so long cold in the tomb, he revived, and gifted with poetic language. This tragedy is the only one of his works that he communicated to me during its progress. We talked over the arrangement of the scenes together. I speedily saw the great mistake we had made, and triumphed in the discovery of the new talent brought to light from that mine of wealth (never, alas, through his untimely death, worked to its depths)—his richly gifted mind.

We suffered a severe affliction in Rome by the loss of our eldest child, who was of such beauty and promise as to cause him deservedly to be the idol of our hearts. We left the capital of the world, anxious for a time to escape a spot associated too intimately with his presence and loss. (Such feelings haunted him when, in "The Cenci", he makes Beatrice speak to Cardinal Camillo of

'that fair blue-eyed child
Who was the lodestar of your life:'—and say—
All see, since his most swift and piteous death,
That day and night, and heaven and earth, and time,
And all the things hoped for or done therein
Are changed to you, through your exceeding grief.')

Some friends of ours were residing in the neighbourhood of Leghorn, and we took a small house, Villa Valsovano, about half-way between the town and Monte Nero, where we remained during the summer. Our villa was situated in the midst of a podere; the peasants sang as they worked beneath our windows, during the heats of a very hot season, and in the evening the water-wheel creaked as the process of irrigation went on, and the fireflies flashed from among the myrtle hedges: Nature was bright, sunshiny, and cheerful, or diversified by storms of a majestic terror, such as we had never before witnessed.

At the top of the house there was a sort of terrace. There is often such in Italy, generally roofed: this one was very small, yet not only roofed but glazed. This Shelley made his study; it looked out on a wide prospect of fertile country, and commanded a view of the near sea. The storms that sometimes varied our day showed themselves most picturesquely as they were driven across the ocean; sometimes the dark lurid clouds dipped towards the waves, and became water-spouts that churned up the waters beneath, as they were chased onward and scattered by the tempest. At other times the dazzling sunlight and heat made it almost intolerable to every other; but Shelley basked in both, and his health and spirits revived under their influence. In this airy cell he wrote the principal part of "The Cenci". He was making a study of Calderon at the time, reading his best tragedies with an accomplished lady living near us, to whom his letter from Leghorn was addressed during the following year. He admired Calderon, both for his poetry and his dramatic genius; but it shows his judgement and originality that, though greatly struck by his first acquaintance with the Spanish poet, none of his peculiarities crept into the composition of "The Cenci"; and there is no trace of his new studies, except in that passage to which he himself alludes as suggested by one in "El Purgatorio de San Patricio".

Shelley wished "The Cenci" to be acted. He was not a playgoer, being of such fastidious taste that he was easily disgusted by the bad filling-up of the inferior parts. While preparing for our departure from England, however, he saw Miss O'Neil several times. She was then in the zenith of her glory; and Shelley was deeply moved by her impersonation of several parts, and by the graceful sweetness, the intense pathos, the sublime vehemence of passion she displayed. She was often in his thoughts as he wrote: and, when he had finished, he became anxious that his tragedy should be acted, and receive the advantage of having this accomplished actress to fill the part of the heroine. With this view he wrote the following letter to a friend in London:

> 'The object of the present letter us to ask a favour of you. I have written a tragedy on a story well known in Italy, and, in my conception, eminently dramatic. I have taken some pains to make my play fit for representation, and those who have already seen it judge favourably. It is written without any of the peculiar feelings and opinions which characterize my other compositions; I have attended simply to the impartial development of such characters as it is probable the persons represented really were, together with the greatest degree of popular effect to be produced by such a development. I send you a translation of the Italian manuscript on which my play is founded; the chief circumstance of which I have touched very delicately; for my principal doubt as to whether it would succeed as an acting play hangs entirely on the question as to whether any such a thing as incest in this shape, however treated, would be admitted on the stage. I think, however, it will

form no objection; considering, first, that the facts are matter of history, and, secondly, the peculiar delicacy with which I have treated it. (In speaking of his mode of treating this main incident, Shelley said that it might be remarked that, in the course of the play, he had never mentioned expressly Cenci's worst crime. Every one knew what it must be, but it was never imaged in words—the nearest allusion to it being that portion of Cenci's curse beginning—"That, if she have a child," etc.)

'I am exceedingly interested in the question of whether this attempt of mine will succeed or not. I am strongly inclined to the affirmative at present; founding my hopes on this—that, as a composition, it is certainly not inferior to any of the modern plays that have been acted, with the exception of "Remorse"; that the interest of the plot is incredibly greater and more real; and that there is nothing beyond what the multitude are contented to believe that they can understand, either in imagery, opinion, or sentiment. I wish to preserve a complete incognito, and can trust to you that, whatever else you do, you will at least favour me on this point. Indeed, this is essential, deeply essential, to its success. After it had been acted, and successfully (could I hope for such a thing), I would own it if I pleased, and use the celebrity it might acquire to my own purposes.

'What I want you to do is to procure for me its presentation at Covent Garden. The principal character, Beatrice, is precisely fitted for Miss O'Neil, and it might even seem to have been written for her (God forbid that I should see her play it—it would tear my nerves to pieces); and in all respects it is fitted only for Covent Garden. The chief male character I confess I should be very unwilling that any one but Kean should play. That is impossible, and I must be contented with an inferior actor.'

The play was accordingly sent to Mr. Harris. He pronounced the subject to be so objectionable that he could not even submit the part to Miss O'Neil for perusal, but expressed his desire that the author would write a tragedy on some other subject, which he would gladly accept. Shelley printed a small edition at Leghorn, to ensure its correctness; as he was much annoyed by the many mistakes that crept into his text when distance prevented him from correcting the press.

Universal approbation soon stamped "The Cenci" as the best tragedy of modern times. Writing concerning it, Shelley said: 'I have been cautious to avoid the introducing faults of youthful composition; diffuseness, a profusion of inapplicable imagery, vagueness, generality, and, as Hamlet says, "words, words".' There is nothing that is not purely dramatic throughout; and the character of Beatrice, proceeding, from vehement struggle, to horror, to deadly resolution, and lastly to the elevated dignity of calm suffering, joined to passionate tenderness and pathos, is touched with hues so vivid and so beautiful that the poet seems to have read intimately the secrets of the noble heart imaged in the lovely countenance of the unfortunate girl. The Fifth Act is a masterpiece. It is the finest thing he ever wrote, and may claim proud comparison not only with any contemporary, but preceding, poet. The varying feelings of Beatrice are expressed with passionate, heart-reaching eloquence. Every character has a voice that echoes truth in its tones. It is curious, to one acquainted with the written story, to mark the success with which the poet has inwoven the real incidents of the tragedy into his scenes, and yet, through the power of poetry, has obliterated all that would otherwise have shown too harsh or too hideous in the picture. His success was a double triumph; and often after he was earnestly entreated to write again in a style that commanded popular favour, while it was not less instinct with truth and genius. But the bent of his mind went the other way; and, even when employed on subjects whose interest depended on character and incident, he would start off in another direction, and leave the delineations of human passion, which he could depict in so able a manner, for fantastic creations of his fancy, or the expression of those opinions and sentiments, with regard to human nature and its destiny, a desire to diffuse which was the master passion of his soul.

NOTE ON THE MASK OF ANARCHY, BY MRS. SHELLEY.

Though Shelley's first eager desire to excite his countrymen to resist openly the oppressions existent during 'the good old times' had faded with early youth, still his warmest sympathies were for the people. He was a republican, and loved a democracy. He looked on all human beings as inheriting an equal right to possess the dearest privileges of our nature; the necessaries of life when fairly earned by labour, and intellectual instruction. His hatred of any despotism that looked upon the people as not to be consulted, or protected from want and ignorance, was intense. He was residing near Leghorn, at Villa Valsovano, writing "The Cenci", when the news of the Manchester Massacre reached us; it roused in him violent emotions of indignation and compassion. The great truth that the many, if accordant and resolute, could control the few, as was shown some years after, made him long to teach his injured countrymen how to resist. Inspired by these feelings, he wrote the "Mask of Anarchy", which he sent to his friend Leigh Hunt, to be inserted in the Examiner, of which he was then the Editor.

'I did not insert it,' Leigh Hunt writes in his valuable and interesting preface to this poem, when he printed it in 1832, 'because I thought that the public at large had not become sufficiently discerning to do justice to the sincerity and kind-heartedness of the spirit that walked in this flaming robe of verse.' Days of outrage have passed away, and with them the exasperation that would cause such an appeal to the many to be injurious. Without being aware of them, they at one time acted on his suggestions, and gained the day. But they rose when human life was respected by the Minister in power; such was not the case during the Administration which excited Shelley's abhorrence.

The poem was written for the people, and is therefore in a more popular tone than usual: portions strike as abrupt and unpolished, but many stanzas are all his own. I heard him repeat, and admired, those beginning

'My Father Time is old and gray,'

before I knew to what poem they were to belong. But the most touching passage is that which describes the blessed effects of liberty; it might make a patriot of any man whose heart was not wholly closed against his humbler fellow-creatures.

NOTE ON PETER BELL THE THIRD, BY MRS. SHELLEY.

In this new edition I have added "Peter Bell the Third". A critique on Wordsworth's "Peter Bell" reached us at Leghorn, which amused Shelley exceedingly, and suggested this poem.

I need scarcely observe that nothing personal to the author of "Peter Bell" is intended in this poem. No man ever admired Wordsworth's poetry more;—he read it perpetually, and taught others to appreciate its beauties. This poem is, like all others written by Shelley, ideal. He conceived the idealism of a poet—a man of lofty and creative genius—quitting the glorious calling of discovering and announcing the beautiful and good, to support and propagate ignorant prejudices and pernicious errors; imparting to the unenlightened, not that ardour for truth and spirit of toleration which Shelley looked on as the sources of the moral improvement and happiness of mankind, but false and injurious opinions, that evil was good, and that ignorance and force were the best allies of purity and virtue. His idea was that a man gifted, even as transcendently as the author of "Peter Bell", with the highest qualities of genius, must, if he fostered such errors, be infected with dulness. This poem was written as a warning—not as a narration of the reality. He was unacquainted personally with Wordsworth, or with Coleridge (to whom he alludes in the fifth part of the poem), and therefore, I repeat, his poem is purely ideal;—it contains something of criticism on the compositions of those great poets, but nothing injurious to the men themselves.

No poem contains more of Shelley's peculiar views with regard to the errors into which many of the wisest have fallen, and the pernicious effects of certain opinions on society. Much of it is beautifully written: and, though, like the burlesque drama of "Swellfoot", it must be looked on as a plaything, it has so much merit and poetry—so much of HIMSELF in it—that it cannot fail to interest greatly, and by right belongs to the world for whose instruction and benefit it was written.

NOTE ON THE WITCH OF ATLAS, BY MRS. SHELLEY.

We spent the summer of 1820 at the Baths of San Giuliano, four miles from Pisa. These baths were of great use to Shelley in soothing his nervous irritability. We made several excursions in the neighbourhood. The country around is fertile, and diversified and rendered picturesque by ranges of near hills and more distant mountains. The peasantry are a handsome intelligent race; and there was a gladsome sunny heaven spread over us, that rendered home and every scene we visited cheerful and bright. During some of the hottest days of August, Shelley made a solitary journey on foot to the summit of Monte San Pellegrino—a mountain of some height, on the top of which there is a chapel, the object, during certain days of the year, of many pilgrimages. The excursion delighted him while it lasted; though he exerted himself too much, and the effect was considerable lassitude and weakness on his return. During the expedition he conceived the idea, and wrote, in the three days immediately succeeding to his return, the "Witch of Atlas". This poem is peculiarly characteristic of his tastes—wildly fanciful, full of brilliant imagery, and discarding human interest and passion, to revel in the fantastic ideas that his imagination suggested.

The surpassing excellence of "The Cenci" had made me greatly desire that Shelley should increase his popularity by adopting subjects that would more suit the popular taste than a poem conceived in the abstract and dreamy spirit of the "Witch of Atlas". It was not only that I wished him to acquire popularity as redounding to his fame; but I believed that he would obtain a greater mastery over his own powers, and greater happiness in his mind, if public applause crowned his endeavours. The few stanzas that precede the poem were addressed to me on my representing these ideas to him. Even now I believe that I was in the right. Shelley did not expect sympathy and approbation from the public; but the want of it took away a portion of the ardour that ought to have sustained him while writing. He was thrown on his own resources, and on the inspiration of his own soul; and wrote because his mind overflowed, without the hope of being appreciated. I had not the most distant wish that he should truckle in opinion, or submit his lofty aspirations for the human race to the low ambition and pride of the many; but I felt sure that, if his poems were more addressed to the common feelings of men, his proper rank among the writers of the day would be acknowledged, and that popularity as a poet would enable his countrymen to do justice to his character and virtues, which in those days it was the mode to attack with the most flagitious calumnies and insulting abuse. That he felt these things deeply cannot be doubted, though he armed himself with the consciousness of acting from a lofty and heroic sense of right. The truth burst from his heart sometimes in solitude, and he would write a few unfinished verses that showed that he felt the sting; among such I find the following:—

> 'Alas! this is not what I thought Life was.
> I knew that there were crimes and evil men,
> Misery and hate; nor did I hope to pass
> Untouched by suffering through the rugged glen.
> In mine own heart I saw as in a glass
> The hearts of others . . . And, when
> I went among my kind, with triple brass
> Of calm endurance my weak breast I armed,
> To bear scorn, fear, and hate—a woful mass!'

I believed that all this morbid feeling would vanish if the chord of sympathy between him and his countrymen were touched. But my persuasions were vain, the mind could not be bent from its natural inclination. Shelley shrunk instinctively from portraying human passion, with its mixture of good and evil, of disappointment and disquiet. Such opened again the wounds of his own heart; and he loved to shelter himself rather in the airiest flights of fancy, forgetting love and hate, and regret and lost hope, in such imaginations as borrowed their hues from sunrise or sunset, from the yellow moonshine or paly twilight, from the aspect of the far ocean or the shadows of the woods,—which celebrated the singing of the winds among the pines, the flow of a murmuring stream, and the thousand harmonious sounds which Nature creates in her solitudes. These are the materials which form the "Witch of Atlas": it is a brilliant congregation of ideas such as his senses gathered, and his fancy coloured, during his rambles in the sunny land he so much loved.

NOTE ON OEDIPUS TYRANNUS, BY MRS. SHELLEY.

In the brief journal I kept in those days, I find recorded, in August, 1820, Shelley 'begins "Swellfoot the Tyrant", suggested by the pigs at the fair of San Giuliano.' This was the period of Queen Caroline's landing in England, and the struggles made by George IV to get rid of her claims; which failing, Lord Castlereagh placed the "Green Bag" on the table of the House of Commons, demanding in the King's name that an enquiry should be instituted into his wife's conduct. These circumstances were the theme of all conversation among the English. We were then at the Baths of San Giuliano. A friend came to visit us on the day when a fair was held in the square, beneath our windows: Shelley read to us his "Ode to Liberty"; and was riotously accompanied by the grunting of a quantity of pigs brought for sale to the fair. He compared it to the 'chorus of frogs' in the satiric drama of Aristophanes; and, it being an hour of merriment, and one ludicrous association suggesting another, he imagined a political-satirical drama on the circumstances of the day, to which the pigs would serve as chorus—and "Swellfoot" was begun. When finished, it was transmitted to England, printed, and published anonymously; but stifled at the very dawn of its existence by the Society for the Suppression of Vice, who threatened to prosecute it, if not immediately withdrawn. The friend who had taken the trouble of bringing it out, of course did not think it worth the annoyance and expense of a contest, and it was laid aside.

Hesitation of whether it would do honour to Shelley prevented my publishing it at first. But I cannot bring myself to keep back anything he ever wrote; for each word is fraught with the peculiar views and sentiments which he believed to be beneficial to the human race, and the bright light of poetry irradiates every thought. The world has a right to the entire compositions of such a man; for it does not live and thrive by the outworn lesson of the dullard or the hypocrite, but by the original free thoughts of men of genius, who aspire to pluck bright truth

> 'from the pale-faced moon;
> Or dive into the bottom of the deep
> Where fathom-line would never touch the ground,
> And pluck up drowned'

truth. Even those who may dissent from his opinions will consider that he was a man of genius, and that the world will take more interest in his slightest word than in the waters of Lethe which are so eagerly prescribed as medicinal for all its wrongs and woe. This drama, however, must not be judged for more than was meant. It is a mere plaything of the imagination; which even may not excite smiles among many, who will not see wit in those combinations of thought which were full of the ridiculous to the author. But, like everything he wrote, it breathes that deep sympathy for the sorrows of humanity, and indignation against its oppressors, which make it worthy of his name.

NOTE ON HELLAS, BY MRS. SHELLEY.

The South of Europe was in a state of great political excitement at the beginning of the year 1821. The Spanish Revolution had been a signal to Italy; secrete societies were formed; and, when Naples rose to declare the Constitution, the call was responded to from Brundusium to the foot of the Alps. To crush these attempts to obtain liberty, early in 1821 the Austrians poured their armies into the Peninsula: at first their coming rather seemed to add energy and resolution to a people long enslaved. The Piedmontese asserted their freedom; Genoa threw off the yoke of the King of Sardinia; and, as if in playful imitation, the people of the little state of Massa and Carrara gave the conge to their sovereign, and set up a republic.

Tuscany alone was perfectly tranquil. It was said that the Austrian minister presented a list of sixty Carbonari to the Grand Duke, urging their imprisonment; and the Grand Duke replied, 'I do not know whether these sixty men are Carbonari, but I know, if I imprison them, I shall directly have sixty thousand start up.' But, though the Tuscans had no desire to disturb the paternal government beneath whose shelter they slumbered, they regarded the progress of the various Italian revolutions with intense interest, and hatred for the Austrian was warm in every bosom. But they had slender hopes; they knew that the Neapolitans would offer no fit resistance to the regular German troops, and that the overthrow of the constitution in Naples would act as a decisive blow against all struggles for liberty in Italy.

We have seen the rise and progress of reform. But the Holy Alliance was alive and active in those days, and few could dream of the peaceful triumph of liberty. It seemed then that the armed assertion of freedom in the South of Europe was the only hope of the liberals, as, if it prevailed, the nations of the north would imitate the example. Happily the reverse has proved the fact. The countries accustomed to the exercise of the privileges of freemen, to a limited extent, have extended, and are extending, these limits. Freedom and knowledge have now a chance of proceeding hand in hand; and, if it continue thus, we may hope for the durability of both. Then, as I have said—in 1821—Shelley, as well as every other lover of liberty, looked upon the struggles in Spain and Italy as decisive of the destinies of the world, probably for centuries to come. The interest he took in the progress of affairs was intense. When Genoa declared itself free, his hopes were at their highest. Day after day he read the bulletins of the Austrian army, and sought eagerly to gather tokens of its defeat. He heard of the revolt of Genoa with emotions of transport. His whole heart and soul were in the triumph of the cause. We were living at Pisa at that time; and several well-informed Italians, at the head of whom we may place the celebrated Vacca, were accustomed to seek for sympathy in their hopes from Shelley: they did not find such for the despair they too generally experienced, founded on contempt for their southern countrymen.

While the fate of the progress of the Austrian armies then invading Naples was yet in suspense, the news of another revolution filled him with exultation. We had formed the acquaintance at Pisa of several Constantinopolitan Greeks, of the family of Prince Caradja, formerly Hospodar of Wallachia; who, hearing that the bowstring, the accustomed finale of his viceroyalty, was on the road to him, escaped with his treasures, and took up his abode in Tuscany. Among these was the gentleman to whom the drama of "Hellas" is dedicated. Prince Mavrocordato was warmed by those aspirations for the independence of his country which filled the hearts of many of his countrymen. He often intimated the possibility of an insurrection in Greece; but we had no idea of its being so near at hand, when, on the 1st of April 1821, he called on Shelley, bringing the proclamation of his cousin, Prince Ypsilanti, and, radiant with exultation and delight, declared that henceforth Greece would be free.

Shelley had hymned the dawn of liberty in Spain and Naples, in two odes dictated by the warmest enthusiasm; he felt himself naturally impelled to decorate with poetry the uprise of the descendants of that people whose works he regarded with deep admiration, and to adopt the vaticinatory character in prophesying their success. "Hellas" was written in a moment of enthusiasm. It is curious to remark how well he overcomes the difficulty of forming a drama out of such scant materials. His prophecies, indeed, came true in their general, not their particular, purport. He did not foresee the death of Lord Londonderry, which was to be the epoch of a change in English politics, particularly as regarded foreign affairs; nor that the navy of his country would fight for instead of against the Greeks, and by the battle of Navarino secure their enfranchisement from the Turks. Almost against reason, as it appeared to him, he resolved to believe that Greece would prove triumphant; and in this spirit, auguring ultimate good, yet grieving over the vicissitudes to be endured in the interval, he composed his drama.

"Hellas" was among the last of his compositions, and is among the most beautiful. The choruses are singularly imaginative, and melodious in their versification. There are some stanzas that beautifully exemplify Shelley's peculiar style; as, for instance, the assertion of the intellectual empire which must be for ever the inheritance of the country of Homer, Sophocles, and Plato:—

> 'But Greece and her foundations are
> Built below the tide of war,
> Based on the crystalline sea
> Of thought and its eternity.'

And again, that philosophical truth felicitously imaged forth—

> 'Revenge and Wrong bring forth their kind,
> The foul cubs like their parents are,
> Their den is in the guilty mind,
> And Conscience feeds them with despair.'

The conclusion of the last chorus is among the most beautiful of his lyrics. The imagery is distinct and majestic; the prophecy, such as poets love to dwell upon, the Regeneration of Mankind—and that regeneration reflecting back splendour on the foregone time, from which it inherits so much of intellectual wealth, and memory of past virtuous deeds, as must render the possession of happiness and peace of tenfold value.

NOTE ON THE EARLY POEMS, BY MRS. SHELLEY.

The remainder of Shelley's Poems will be arranged in the order in which they were written. Of course, mistakes will occur in placing some of the shorter ones; for, as I have said, many of these were thrown aside, and I never saw them till I had the misery of looking over his writings after the hand that traced them was dust; and some were in the hands of others, and I never saw them till now. The subjects of the poems are often to me an unerring guide; but on other occasions I can only guess, by finding them in the pages of the same manuscript book that contains poems with the date of whose composition I am fully conversant. In the present arrangement all his poetical translations will be placed together at the end.

The loss of his early papers prevents my being able to give any of the poetry of his boyhood. Of the few I give as "Early Poems", the greater part were published with "Alastor"; some of them were written previously, some at the same period. The poem beginning 'Oh, there are spirits in the air' was addressed in idea to Coleridge, whom he never knew; and at whose character he could only guess imperfectly, through his writings, and accounts he heard of him from some who knew him well. He regarded his change of opinions as rather an act of will than conviction, and believed that in his inner heart he would be haunted by what Shelley considered the better and holier aspirations of his youth. The summer evening that suggested to him the poem written in the churchyard of Lechlade occurred during his voyage up the Thames in 1815. He had been advised by a physician to live as much as possible in the open air; and a fortnight of a bright warm July was spent in tracing the Thames to its source. He never spent a season more tranquilly than the summer of 1815. He had just recovered from a severe pulmonary attack; the weather was warm and pleasant. He lived near Windsor Forest; and his life was spent under its shades or on the water, meditating subjects for verse. Hitherto, he had chiefly aimed at extending his political doctrines, and attempted so to do by appeals in prose essays to the people, exhorting them to claim their rights; but he had now begun to feel that the time for action was not ripe in England, and that the pen was the only instrument wherewith to prepare the way for better things.

In the scanty journals kept during those years I find a record of the books that Shelley read during several years. During the years of 1814 and 1815 the list is extensive. It includes, in Greek, Homer, Hesiod, Theocritus, the histories of Thucydides and Herodotus, and Diogenes Laertius. In Latin, Petronius, Suetonius, some of the works of Cicero, a large proportion of those of Seneca and Livy. In English, Milton's poems, Wordsworth's "Excursion", Southey's "Madoc" and "Thalaba", Locke "On the Human Understanding", Bacon's "Novum Organum". In Italian, Ariosto, Tasso, and Alfieri. In French, the "Reveries d'un Solitaire" of Rousseau. To these may be added several modern books of travel. He read few novels.

NOTE ON POEMS OF 1816, BY MRS. SHELLEY.

Shelley wrote little during this year. The poem entitled "The Sunset" was written in the spring of the year, while still residing at Bishopsgate. He spent the summer on the shores of the Lake of Geneva. The "Hymn to Intellectual Beauty" was conceived during his voyage round the lake with Lord Byron. He occupied himself during this voyage by reading the "Nouvelle Heloise" for the first time. The reading it on the very spot where the scenes are laid added to the interest; and he was at once surprised and charmed by the passionate eloquence and earnest enthralling interest that pervade this work. There was something in the character of Saint-Preux, in his abnegation of self, and in the worship he paid to Love, that coincided with Shelley's own disposition; and, though differing in many of the views and shocked by others, yet the effect of the whole was fascinating and delightful.

"Mont Blanc" was inspired by a view of that mountain and its surrounding peaks and valleys, as he lingered on the Bridge of Arve on his way through the Valley of Chamouni. Shelley makes the following mention of this poem in his publication of the "History of a Six Weeks' Tour, and Letters from Switzerland": 'The poem entitled "Mont Blanc" is written by the author of the two letters from Chamouni and Vevai. It was composed under the immediate impression of the deep and powerful feelings excited by the objects which it attempts to describe; and, as an undisciplined overflowing of the soul, rests its claim to approbation on an attempt to imitate the untamable wildness and inaccessible solemnity from which those feelings sprang.'

This was an eventful year, and less time was given to study than usual. In the list of his reading I find, in Greek, Theocritus, the "Prometheus" of Aeschylus, several of Plutarch's "Lives", and the works of Lucian. In Latin, Lucretius, Pliny's "Letters", the "Annals" and "Germany" of Tacitus. In French, the "History of the French Revolution" by Lacretelle. He read for the first time, this year, Montaigne's "Essays", and regarded them ever after as one of the most delightful and instructive books in the world. The list is scanty in English works: Locke's "Essay", "Political Justice", and Coleridge's "Lay Sermon", form nearly the whole. It was his frequent habit to read aloud to me in the evening; in this way we read, this year, the New Testament, "Paradise Lost", Spenser's "Faery Queen", and "Don Quixote".

NOTE ON POEMS OF 1817, BY MRS. SHELLEY.

The very illness that oppressed, and the aspect of death which had approached so near Shelley, appear to have kindled to yet keener life the Spirit of Poetry in his heart. The restless thoughts kept awake by pain clothed themselves in verse. Much was composed during this year. The "Revolt of Islam", written and printed, was a great effort—"Rosalind and Helen" was begun—and the fragments and poems I can trace to the same period show how full of passion and reflection were his solitary hours.

In addition to such poems as have an intelligible aim and shape, many a stray idea and transitory emotion found imperfect and abrupt expression, and then again lost themselves in silence. As he never wandered without a book and without implements of writing, I find many such, in his manuscript books, that scarcely bear record; while some of them, broken and vague as they are, will appear valuable to those who love Shelley's mind, and desire to trace its workings.

He projected also translating the "Hymns" of Homer; his version of several of the shorter ones remains, as well as that to Mercury already published in the "Posthumous Poems". His readings this year were chiefly Greek. Besides the "Hymns" of Homer and the "Iliad", he read the dramas of Aeschylus and Sophocles, the "Symposium" of Plato, and Arrian's "Historia Indica". In Latin, Apuleius alone is named. In English, the Bible was his constant study; he read a great portion of it aloud in the evening. Among these evening readings I find also mentioned the "Faerie

Queen"; and other modern works, the production of his contemporaries, Coleridge, Wordsworth, Moore and Byron.

His life was now spent more in thought than action—he had lost the eager spirit which believed it could achieve what it projected for the benefit of mankind. And yet in the converse of daily life Shelley was far from being a melancholy man. He was eloquent when philosophy or politics or taste were the subjects of conversation. He was playful; and indulged in the wild spirit that mocked itself and others—not in bitterness, but in sport. The author of "Nightmare Abbey" seized on some points of his character and some habits of his life when he painted Scythrop. He was not addicted to 'port or madeira,' but in youth he had read of 'Illuminati and Eleutherarchs,' and believed that he possessed the power of operating an immediate change in the minds of men and the state of society. These wild dreams had faded; sorrow and adversity had struck home; but he struggled with despondency as he did with physical pain. There are few who remember him sailing paper boats, and watching the navigation of his tiny craft with eagerness—or repeating with wild energy "The Ancient Mariner", and Southey's "Old Woman of Berkeley"; but those who do will recollect that it was in such, and in the creations of his own fancy when that was most daring and ideal, that he sheltered himself from the storms and disappointments, the pain and sorrow, that beset his life.

No words can express the anguish he felt when his elder children were torn from him. In his first resentment against the Chancellor, on the passing of the decree, he had written a curse, in which there breathes, besides haughty indignation, all the tenderness of a father's love, which could imagine and fondly dwell upon its loss and the consequences.

At one time, while the question was still pending, the Chancellor had said some words that seemed to intimate that Shelley should not be permitted the care of any of his children, and for a moment he feared that our infant son would be torn from us. He did not hesitate to resolve, if such were menaced, to abandon country, fortune, everything, and to escape with his child; and I find some unfinished stanzas addressed to this son, whom afterwards we lost at Rome, written under the idea that we might suddenly be forced to cross the sea, so to preserve him. This poem, as well as the one previously quoted, were not written to exhibit the pangs of distress to the public; they were the spontaneous outbursts of a man who brooded over his wrongs and woes, and was impelled to shed the grace of his genius over the uncontrollable emotions of his heart. I ought to observe that the fourth verse of this effusion is introduced in "Rosalind and Helen". When afterwards this child died at Rome, he wrote, a propos of the English burying-ground in that city: 'This spot is the repository of a sacred loss, of which the yearnings of a parent's heart are now prophetic; he is rendered immortal by love, as his memory is by death. My beloved child lies buried here. I envy death the body far less than the oppressors the minds of those whom they have torn from me. The one can only kill the body, the other crushes the affections.'

NOTE ON POEMS OF 1818, BY MRS. SHELLEY.

We often hear of persons disappointed by a first visit to Italy. This was not Shelley's case. The aspect of its nature, its sunny sky, its majestic storms, of the luxuriant vegetation of the country, and the noble marble-built cities, enchanted him. The sight of the works of art was full enjoyment and wonder. He had not studied pictures or statues before; he now did so with the eye of taste, that referred not to the rules of schools, but to those of Nature and truth. The first entrance to Rome opened to him a scene of remains of antique grandeur that far surpassed his expectations; and the unspeakable beauty of Naples and its environs added to the impression he received of the transcendent and glorious beauty of Italy.

Our winter was spent at Naples. Here he wrote the fragments of "Marenghi" and "The Woodman and the Nightingale", which he afterwards threw aside. At this time, Shelley suffered greatly in health. He put himself under the care of a medical man, who promised great things, and made him endure severe bodily pain, without any good results. Constant and poignant physical suffering exhausted him; and though he preserved the appearance of cheerfulness, and often greatly enjoyed our wanderings in the environs of Naples, and our excursions on its sunny sea, yet many hours were passed when his thoughts, shadowed by illness, became gloomy,—and then he escaped to solitude, and in verses, which he hid from fear of wounding me, poured forth morbid but too natural bursts of discontent and sadness. One looks back with unspeakable regret and gnawing remorse to such periods; fancying that, had one been more alive to the nature of his feelings, and more attentive to soothe them, such would not have existed. And yet, enjoying as he appeared to do every sight or influence of earth or sky, it was difficult to imagine that any melancholy he showed was aught but the effect of the constant pain to which he was a martyr.

We lived in utter solitude. And such is often not the nurse of cheerfulness; for then, at least with those who have been exposed to adversity, the mind broods over its sorrows too intently; while the society of the enlightened, the witty, and the wise, enables us to forget ourselves by making us the sharers of the thoughts of others, which is a portion of the philosophy of happiness. Shelley never liked society in numbers,—it harassed and wearied him; but neither did he like loneliness, and usually, when alone, sheltered himself against memory and reflection in a book. But, with one or two whom he loved, he gave way to wild and joyous spirits, or in more serious conversation expounded his opinions with vivacity and eloquence. If an argument arose, no man ever argued better. He was clear, logical, and earnest, in supporting his own views; attentive, patient, and impartial, while listening to those on the adverse side. Had not a wall of prejudice been raised at this time between him and his countrymen, how many would have sought the acquaintance of one whom to know was to love and to revere! How many of the more enlightened of his contemporaries have since regretted that they did not seek him! how very few knew his worth while he lived! and, of those few, several were withheld by timidity or envy from declaring their sense of it. But no man was ever more enthusiastically loved—more looked up to, as one superior to his fellows in intellectual endowments and moral worth, by the few who knew him well, and had sufficient nobleness of soul to appreciate his superiority. His excellence is now acknowledged; but, even while admitted, not duly appreciated. For who, except those who were acquainted with him, can imagine his unwearied benevolence, his generosity, his systematic forbearance? And still less is his vast superiority in intellectual attainments sufficiently understood—his sagacity, his clear understanding, his learning, his prodigious memory. All these as displayed in conversation, were known to few while he lived, and are now silent in the tomb:

> 'Ahi orbo mondo ingrato!
> Gran cagion hai di dever pianger meco;
> Che quel ben ch' era in te, perdut' hai seco.'

NOTE ON POEMS OF 1819, BY MRS. SHELLEY.

Shelley loved the People; and respected them as often more virtuous, as always more suffering, and therefore more deserving of sympathy, than the great. He believed that a clash between the two classes of society was inevitable, and he eagerly ranged himself on the people's side. He had an idea of publishing a series of poems adapted expressly to commemorate their circumstances and wrongs. He wrote a few; but, in those days of prosecution for libel, they could not be printed. They are not among the best of his productions, a writer being always shackled when he endeavours to write down to the comprehension of those who could not understand or feel a highly imaginative style; but they show his earnestness, and with what heart-felt compassion he went home to the direct point of injury—that oppression is detestable as being the parent of starvation, nakedness, and ignorance. Besides these outpourings of compassion and indignation, he had meant to adorn the cause he loved with loftier poetry of glory and triumph: such is the scope of the "Ode to the Assertors of Liberty". He sketched also a new version of our national anthem, as addressed to Liberty.

NOTE ON POEMS OF 1820, BY MRS. SHELLEY.

We spent the latter part of the year 1819 in Florence, where Shelley passed several hours daily in the Gallery, and made various notes on its ancient works of art. His thoughts were a good deal taken up also by the project of a steamboat, undertaken by a friend, an engineer, to ply between Leghorn and Marseilles, for which he supplied a sum of money. This was a sort of plan to delight Shelley, and he was greatly disappointed when it was thrown aside.

There was something in Florence that disagreed excessively with his health, and he suffered far more pain than usual; so much so that we left it sooner than we intended, and removed to Pisa, where we had some friends, and, above all, where we could consult the celebrated Vacca as to the cause of Shelley's sufferings. He, like every other medical man, could only guess at that, and gave little hope of immediate relief; he enjoined him to abstain from all physicians and medicine, and to leave his complaint to Nature. As he had vainly consulted medical men of the highest repute in England, he was easily persuaded to adopt this advice. Pain and ill-health followed him to the end; but the residence at Pisa agreed with him better than any other, and there in consequence we remained.

In the Spring we spent a week or two near Leghorn, borrowing the house of some friends who were absent on a journey to England. It was on a beautiful summer evening, while wandering among the lanes whose myrtle-hedges were the bowers of the fire-flies, that we heard the carolling of the skylark which inspired one of the most beautiful of his poems. He addressed the letter to Mrs. Gisborne from this house, which was hers: he had made his study of the workshop of her son, who was an engineer. Mrs. Gisborne had been a friend of my father in her younger days. She was a lady of great accomplishments, and charming from her frank and affectionate nature. She had the most intense love of knowledge, a delicate and trembling sensibility, and preserved freshness of mind after a life of considerable adversity. As a favourite friend of my father, we had sought her with eagerness; and the most open and cordial friendship was established between us.

Our stay at the Baths of San Giuliano was shortened by an accident. At the foot of our garden ran the canal that communicated between the Serchio and the Arno. The Serchio overflowed its banks, and, breaking its bounds, this canal also overflowed; all this part of the country is below the level of its rivers, and the consequence was that it was speedily flooded. The rising waters filled the Square of the Baths, in the lower part of which our house was situated. The canal overflowed in the garden behind; the rising waters on either side at last burst open the doors, and, meeting in the house, rose to the height of six feet. It was a picturesque sight at night to see the peasants driving the cattle from the plains below to the hills above the Baths. A fire was kept up to guide them across the ford; and the forms of the men and the animals showed in dark relief against the red glare of the flame, which was reflected again in the waters that filled the Square.

We then removed to Pisa, and took up our abode there for the winter. The extreme mildness of the climate suited Shelley, and his solitude was enlivened by an intercourse with several intimate friends. Chance cast us strangely enough on this quiet half-unpeopled town; but its very peace suited Shelley. Its river, the near mountains, and not distant sea, added to its attractions, and were the objects of many delightful excursions. We feared the south of Italy, and a hotter climate, on account of our child; our former bereavement inspiring us with terror. We seemed to take root here, and moved little afterwards; often, indeed, entertaining projects for visiting other parts of Italy, but still delaying. But for our fears on account of our child, I believe we should have wandered over the world, both being passionately fond of travelling. But human life, besides its great unalterable necessities, is ruled by a thousand lilliputian ties that shackle at the time, although it is difficult to account afterwards for their influence over our destiny.

NOTE ON POEMS OF 1821, BY MRS. SHELLEY.

My task becomes inexpressibly painful as the year draws near that which sealed our earthly fate, and each poem, and each event it records, has a real or mysterious connection with the fatal catastrophe. I feel that I am incapable of putting on paper the history of those times. The heart of the man, abhorred of the poet, who could

> 'peep and botanize
> Upon his mother's grave,'

does not appear to me more inexplicably framed than that of one who can dissect and probe past woes, and repeat to the public ear the groans drawn from them in the throes of their agony.

The year 1821 was spent in Pisa, or at the Baths of San Giuliano. We were not, as our wont had been, alone; friends had gathered round us. Nearly all are dead, and, when Memory recurs to the past, she wanders among tombs. The genius, with all his blighting errors and mighty powers; the companion of Shelley's ocean-wanderings, and the sharer of his fate, than whom no man ever existed more gentle, generous, and fearless; and others, who found in Shelley's society, and in his great knowledge and warm sympathy, delight, instruction, and solace; have joined him beyond the grave. A few survive who have felt life a desert since he left it. What misfortune can equal death? Change can convert every other into a blessing, or heal its sting—death alone has no cure. It shakes the foundations of the earth on which we tread; it destroys its beauty; it casts down our shelter; it exposes us bare to desolation. When those we love have passed into eternity, 'life is the desert and the solitude' in which we are forced to linger—but never find comfort more.

There is much in the "Adonais" which seems now more applicable to Shelley himself than to the young and gifted poet whom he mourned. The poetic view he takes of death, and the lofty scorn he displays towards his calumniators, are as a prophecy on his own destiny when received among immortal names, and the poisonous breath of critics has vanished into emptiness before the fame he inherits.

Shelley's favourite taste was boating; when living near the Thames or by the Lake of Geneva, much of his life was spent on the water. On the shore of every lake or stream or sea near which he dwelt, he had a boat moored. He had latterly enjoyed this pleasure again. There are no pleasure-boats on the Arno; and the shallowness of its waters (except in winter-time, when the stream is too turbid and impetuous for boating) rendered it difficult to get any skiff light enough to float. Shelley, however, overcame the difficulty; he, together with a friend, contrived a boat such as the huntsmen carry about with them in the Maremma, to cross the sluggish but deep streams that intersect the forests,—a boat of laths and pitched canvas. It held three persons; and he was often seen on the Arno in it, to the horror of the Italians, who remonstrated on the danger, and could not understand how anyone could take pleasure in an exercise that risked life. 'Ma va per la vita!' they exclaimed. I little thought how true their words would prove. He once ventured, with a friend, on the glassy sea of a calm day, down the Arno and round the coast to Leghorn, which, by keeping close in shore, was very practicable. They returned to Pisa by the canal, when, missing the direct cut, they got entangled among weeds, and the boat upset; a wetting was all the harm done, except that the intense cold of his drenched clothes made Shelley faint. Once I went down with him to the mouth of the Arno, where the stream, then high and swift, met the tideless sea, and disturbed its sluggish waters. It was a waste and dreary scene; the desert sand stretched into a point surrounded by waves that broke idly though perpetually around; it was a scene very similar to Lido, of which he had said—

> 'I love all waste
> And solitary places; where we taste
> The pleasure of believing what we see
> Is boundless, as we wish our souls to be:
> And such was this wide ocean, and this shore
> More barren than its billows.'

Our little boat was of greater use, unaccompanied by any danger, when we removed to the Baths. Some friends lived at the village of Pugnano, four miles off, and we went to and fro to see them, in our boat, by the canal; which, fed by the Serchio, was, though an artificial, a full and picturesque stream, making its way under verdant banks, sheltered by trees that dipped their boughs into the murmuring waters. By day, multitudes of Ephemera darted to and fro on the surface; at night, the fireflies came out among the shrubs on the banks; the cicale at noon-day kept up their hum; the aziola cooed in the quiet evening. It was a pleasant summer, bright in all but Shelley's health and inconstant spirits; yet he enjoyed himself greatly, and became more and more attached to the part of the country were chance appeared to cast us. Sometimes he projected taking a farm situated on the height of one of the near hills, surrounded by chestnut and pine woods, and overlooking a wide extent of country: or settling still farther in the maritime Apennines, at Massa. Several of his slighter and unfinished poems were inspired by these scenes, and by the companions around us. It is the nature of that poetry, however, which overflows from the soul oftener to express sorrow and regret than joy; for it is when oppressed by the weight of life, and away from those he loves, that the poet has recourse to the solace of expression in verse.

Still, Shelley's passion was the ocean; and he wished that our summers, instead of being passed among the hills near Pisa, should be spent on the shores of the sea. It was very difficult to find a spot. We shrank from Naples from a fear that the heats would disagree with Percy: Leghorn had lost its only attraction, since our friends who had resided there were returned to England; and, Monte Nero being the resort of many English, we did not wish to find ourselves in the midst of a colony of chance travellers. No one then thought it possible to reside at Via Reggio, which latterly has become a summer resort. The low lands and bad air of Maremma stretch the whole length of the western shores of the Mediterranean, till broken by the rocks and hills of Spezia. It was a vague idea, but Shelley suggested an excursion to Spezia, to see whether it would be feasible to spend a summer there. The beauty of the bay enchanted him. We saw no house to suit us; but the notion took root, and many circumstances, enchained as by fatality, occurred to urge him to execute it.

He looked forward this autumn with great pleasure to the prospect of a visit from Leigh Hunt. When Shelley visited Lord Byron at Ravenna, the latter had suggested his coming out, together with the plan of a periodical work in which they should all join. Shelley saw a prospect of good for the fortunes of his friend, and pleasure in his society; and instantly exerted himself to have the plan executed. He did not intend himself joining in the work: partly from pride, not wishing to have the air of acquiring readers for his poetry by associating it with the compositions of more popular writers; and also because he might feel shackled in the free expression of his opinions, if any friends were to be compromised. By those opinions, carried even to their outermost extent, he wished to live and die, as being in his conviction not only true, but such as alone would conduce to the moral improvement and happiness of mankind. The sale of the work might meanwhile, either really or supposedly, be injured by the free expression of his thoughts; and this evil he resolved to avoid.

NOTE ON POEMS OF 1822, BY MRS. SHELLEY.

This morn thy gallant bark
Sailed on a sunny sea:
'Tis noon, and tempests dark
Have wrecked it on the lee.
Ah woe! ah woe!
By Spirits of the deep
Thou'rt cradled on the billow
To thy eternal sleep.

Thou sleep'st upon the shore
Beside the knelling surge,
And Sea-nymphs evermore
Shall sadly chant thy dirge.
They come, they come,
The Spirits of the deep,—
While near thy seaweed pillow
My lonely watch I keep.

From far across the sea
I hear a loud lament,
By Echo's voice for thee
From Ocean's caverns sent.
O list! O list!
The Spirits of the deep!

They raise a wail of sorrow,
While I forever weep.

With this last year of the life of Shelley these Notes end. They are not what I intended them to be. I began with energy, and a burning desire to impart to the world, in worthy language, the sense I have of the virtues and genius of the beloved and the lost; my strength has failed under the task. Recurrence to the past, full of its own deep and unforgotten joys and sorrows, contrasted with succeeding years of painful and solitary struggle, has shaken my health. Days of great suffering have followed my attempts to write, and these again produced a weakness and languor that spread their sinister influence over these notes. I dislike speaking of myself, but cannot help apologizing to the dead, and to the public, for not having executed in the manner I desired the history I engaged to give of Shelley's writings. (I at one time feared that the correction of the press might be less exact through my illness; but I believe that it is nearly free from error. Some asterisks occur in a few pages, as they did in the volume of "Posthumous Poems", either because they refer to private concerns, or because the original manuscript was left imperfect. Did any one see the papers from which I drew that volume, the wonder would be how any eyes or patience were capable of extracting it from so confused a mass, interlined and broken into fragments, so that the sense could only be deciphered and joined by guesses which might seem rather intuitive than founded on reasoning. Yet I believe no mistake was made.)

The winter of 1822 was passed in Pisa, if we might call that season winter in which autumn merged into spring after the interval of but few days of bleaker weather. Spring sprang up early, and with extreme beauty. Shelley had conceived the idea of writing a tragedy on the subject of Charles I. It was one that he believed adapted for a drama; full of intense interest, contrasted character, and busy passion. He had recommended it long before, when he encouraged me to attempt a play. Whether the subject proved more difficult than he anticipated, or whether in fact he could not bend his mind away from the broodings and wanderings of thought, divested from human interest, which he best loved, I cannot tell; but he proceeded slowly, and threw it aside for one of the most mystical of his poems, the "Triumph of Life", on which he was employed at the last.

His passion for boating was fostered at this time by having among our friends several sailors. His favourite companion, Edward Ellerker Williams, of the 8th Light Dragoons, had begun his life in the navy, and had afterwards entered the army; he had spent several years in India, and his love for adventure and manly exercises accorded with Shelley's taste. It was their favourite plan to build a boat such as they could manage themselves, and, living on the sea-coast, to enjoy at every hour and season the pleasure they loved best. Captain Roberts, R.N., undertook to build the boat at Genoa, where he was also occupied in building the "Bolivar" for Lord Byron. Ours was to be an open boat, on a model taken from one of the royal dockyards. I have since heard that there was a defect in this model, and that it was never seaworthy. In the month of February, Shelley and his friend went to Spezia to seek for houses for us. Only one was to be found at all suitable; however, a trifle such as not finding a house could not stop Shelley; the one found was to serve for all. It was unfurnished; we sent our furniture by sea, and with a good deal of precipitation, arising from his impatience, made our removal. We left Pisa on the 26th of April.

The Bay of Spezia is of considerable extent, and divided by a rocky promontory into a larger and smaller one. The town of Lerici is situated on the eastern point, and in the depth of the smaller bay, which bears the name of this town, is the village of San Terenzo. Our house, Casa Magni, was close to this village; the sea came up to the door, a steep hill sheltered it behind. The proprietor of the estate on which it was situated was insane; he had begun to erect a large house at the summit of the hill behind, but his malady prevented its being finished, and it was falling into ruin. He had (and this to the Italians had seemed a glaring symptom of very decided madness) rooted up the olives on the hillside, and planted forest trees. These were mostly young, but the plantation was more in English taste than I ever elsewhere saw in Italy; some fine walnut and ilex trees intermingled their dark massy foliage, and formed groups which still haunt my memory, as then they satiated the eye with a sense of loveliness. The scene was indeed of unimaginable beauty. The blue extent of waters, the almost landlocked bay, the near castle of Lerici shutting it in to the east, and distant Porto Venere to the west; the varied forms of the precipitous rocks that bound in the beach, over which there was only a winding rugged footpath towards Lerici, and none on the other side; the tideless sea leaving no sands nor shingle, formed a picture such as one sees in Salvator Rosa's landscapes only. Sometimes the sunshine vanished when the sirocco raged—the 'ponente' the wind was called on that shore. The gales and squalls that hailed our first arrival surrounded the bay with foam; the howling wind swept round our exposed house, and the sea roared unremittingly, so that we almost fancied ourselves on board ship. At other times sunshine and calm invested sea and sky, and the rich tints of Italian heaven bathed the scene in bright and ever-varying tints.

The natives were wilder than the place. Our near neighbours of San Terenzo were more like savages than any people I ever before lived among. Many a night they passed on the beach, singing, or rather howling; the women dancing about among the waves that broke at their feet, the men leaning against the rocks and joining in their loud wild chorus. We could get no provisions nearer than Sarzana, at a distance of three miles and a half off, with the torrent of the Magra between; and even there the supply was very deficient. Had we been wrecked on an island of the South Seas, we could scarcely have felt ourselves farther from civilisation and comfort; but, where the sun shines, the latter becomes an unnecessary luxury, and we had enough society among ourselves. Yet I confess housekeeping became rather a toilsome task, especially as I was suffering in my health, and could not exert myself actively.

At first the fatal boat had not arrived, and was expected with great impatience. On Monday, 12th May, it came. Williams records the long-wished-for fact in his journal: 'Cloudy and threatening weather. M. Maglian called; and after dinner, and while walking with him on the terrace, we discovered a strange sail coming round the point of Porto Venere, which proved at length to be Shelley's boat. She had left Genoa on Thursday last, but had been driven back by the prevailing bad winds. A Mr. Heslop and two English seamen brought her round, and they speak most highly of her performances. She does indeed excite my surprise and admiration. Shelley and I walked to Lerici, and made a stretch off the land to try her: and I find she fetches whatever she looks at. In short, we have now a perfect plaything for the summer.'—It was thus that short-sighted mortals welcomed Death, he having disguised his grim form in a pleasing mask! The time of the friends was now spent on the sea; the weather became fine, and our whole party often passed the evenings on the water when the wind promised pleasant sailing. Shelley and Williams made longer excursions; they sailed several times to Massa. They had engaged one of the seamen who brought her round, a boy, by name Charles Vivian; and they had not the slightest apprehension of danger. When the weather was unfavourable, they employed themselves with alterations in the rigging, and by building a boat of canvas and reeds, as light as possible, to have on board the other for the convenience of landing in waters too shallow for the larger vessel. When Shelley was on board, he had his papers with him; and much of the "Triumph of Life" was written as he sailed or weltered on that sea which was soon to engulf him.

The heats set in in the middle of June; the days became excessively hot. But the sea-breeze cooled the air at noon, and extreme heat always put Shelley in spirits. A long drought had preceded the heat; and prayers for rain were being put up in the churches, and processions of relics for the same effect took place in every town. At this time we received letters announcing the arrival of Leigh Hunt at Genoa. Shelley was very eager to see him. I was confined to my room by severe illness, and could not move; it was agreed that Shelley and Williams should go to Leghorn in the boat. Strange that no fear of danger crossed our minds! Living on the sea-shore, the ocean became as a plaything: as a child may sport with a lighted stick, till a spark inflames a forest, and spreads destruction over all, so did we fearlessly and blindly tamper with danger, and make a game of the terrors of the ocean. Our Italian neighbours, even, trusted themselves as far as Massa in the skiff; and the running down the line of coast to Leghorn gave no more notion of peril than a fair-weather inland navigation would have done to those who had never seen the sea. Once, some months before, Trelawny had raised a warning voice as to the difference of our calm bay and the open sea beyond; but Shelley and his friend, with their one sailor-boy, thought themselves a match for the storms of the Mediterranean, in a boat which they looked upon as equal to all it was put to do.

On the 1st of July they left us. If ever shadow of future ill darkened the present hour, such was over my mind when they went. During the whole of our stay at Lerici, an intense presentiment of coming evil brooded over my mind, and covered this beautiful place and genial summer with the shadow of coming misery. I had vainly struggled with these emotions—they seemed accounted for by my illness; but at this hour of separation they recurred with renewed violence. I did not anticipate danger for them, but a vague expectation of evil shook me to agony, and I could scarcely bring myself to let them go. The day was calm and clear; and, a fine breeze rising at twelve, they weighed for Leghorn. They made the run of about fifty miles in seven hours and a half. The "Bolivar" was in port; and, the regulations of the Health-office not permitting them to go on shore after sunset, they borrowed cushions from the larger vessel, and slept on board their boat.

They spent a week at Pisa and Leghorn. The want of rain was severely felt in the country. The weather continued sultry and fine. I have heard that Shelley all this time was in brilliant spirits. Not long before, talking of presentiment, he had said the only one that he ever found infallible was the certain advent of some evil fortune when he felt peculiarly joyous. Yet, if ever fate whispered of coming disaster, such inaudible but not unfelt prognostics hovered around us. The beauty of the place seemed unearthly in its excess: the distance we were at from all signs of civilization, the sea at our feet, its murmurs or its roaring for ever in our ears,—all these things led the mind to brood over strange thoughts, and, lifting it from everyday life, caused it to be familiar with the unreal. A sort of spell surrounded us; and each day, as the voyagers did not return, we grew restless and disquieted, and yet, strange to say, we were not fearful of the most apparent danger.

The spell snapped; it was all over; an interval of agonizing doubt—of days passed in miserable journeys to gain tidings, of hopes that took firmer root even as they were more baseless—was changed to the certainty of the death that eclipsed all happiness for the survivors for evermore.

There was something in our fate peculiarly harrowing. The remains of those we lost were cast on shore; but, by the quarantine-laws of the coast, we were not permitted to have possession of them—the law with respect to everything cast on land by the sea being that such should be burned, to prevent the possibility of any remnant bringing the plague into Italy; and no representation could alter the law. At length, through the kind and unwearied exertions of Mr. Dawkins, our Charge d'Affaires at Florence, we gained permission to receive the ashes after the bodies were consumed. Nothing could equal the zeal of Trelawny in carrying our wishes into effect. He was indefatigable in his exertions, and full of forethought and sagacity in his arrangements. It was a fearful task; he stood before us at last, his hands scorched and blistered by the flames of the funeral-pyre, and by touching the burnt relics as he placed them in the receptacles prepared for the purpose. And there, in compass of that small case, was gathered all that remained on earth of him whose genius and virtue were a crown of glory to the world—whose love had been the source of happiness, peace, and good,—to be buried with him!

The concluding stanzas of the "Adonais" pointed out where the remains ought to be deposited; in addition to which our beloved child lay buried in the cemetery at Rome. Thither Shelley's ashes were conveyed; and they rest beneath one of the antique weed-grown towers that recur at intervals in the circuit of the massy ancient wall of Rome. He selected the hallowed place himself; there is

'the sepulchre,
Oh, not of him, but of our joy!—

* * * * *

And gray walls moulder round, on which dull Time
Feeds, like slow fire upon a hoary brand;
And one keen pyramid with wedge sublime,
Pavilioning the dust of him who planned
This refuge for his memory, doth stand
Like flame transformed to marble; and beneath,
A field is spread, on which a newer band
Have pitched in Heaven's smile their camp of death,
Welcoming him we lose with scarce extinguished breath.'

Could sorrow for the lost, and shuddering anguish at the vacancy left behind, be soothed by poetic imaginations, there was something in Shelley's fate to mitigate pangs which yet, alas! could not be so mitigated; for hard reality brings too miserably home to the mourner all that is lost of happiness, all of lonely unsolaced struggle that remains. Still, though dreams and hues of poetry cannot blunt grief, it invests his fate with a sublime fitness, which those less nearly allied may regard with complacency. A year before he had poured into verse all such ideas about death as give it a glory of its own. He had, as it now seems, almost anticipated his own destiny; and, when the mind figures his skiff wrapped from sight by the thunder-storm, as it was last seen upon the purple sea, and then, as the cloud of the tempest passed away, no sign remained of where it had been (Captain Roberts watched the vessel with his glass from the top of the lighthouse of Leghorn, on its homeward track. They were off Via Reggio, at some distance from shore, when a storm was driven over the sea. It enveloped them and several larger vessels in darkness. When the cloud passed onwards, Roberts looked again, and saw every other vessel sailing on the ocean except their little schooner, which had vanished. From that time he could scarcely doubt the fatal truth; yet we fancied that they might have been driven towards Elba or Corsica, and so be saved. The observation made as to the spot where the boat disappeared caused it to be found, through the exertions of Trelawny for that effect. It had gone down in ten fathom water; it had not capsized, and, except such things as had floated from her, everything was found on board exactly as it had been placed when they sailed. The boat itself was uninjured. Roberts possessed himself of her, and decked her; but she proved not seaworthy, and her shattered planks now lie rotting on the shore of one of the Ionian islands, on which she was wrecked.)—who but will regard as a prophecy the last stanza of the "Adonais"?

> 'The breath whose might I have invoked in song
> Descends on me; my spirit's bark is driven,
> Far from the shore, far from the trembling throng
> Whose sails were never to the tempest given;
> The massy earth and sphered skies are riven!
> I am borne darkly, fearfully, afar;
> Whilst burning through the inmost veil of Heaven,
> The soul of Adonais, like a star,
> Beacons from the abode where the Eternal are.'

Putney, May 1, 1839.

MATHILDA

Edited by ELIZABETH NITCHIE

PREFACE

This volume prints for the first time the full text of Mary Shelley's novelette *Mathilda* together with the opening pages of its rough draft, *The Fields of Fancy*. They are transcribed from the microfilm of the notebooks belonging to Lord Abinger which is in the library of Duke University.

The text follows Mary Shelley's manuscript exactly except for the omission of mere corrections by the author, most of which are negligible; those that are significant are included and explained in the notes. Footnotes indicated by an asterisk are Mrs. Shelley's own notes. She was in general a fairly good speller, but certain words, especially those in which there was a question of doubling or not doubling a letter, gave her trouble: untill (though occasionally she deleted the final *l* or wrote the word correctly), agreable, occured, confering, buble, meaness, receeded, as well as hopless, lonly, seperate, extactic, sacrifise, desart, and words ending in -ance or -ence. These and other mispellings (even those of proper names) are reproduced without change or comment. The use of *sic* and of square brackets is reserved to indicate evident slips of the pen, obviously incorrect, unclear, or incomplete phrasing and punctuation, and my conjectures in emending them.

I am very grateful to the library of Duke University and to its librarian, Dr. Benjamin E. Powell, not only for permission to transcribe and publish this work by Mary Shelley but also for the many courtesies shown to me when they welcomed me as a visiting scholar in 1956. To Lord Abinger also my thanks are due for adding his approval of my undertaking, and to the Curators of the Bodleian Library for permiting me to use and to quote from the papers in the reserved Shelley Collection. Other libraries and individuals helped me while I was editing *Mathilda*: the Enoch Pratt Free Library of Baltimore, whose Literature and Reference Departments went to endless trouble for me; the Julia Rogers Library of Goucher College and its staff; the library of the University of Pennsylvania; Miss R. Glynn Grylls (Lady Mander); Professor Lewis Patton of Duke University; Professor Frederick L. Jones of the University of Pennsylvania; and many other persons who did me favors that seemed to them small but that to me were very great.

I owe much also to previous books by and about the Shelleys. Those to which I have referred more than once in the introduction and notes are here given with the abbreviated form which I have used:

Frederick L. Jones, ed. *The Letters of Mary W. Shelley*, 2 vols. Norman: University of Oklahoma Press, 1944 (*Letters*)

—*Mary Shelley's Journal*. Norman: University of Oklahoma Press, 1947 (*Journal*)

Roger Ingpen and W.E. Peck, eds. *The Complete Works of Percy Bysshe Shelley*, Julian Edition, 10 vols. London, 1926-1930 (Julian *Works*)

Newman Ivey White. *Shelley*, 2 vols. New York: Knopf, 1940 (White, *Shelley*)

Elizabeth Nitchie. *Mary Shelley, Author of "Frankenstein."* New Brunswick: Rutgers University Press, 1953 (Nitchie, *Mary Shelley*)

Elizabeth Nitchie
May, 1959

INTRODUCTION

Of all the novels and stories which Mary Wollstonecraft Shelley left in manuscript,[i] only one novelette, *Mathilda*, is complete. It exists in both rough draft and final copy. In this story, as in all Mary Shelley's writing, there is much that is autobiographical: it would be hard to find a more self-revealing work. For an understanding of Mary's character, especially as she saw herself, and of her attitude toward Shelley and toward Godwin in 1819, this tale is an important document. Although the main narrative, that of the father's incestuous love for his daughter, his suicide, and Mathilda's consequent withdrawal from society to a lonely heath, is not in any real sense autobiographical, many elements in it are drawn from reality. The three main characters are clearly Mary herself, Godwin, and Shelley, and their relations can easily be reassorted to correspond with actuality.

Highly personal as the story was, Mary Shelley hoped that it would be published, evidently believing that the characters and the situations were sufficiently disguised. In May of 1820 she sent it to England by her friends, the Gisbornes, with a request that her father would arrange for its publication. But *Mathilda*, together with its rough draft entitled *The Fields of Fancy*, remained unpublished among the Shelley papers. Although Mary's references to it in her letters and journal aroused some curiosity among scholars, it also remained unexamined until comparatively recently.

This seeming neglect was due partly to the circumstances attending the distribution of the family papers after the deaths of Sir Percy and Lady Shelley. One part of them went to the Bodleian Library to become a reserved collection which, by the terms of Lady Shelley's will, was opened to scholars only under definite restrictions. Another part went to Lady Shelley's niece and, in turn, to her heirs, who for a time did not make the manuscripts available for study. A third part went to Sir John Shelley-Rolls, the poet's grand-nephew, who released much important Shelley material, but not all the scattered manuscripts. In this division, the two notebooks containing the finished draft of *Mathilda* and a portion of *The Fields of Fancy* went to Lord Abinger, the notebook containing the remainder of the rough draft to the Bodleian Library, and some loose sheets containing additions and revisions to Sir John Shelley-Rolls. Happily all the manuscripts are now accessible to scholars, and it is possible to publish the full text of *Mathilda* with such additions from *The Fields of Fancy* as are significant.[ii]

The three notebooks are alike in format.[iii] One of Lord Abinger's notebooks contains the first part of *The Fields of Fancy*, Chapter 1 through the beginning of Chapter 10, 116 pages. The concluding portion occupies the first fifty-four pages of the Bodleian notebook. There is then a blank page, followed by three and a half pages, scored out, of what seems to be a variant of the end of Chapter 1 and the beginning of Chapter 2. A revised and expanded version of the first part of Mathilda's narrative follows (Chapter 2 and the beginning of Chapter 3), with a break between the account of her girlhood in Scotland and the brief description of her father after his return. Finally there are four pages of a new opening, which was used in *Mathilda*. This is an extremely rough draft: punctuation is largely confined to the dash, and there are many corrections and alterations. The Shelley-Rolls fragments, twenty-five sheets or slips of paper, usually represent additions to or revisions of *The Fields of Fancy*: many of them are numbered, and some are keyed into the manuscript in Lord Abinger's notebook. Most of the changes were incorporated in *Mathilda*.

The second Abinger notebook contains the complete and final draft of *Mathilda*, 226 pages. It is for the most part a fair copy. The text is punctuated and there are relatively few corrections, most of them, apparently the result of a final rereading, made to avoid the repetition of words. A few additions are written in the margins. On several pages slips of paper containing evident revisions (quite possibly originally among the Shelley-Rolls fragments) have been pasted over the corresponding lines of the text. An occasional passage is scored out and some words and phrases are crossed out to make way for a revision. Following page 216, four sheets containing the conclusion of the story are cut out of the notebook. They appear, the pages numbered 217 to 223, among the Shelley-Rolls fragments. A revised version, pages 217 to 226, follows the cut.[iv]

The mode of telling the story in the final draft differs radically from that in the rough draft. In *The Fields of Fancy* Mathilda's history is set in a fanciful framework. The author is transported by the fairy Fantasia to the Elysian Fields, where she listens to the discourse of Diotima and meets Mathilda. Mathilda tells her story, which closes with her death. In the final draft this unrealistic and largely irrelevant framework is discarded: Mathilda, whose death is approaching, writes out for her friend Woodville the full details of her tragic history which she had never had the courage to tell him in person.

The title of the rough draft, *The Fields of Fancy*, and the setting and framework undoubtedly stem from Mary Wollstonecraft's unfinished tale, *The Cave of Fancy*, in which one of the souls confined in the center of the earth to purify themselves from the dross of their earthly existence tells to Sagesta (who may be compared with Diotima) the story of her ill-fated love for a man whom she hopes to rejoin after her purgation is completed.[v] Mary was completely familiar with her mother's works. This title was, of course, abandoned when the framework was abandoned, and the name of the heroine was substituted. Though it is worth noticing that Mary chose a name with the same initial letter as her own, it was probably taken from Dante. There are several references in the story to the cantos of the *Purgatorio* in which Mathilda appears. Mathilda's father is never named, nor is Mathilda's surname given. The name of the poet went through several changes: Welford, Lovel, Herbert, and finally Woodville.

The evidence for dating *Mathilda* in the late summer and autumn of 1819 comes partly from the manuscript, partly from Mary's journal. On the pages succeeding the portions of *The Fields of Fancy* in the Bodleian notebook are some of Shelley's drafts of verse and prose, including parts of *Prometheus Unbound* and of *Epipsychidion*, both in Italian, and of the preface to the latter in English, some prose fragments, and extended portions of the *Defence of Poetry*. Written from the other end of the book are the *Ode to Naples* and *The Witch of Atlas*. Since these all belong to the years 1819, 1820, and 1821, it is probable that Mary finished her rough draft some time in 1819, and that when she had copied her story, Shelley took over the notebook. Chapter 1 of *Mathilda* in Lord Abinger's notebook is headed, "Florence Nov. 9th. 1819." Since the whole of Mathilda's story takes place in England and Scotland, the date must be that of the manuscript. Mary was in Florence at that time.

These dates are supported by entries in Mary's journal which indicate that she began writing *Mathilda*, early in August, while the Shelleys were living in the Villa Valosano, near Leghorn. On August 4, 1819, after a gap of two months from the time of her little son's death, she resumed her diary. Almost every day thereafter for a month she recorded, "Write," and by September 4, she was saying, "Copy." On September 12 she wrote, "Finish copying my Tale." The next entry to indicate literary activity is the one word, "write," on November 8. On the 12th Percy Florence was born, and Mary did no more writing until March, when she was working on *Valperga*. It is probable, therefore, that Mary wrote and copied *Mathilda* between August 5 and September 12, 1819, that she did some revision on November 8 and finally dated the manuscript November 9.

The subsequent history of the manuscript is recorded in letters and journals. When the Gisbornes went to England on May 2, 1820, they took *Mathilda* with them; they read it on the journey and recorded their admiration of it in their journal.[vi] They were to show it to Godwin and get his advice about publishing it. Although Medwin heard about the story when he was with the Shelleys in 1820[vii] and Mary read it—perhaps from the rough draft—to Edward and Jane Williams in the summer of 1821,[viii] this manuscript apparently stayed in Godwin's hands. He evidently did not share the Gisbornes' enthusiasm: his approval was qualified. He thought highly of certain parts of it, less highly of others; and he regarded the subject as "disgusting and detestable," saying that the story would need a preface to prevent readers "from being tormented by the apprehension . . . of the fall of the heroine,"—that is, if it was ever published.[ix] There is, however, no record of his having made any attempt to get it into print. From January 18 through June 2, 1822, Mary repeatedly asked Mrs. Gisborne to retrieve the manuscript and have it copied for her, and Mrs. Gisborne invariably reported her failure to do so. The last references to the story are after Shelley's death in an unpublished journal entry and two of Mary's letters. In her journal for October 27, 1822, she told of the solace for her misery she had once found in writing *Mathilda*. In one letter to Mrs. Gisborne she compared the journey of herself and Jane to Pisa and Leghorn to get news of Shelley and Williams to that of Mathilda in search of her father, "driving—(like Matilda), towards the *sea* to learn if we were to be for ever doomed to misery."[x] And on May 6, 1823, she wrote, "Matilda foretells even many small circumstances most truly—and the whole of it is a monument of what now is."[xi]

These facts not only date the manuscript but also show Mary's feeling of personal involvement in the story. In the events of 1818-1819 it is possible to find the basis for this morbid tale and consequently to assess its biographical significance.

On September 24, 1818, the Shelleys' daughter, Clara Everina, barely a year old, died at Venice. Mary and her children had gone from Bagni di Lucca to Este to join Shelley at Byron's villa. Clara was not well when they started, and she grew worse on the journey. From Este Shelley and Mary took her to Venice to consult a physician, a trip which was beset with delays and difficulties. She died almost as soon as they arrived. According to Newman Ivey White,[xii] Mary, in the unreasoning agony of her grief, blamed Shelley for the child's death and for a time felt toward him an extreme physical antagonism which subsided into apathy and spiritual alienation. Mary's black moods made her difficult to live with, and Shelley himself fell into deep dejection. He expressed his sense of their estrangement in some of the lyrics of 1818—"all my saddest poems." In one fragment of verse, for example, he lamented that Mary had left him "in this dreary world alone."

> Thy form is here indeed—a lovely one—
> But thou art fled, gone down the dreary road,
> That leads to Sorrow's most obscure abode.
> Thou sittest on the hearth of pale despair,
>   Where
> For thine own sake I cannot follow thee.

Professor White believed that Shelley recorded this estrangement only "in veiled terms" in *Julian and Maddalo* or in poems that he did not show to Mary, and that Mary acknowledged it only after Shelley's death, in her poem "The Choice" and in her editorial notes on his poems of that year. But this unpublished story, written after the death of their other child William, certainly contains, though also in veiled terms, Mary's immediate recognition and remorse. Mary well knew, I believe, what she was doing to Shelley. In an effort to purge her own emotions and to acknowledge her fault, she poured out on the pages of *Mathilda* the suffering and the loneliness, the bitterness and the self-recrimination of the past months.

The biographical elements are clear: Mathilda is certainly Mary herself; Mathilda's father is Godwin; Woodville is an idealized Shelley.

Like Mathilda Mary was a woman of strong passions and affections which she often hid from the world under a placid appearance. Like Mathilda's, Mary's mother had died a few days after giving her birth. Like Mathilda she spent part of her girlhood in Scotland. Like Mathilda she met and loved a poet of "exceeding beauty," and—also like Mathilda—in that sad year she had treated him ill, having become "captious and unreasonable" in her sorrow. Mathilda's loneliness, grief, and remorse can be paralleled in Mary's later journal and in "The Choice." This story was the outlet for her emotions in 1819.

Woodville, the poet, is virtually perfect, "glorious from his youth," like "an angel with winged feet"—all beauty, all goodness, all gentleness. He is also successful as a poet, his poem written at the age of twenty-three having been universally acclaimed. Making allowance for Mary's exaggeration and wishful thinking, we easily recognize Shelley: Woodville has his poetic ideals, the charm of his conversation, his high moral qualities, his sense of dedication and responsibility to those he loved and to all humanity. He is Mary's earliest portrait of her husband, drawn in a year when she was slowly returning to him from "the hearth of pale despair."

The early circumstances and education of Godwin and of Mathilda's father were different. But they produced similar men, each extravagant, generous, vain, dogmatic. There is more of Godwin in this tale than the account of a great man ruined by character and circumstance. The relationship between father and daughter, before it was destroyed by the father's unnatural passion, is like that between Godwin and Mary. She herself called her love for him "excessive and romantic."[xiii] She may well have been recording, in Mathilda's sorrow over her alienation from her father and her loss of him by death, her own grief at a spiritual separation from Godwin through what could only seem to her his cruel lack of sympathy. He had accused her of being cowardly and insincere in her grief over Clara's death[xiv] and later he belittled her loss of William.[xv] He had also called Shelley "a disgraceful and flagrant person" because of Shelley's refusal to send him more money.[xvi] No wonder if Mary felt that, like Mathilda, she had lost a beloved but cruel father.

Thus Mary took all the blame for the rift with Shelley upon herself and transferred the physical alienation to the break in sympathy with Godwin.

That she turned these facts into a story of incest is undoubtedly due to the interest which she and Shelley felt in the subject at this time. They regarded it as a dramatic and effective theme. In August of 1819 Shelley completed *The Cenci*. During its progress he had talked over with Mary the arrangement of scenes; he had even suggested at the outset that she write the tragedy herself. And about a year earlier he had been urging upon her a translation of Alfieri's *Myrrha*. Thomas Medwin, indeed, thought that the story which she was writing in 1819 was specifically based on *Myrrha*. That she was thinking of that tragedy while writing *Mathilda* is evident from her effective use of it at one of the crises in the tale. And perhaps she was remembering her own handling of the theme when she wrote the biographical sketch of Alfieri for Lardner's *Cabinet Cyclopaedia* nearly twenty years later. She then spoke of the difficulties inherent in such a subject, "inequality of age adding to the unnatural incest. To shed any interest over such an attachment, the dramatist ought to adorn the father with such youthful attributes as would be by no means contrary to probability."[xvii] This she endeavored to do in *Mathilda* (aided indeed by the fact that the situation was the reverse of that in *Myrrha*). Mathilda's father was young: he married before he was twenty. When he returned to Mathilda, he still showed "the ardour and freshness of feeling incident to youth." He lived in the past and saw his dead wife reincarnated in his daughter. Thus Mary attempts to validate the situation and make it "by no means contrary to probability."

Mathilda offers a good example of Mary Shelley's methods of revision. A study of the manuscript shows that she was a careful workman, and that in polishing this bizarre story she strove consistently for greater credibility and realism, more dramatic (if sometimes melodramatic) presentation of events, better motivation, conciseness, and exclusion of purple passages. In the revision and rewriting, many additions were made, so that *Mathilda* is appreciably longer than *The Fields of Fancy*. But the additions are usually improvements: a much fuller account of Mathilda's father and mother and of their marriage, which makes of them something more than lay figures and to a great extent explains the tragedy; development of the character of the Steward, at first merely the servant who accompanies Mathilda in her search for her father, into the sympathetic confidant whose responses help to dramatise the situation; an added word or short phrase that marks Mary Shelley's penetration into the motives and actions of both Mathilda and her father. Therefore *Mathilda* does not impress the reader as being longer than *The Fields of Fancy* because it better sustains his interest. And with all the additions there are also effective omissions of the obvious, of the tautological, of the artificially elaborate.[xviii]

The finished draft, *Mathilda*, still shows Mary Shelley's faults as a writer: verbosity, loose plotting, somewhat stereotyped and extravagant characterization. The reader must be tolerant of its heroine's overwhelming lamentations. But she is, after all, in the great tradition of romantic heroines: she compares her own weeping to that of Boccaccio's Ghismonda over the heart of Guiscardo. If the reader can accept Mathilda on her own terms, he will find not only biographical interest in her story but also intrinsic merits: a feeling for character and situation and phrasing that is often vigorous and precise.

MATHILDA[1]

CHAP. I

Florence. Nov. 9th 1819

It is only four o'clock; but it is winter and the sun has already set: there are no clouds in the clear, frosty sky to reflect its slant beams, but the air itself is tinged with a slight roseate colour which is again reflected on the snow that covers the ground. I live in a lone cottage on a solitary, wide heath: no voice of life reaches me. I see the desolate plain covered with white, save a few black patches that the noonday sun has made at the top of those sharp pointed hillocks from which the snow, sliding as it fell, lay thinner than on the plain ground: a few birds are pecking at the hard ice that covers the pools—for the frost has been of long continuance.[2]

I am in a strange state of mind.[3] I am alone—quite alone—in the world—the blight of misfortune has passed over me and withered me; I know that I am about to die and I feel happy—joyous.—I feel my pulse; it beats fast: I place my thin hand on my cheek; it burns: there is a slight, quick spirit within me which is now emitting its last sparks. I shall never see the snows of another winter—I do believe that I shall never again feel the vivifying warmth of another summer sun; and it is in this persuasion that I begin to write my tragic history. Perhaps a history such as mine had better die with me, but a feeling that I cannot define leads me on and I am too weak both in body and mind to resist the slightest impulse. While life was strong within me I thought indeed that there was a sacred horror in my tale that rendered it unfit for utterance, and now about to die I pollute its mystic terrors. It is as the wood of the Eumenides none but the dying may enter; and Oedipus is about to die.[4]

What am I writing?—I must collect my thoughts. I do not know that any will peruse these pages except you, my friend, who will receive them at my death. I do not address them to you alone because it will give me pleasure to dwell upon our friendship in a way that would be needless if you alone read what I shall write. I shall relate my tale therefore as if I wrote for strangers. You have often asked me the cause of my solitary life; my tears; and above all of my impenetrable and unkind silence. In life I dared not; in death I unveil the mystery. Others will toss these pages lightly over: to you, Woodville, kind, affectionate friend, they will be dear—the precious memorials of a heart-broken girl who, dying, is still warmed by gratitude towards you:[5] your tears will fall on the words that record my misfortunes; I know they will—and while I have life I thank you for your sympathy.

But enough of this. I will begin my tale: it is my last task, and I hope I have strength sufficient to fulfill it. I record no crimes; my faults may easily be pardoned; for they proceeded not from evil motive but from want of judgement; and I believe few would say that they could, by a different conduct and superior wisdom, have avoided the misfortunes to which I am the victim. My fate has been governed by necessity, a hideous necessity. It required hands stronger than mine; stronger I do believe than any human force to break the thick, adamantine chain that has bound me, once breathing nothing but joy, ever possessed by a warm love & delight in goodness,—to misery only to be ended, and now about to be ended, in death. But I forget myself, my tale is yet untold. I will pause a few moments, wipe my dim eyes, and endeavour to lose the present obscure but heavy feeling of unhappiness in the more acute emotions of the past.[6]

I was born in England. My father was a man of rank:[7] he had lost his father early, and was educated by a weak mother with all the indulgence she thought due to a nobleman of wealth. He was sent to Eton and afterwards to college; & allowed from childhood the free use of large sums of money; thus enjoying from his earliest youth the independance which a boy with these advantages, always acquires at a public school.

Under the influence of these circumstances his passions found a deep soil wherein they might strike their roots and flourish either as flowers or weeds as was their nature. By being always allowed to act for himself his character became strongly and early marked and exhibited a various surface on which a quick sighted observer might see the seeds of virtues and of misfortunes. His careless extravagance, which made him squander immense sums of money to satisfy passing whims, which from their apparent energy he dignified with the name of passions, often displayed itself in unbounded generosity. Yet while he earnestly occupied himself about the wants of others his own desires were gratified to their fullest extent. He gave his money, but none of his own wishes were sacrifised to his gifts; he gave his time, which he did not value, and his affections which he was happy in any manner to have called into action.

I do not say that if his own desires had been put in competition with those of others that he would have displayed undue selfishness, but this trial was never made. He was nurtured in prosperity and attended by all its advantages; every one loved him and wished to gratify him. He was ever employed in promoting the pleasures of his companions—but their pleasures were his; and if he bestowed more attention upon the feelings of others than is usual with schoolboys it was because his social temper could never enjoy itself if every brow was not as free from care as his own.

While at school, emulation and his own natural abilities made him hold a conspicuous rank in the forms among his equals; at college he discarded books; he believed that he had other lessons to learn than those which they could teach him. He was now to enter into life and he was still young enough to consider study as a school-boy shackle, employed merely to keep the unruly out of mischief but as having no real connexion with life—whose wisdom of riding—gaming &c. he considered with far deeper interest—So he quickly entered into all college follies although his heart was too well moulded to be contaminated by them—it might be light but it was never cold. He was a sincere and sympathizing friend—but he had met with none who superior or equal to himself could aid him in unfolding his mind, or make him seek for fresh stores of thought by exhausting the old ones. He felt himself superior in quickness of judgement to those around him: his talents, his rank and wealth made him the chief of his party, and in that station he rested not only contented but glorying, conceiving it to be the only ambition worthy for him to aim at in the world.

By a strange narrowness of ideas he viewed all the world in connexion only as it was or was not related to his little society. He considered queer and out of fashion all opinions that were exploded by his circle of intimates, and he became at the same time dogmatic and yet fearful of not coinciding with the only sentiments he could consider orthodox. To the generality of spectators he appeared careless of censure, and with high disdain to throw aside all dependance on public prejudices; but at the same time that he strode with a triumphant stride over the rest of the world, he cowered, with self disguised lowliness, to his own party, and although its [chi]ef never dared express an opinion or a feeling until he was assured that it would meet with the approbation of his companions.

Yet he had one secret hidden from these dear friends; a secret he had nurtured from his earliest years, and although he loved his fellow collegiates he would not trust it to the delicacy or sympathy of any one among them. He loved. He feared that the intensity of his passion might become the subject of their ridicule; and he could not bear that they should blaspheme it by considering that trivial and transitory which he felt was the life of his life.

There was a gentleman of small fortune who lived near his family mansion who had three lovely daughters. The eldest was far the most beautiful, but her beauty was only an addition to her other qualities—her understanding was clear & strong and her disposition angelically gentle. She and my father had been playmates from infancy: Diana, even in her childhood had been a favourite with his mother; this partiality encreased with the years of this beautiful and lively girl and thus during his school & college vacations[8] they were perpetually together. Novels and all the various methods by which youth in civilized life are led to a knowledge of the existence of passions before they really feel them, had produced a strong effect on him who was so peculiarly susceptible of every impression. At eleven years of age Diana was his favourite playmate but he already talked the language of love. Although she was elder than he by nearly two years the nature of her education made her more childish at least in the knowledge and expression of feeling; she received his warm protestations with innocence, and returned them unknowing of what they meant. She had read no novels and associated only with her younger sisters, what could she know of the difference between love and friendship? And when the development of her understanding disclosed the true nature of this intercourse to her, her affections were already engaged to her friend, and all she feared was lest other attractions and fickleness might make him break his infant vows.

But they became every day more ardent and tender. It was a passion that had grown with his growth; it had become entwined with every faculty and every sentiment and only to be lost with life. None knew of their love except their own two hearts; yet although in all things else, and even in this he dreaded the censure of his companions, for thus truly loving one inferior to him in fortune, nothing was ever able for a moment to shake his purpose of uniting himself to her as soon as he could muster courage sufficient to meet those difficulties he was determined to surmount.

Diana was fully worthy of his deepest affection. There were few who could boast of so pure a heart, and so much real humbleness of soul joined to a firm reliance on her own integrity and a belief in that of others. She had from her birth lived a retired life. She had lost her mother when very young, but her father had devoted himself to the care of her education—He had many peculiar ideas which influenced the system he had adopted with regard to her—She was well acquainted with the heroes of Greece and Rome or with those of England who had lived some hundred years ago, while she was nearly ignorant of the passing events of the day: she had read few authors who had written during at least the last fifty years but her reading with this exception was very extensive. Thus although she appeared to be less initiated in the mysteries of life and society than he her knowledge was of a deeper kind and laid on firmer foundations; and if even her beauty and sweetness had not fascinated him her understanding would ever have held his in thrall. He looked up to her as his guide, and such was his adoration that he delighted to augment to his own mind the sense of inferiority with which she sometimes impressed him.[9]

When he was nineteen his mother died. He left college on this event and shaking off for a while his old friends he retired to the neighbourhood of his Diana and received all his consolation from her sweet voice and dearer caresses. This short seperation from his companions gave him courage to assert his independance. He had a feeling that however they might express ridicule of his intended marriage they would not dare display it when it had taken place; therefore seeking the consent of his guardian which with some difficulty he obtained, and of the father of his mistress which was more easily given, without acquainting any one else of his intention, by the time he had attained his twentieth birthday he had become the husband of Diana.

He loved her with passion and her tenderness had a charm for him that would not permit him to think of aught but her. He invited some of his college friends to see him but their frivolity disgusted him. Diana had torn the veil which had before kept him in his boyhood: he was become a man and he was surprised how he could ever have joined in the cant words and ideas of his fellow collegiates or how for a moment he had feared the censure of such as these. He discarded his old friendships not from fickleness but because they were indeed unworthy of him. Diana filled up all his heart: he felt as if by his union with her he had received a new and better soul. She was his monitress as he learned what were the true ends of life. It was through her beloved lessons that he cast off his old pursuits and gradually formed himself to become one among his fellow men; a distinguished member of society, a Patriot; and an enlightened lover of truth and virtue.—He loved her for her beauty and for her amiable disposition but he seemed to love her more for what he considered her superior wisdom. They studied, they rode together; they were never seperate and seldom admitted a third to their society.

Thus my father, born in affluence, and always prosperous, clombe without the difficulty and various disappointments that all human beings seem destined to encounter, to the very topmost pinacle of happiness: Around him was sunshine, and clouds whose shapes of beauty made the prospect divine concealed from him the barren reality which lay hidden below them. From this dizzy point he was dashed at once as he unawares congratulated himself on his felicity. Fifteen months after their marriage I was born, and my mother died a few days after my birth.

A sister of my father was with him at this period. She was nearly fifteen years older than he, and was the offspring of a former marriage of his father. When the latter died this sister was taken by her maternal relations: they had seldom seen one another, and were quite unlike in disposition. This aunt, to whose care I was afterwards consigned, has often related to me the effect that this catastrophe had on my father's strong and susceptible character. From the moment of my mother's death untill his departure she never heard him utter a single word: buried in the deepest melancholy he took no notice of any one; often for hours his eyes streamed tears or a more fearful gloom overpowered him. All outward things seemed to have lost their existence relatively to him and only one circumstance could in any degree recall him from his motionless and mute despair: he would never see me. He seemed insensible to the presence of any one else, but if, as a trial to awaken his sensibility, my aunt brought me into the room he would instantly rush out with every symptom of fury and distraction. At the end of a month he suddenly quitted his house and, unatteneded by any servant, departed from that part of the country without by word or writing informing any one of his intentions. My aunt was only relieved of her anxiety concerning his fate by a letter from him dated Hamburgh.

How often have I wept over that letter which untill I was sixteen was the only relick I had to remind me of my parents. "Pardon me," it said, "for the uneasiness I have unavoidably given you: but while in that unhappy island, where every thing breathes *her* spirit whom I have lost for ever, a spell held me. It is broken: I have quitted England for many years, perhaps for ever. But to convince you that selfish feeling does not entirely engross me I shall remain in this town untill you have made by letter every arrangement that you judge necessary. When I leave this place do not expect to hear from me: I must break all ties that at present exist. I shall become a wanderer, a miserable outcast—alone! alone!"—In another part of the letter he mentioned me—"As for that unhappy little being whom I could not see, and hardly dare mention, I leave her under your protection. Take care of her and cherish her: one day I may claim her at your hands; but futurity is dark, make the present happy to her."

My father remained three months at Hamburgh; when he quitted it he changed his name, my aunt could never discover that which he adopted and only by faint hints, could conjecture that he had taken the road of Germany and Hungary to Turkey.[10]

Thus this towering spirit who had excited interest and high expectation in all who knew and could value him became at once, as it were, extinct. He existed from this moment for himself only. His friends remembered him as a brilliant vision which would never again return to them. The memory of what he had been faded away as years passed; and he who before had been as a part of themselves and of their hopes was now no longer counted among the living.

CHAPTER II

I now come to my own story. During the early part of my life there is little to relate, and I will be brief; but I must be allowed to dwell a little on the years of my childhood that it may be apparent how when one hope failed all life was to be a blank; and how when the only affection I was permitted to cherish was blasted my existence was extinguished with it.

I have said that my aunt was very unlike my father. I believe that without the slightest tinge of a bad heart she had the coldest that ever filled a human breast: it was totally incapable of any affection. She took me under her protection because she considered it her duty; but she had too long lived alone and undisturbed by the noise and prattle of children to allow that I should disturb her quiet. She had never been married; and for the last five years had lived perfectly alone on an estate, that had descended to her through her mother, on the shores of Loch Lomond in Scotland. My father had expressed a wish in his letters that she should reside with me at his family mansion which was situated in a beautiful country near Richmond in Yorkshire. She would not consent to this proposition, but as soon as she had arranged the affairs which her brother's departure had caused to fall to her care, she quitted England and took me with her to her scotch estate.

The care of me while a baby, and afterwards untill I had reached my eighth year devolved on a servant of my mother's, who had accompanied us in our retirement for that purpose. I was placed in a remote part of the house, and only saw my aunt at stated hours. These occurred twice a day; once about noon she came to my nursery, and once after her dinner I was taken to her. She never caressed me, and seemed all the time I staid in the room to fear that I should annoy her by some childish freak. My good nurse always schooled me with the greatest care before she ventured into the parlour—and the awe my aunt's cold looks and few constrained words inspired was so great that I seldom disgraced her lessons or was betrayed from the exemplary stillness which I was taught to observe during these short visits.[11]

Under my good nurse's care I ran wild about our park and the neighbouring fields. The offspring of the deepest love I displayed from my earliest years the greatest sensibility of disposition. I cannot say with what passion I loved every thing even the inanimate objects that surrounded me. I believe that I bore an individual attachment to every tree in our park; every animal that inhabited it knew me and I loved them. Their occasional deaths filled my infant heart with anguish. I cannot number the birds that I have saved during the long and severe winters of that climate; or the hares and rabbits that I have defended from the attacks of our dogs, or have nursed when accidentally wounded.

When I was seven years of age my nurse left me. I now forget the cause of her departure if indeed I ever knew it. She returned to England, and the bitter tears she shed at parting were the last I saw flow for love of me for many years. My grief was terrible: I had no friend but her in the whole world. By degrees I became reconciled to solitude but no one supplied her place in my affections. I lived in a desolate country where

>   —there were none to praise
>   And very few to love.[A]

It is true that I now saw a little more of my aunt, but she was in every way an unsocial being; and to a timid child she was as a plant beneath a thick covering of ice; I should cut my hands in endeavouring to get at it. So I was entirely thrown upon my own resources. The neighbouring minister was engaged to give me lessons in reading, writing and french, but he was without family and his manners even to me were always perfectly characteristic of the profession in the exercise of whose functions he chiefly shone, that of a schoolmaster. I sometimes strove to form friendships with the most attractive of the girls who inhabited the neighbouring village; but I believe I should never have succeeded [even] had not my aunt interposed her authority to prevent all intercourse between me and the peasantry; for she was fearful lest I should acquire the scotch accent and dialect; a little of it I had, although great pains was taken that my tongue should not disgrace my English origin.

As I grew older my liberty encreased with my desires, and my wanderings extended from our park to the neighbouring country. Our house was situated on the shores of the lake and the lawn came down to the water's edge. I rambled amidst the wild scenery of this lovely country and became a complete mountaineer: I passed hours on the steep brow of a mountain that overhung a waterfall or rowed myself in a little skiff to some one of the islands. I wandered for ever about these lovely solitudes, gathering flower after flower

>Ond' era pinta tutta la mia via[B]

singing as I might the wild melodies of the country, or occupied by pleasant day dreams. My greatest pleasure was the enjoyment of a serene sky amidst these verdant woods: yet I loved all the changes of Nature; and rain, and storm, and the beautiful clouds of heaven brought their delights with them. When rocked by the waves of the lake my spirits rose in triumph as a horseman feels with pride the motions of his high fed steed.

But my pleasures arose from the contemplation of nature alone, I had no companion: my warm affections finding no return from any other human heart were forced to run waste on inanimate objects.[12] Sometimes indeed I wept when my aunt received my caresses with repulsive coldness, and when I looked round and found none to love; but I quickly dried my tears. As I grew older books in some degree supplied the place of human intercourse: the library of my aunt was very small; Shakespear, Milton, Pope and Cowper were the strangley assorted poets of her collection; and among the prose authors a translation of Livy and Rollin's ancient history were my chief favourites although as I emerged from childhood I found others highly interesting which I had before neglected as dull.

When I was twelve years old it occurred to my aunt that I ought to learn music; she herself played upon the harp. It was with great hesitation that she persuaded herself to undertake my instruction; yet believing this accomplishment a necessary part of my education, and balancing the evils of this measure or of having some one in the house to instruct me she submitted to the inconvenience. A harp was sent for that my playing might not interfere with hers, and I began: she found me a docile and when I had conquered the first rudiments a very apt scholar. I had acquired in my harp a companion in rainy days; a sweet soother of my feelings when any untoward accident ruffled them: I often addressed it as my only friend; I could pour forth to it my hopes and loves, and I fancied that its sweet accents answered me. I have now mentioned all my studies.

I was a solitary being, and from my infant years, ever since my dear nurse left me, I had been a dreamer. I brought Rosalind and Miranda and the lady of Comus to life to be my companions, or on my isle acted over their parts imagining myself to be in their situations. Then I wandered from the fancies of others and formed affections and intimacies with the aerial creations of my own brain—but still clinging to reality I gave a name to these conceptions and nursed them in the hope of realization. I clung to the memory of my parents; my mother I should never see, she was dead: but the idea of [my] unhappy, wandering father was the idol of my imagination. I bestowed on him all my affections; there was a miniature of him that I gazed on continually; I copied his last letter and read it again and again. Sometimes it made me weep; and at other [times] I repeated with transport those words,—"One day I may claim her at your hands." I was to be his consoler, his companion in after years. My favourite vision was that when I grew up I would leave my aunt, whose coldness lulled my conscience, and disguised like a boy I would seek my father through the world. My imagination hung upon the scene of recognition; his miniature, which I should continually wear exposed on my breast, would be the means and I imaged the moment to my mind a thousand and a thousand times, perpetually varying the circumstances. Sometimes it would be in a desart; in a populous city; at a ball; we should perhaps meet in a vessel; and his first words constantly were, "My daughter, I love thee"! What extactic moments have I passed in these dreams! How many tears I have shed; how often have I laughed aloud.[13]

This was my life for sixteen years. At fourteen and fifteen I often thought that the time was come when I should commence my pilgrimage, which I had cheated my own mind into believing was my imperious duty: but a reluctance to quit my Aunt; a remorse for the grief which, I could not conceal from myself, I should occasion her for ever withheld me. Sometimes when I had planned the next morning for my escape a word of more than usual affection from her lips made me postpone my resolution. I reproached myself bitterly for what I called a culpable weakness; but this weakness returned upon me whenever the critical moment approached, and I never found courage to depart.[14]

CHAPTER III

It was on my sixteenth birthday that my aunt received a letter from my father. I cannot describe the tumult of emotions that arose within me as I read it. It was dated from London; he had returned![15] I could only relieve my transports by tears, tears of unmingled joy. He had returned, and he wrote to know whether my aunt would come to London or whether he should visit her in Scotland. How delicious to me were the words of his letter that concerned me: "I cannot tell you," it said, "how ardently I desire to see my Mathilda. I look on her as the creature who will form the happiness of my future life: she is all that exists on earth that interests me. I can hardly prevent myself from hastening immediately to you but I am necessarily detained a week and I write because if you come here I may see you somewhat sooner." I read these words with devouring eyes; I kissed them, wept over them and exclaimed, "He will love me!"—

My aunt would not undertake so long a journey, and in a fortnight we had another letter from my father, it was dated Edinburgh: he wrote that he should be with us in three days. "As he approached his desire of seeing me," he said, "became more and more ardent, and he felt that the moment when he should first clasp me in his arms would be the happiest of his life."

How irksome were these three days to me! All sleep and appetite fled from me; I could only read and re-read his letter, and in the solitude of the woods imagine the moment of our meeting. On the eve of the third day I retired early to my room; I could not sleep but paced all night about my chamber and, as you may in Scotland at midsummer, watched the crimson track of the sun as it almost skirted the northern horizon. At day break I hastened to the woods; the hours past on while I indulged in wild dreams that gave wings to the slothful steps of time, and beguiled my eager impatience. My father was expected at noon but when I wished to return to me[e]t him I found that I had lost my way: it seemed that in every attempt to find it I only became more involved in the intracacies of the woods, and the trees hid all trace by which I might be guided.[16] I grew impatient, I wept; and wrung my hands but still I could not discover my path.

It was past two o'clock when by a sudden turn I found myself close to the lake near a cove where a little skiff was moored—It was not far from our house and I saw my father and aunt walking on the lawn. I jumped into the boat, and well accustomed to such feats, I pushed it from shore, and exerted all my strength to row swiftly across. As I came, dressed in white, covered only by my tartan *rachan*, my hair streaming on my shoulders, and shooting across with greater speed that it could be supposed I could give to my boat, my father has often told me that I looked more like a spirit than a human maid. I approached the shore, my father held the boat, I leapt lightly out, and in a moment was in his arms.

And now I began to live. All around me was changed from a dull uniformity to the brightest scene of joy and delight. The happiness I enjoyed in the company of my father far exceeded my sanguine expectations. We were for ever together; and the subjects of our conversations were inexhaustible. He had passed the sixteen years of absence among nations nearly unknown to Europe; he had wandered through Persia, Arabia and the north of India and had penetrated among the habitations of the natives with a freedom permitted to few Europeans. His relations of their manners, his anecdotes and descriptions of scenery whiled away delicious hours, when we were tired of talking of our own plans of future life.

The voice of affection was so new to me that I hung with delight upon his words when he told me what he had felt concerning me during these long years of apparent forgetfulness. "At first"—said he, "I could not bear to think of my poor little girl; but afterwards as grief wore off and hope again revisited me I could only turn to her, and amidst cities and desarts her little fairy form, such as I imagined it, for ever flitted before me. The northern breeze as it refreshed me was sweeter and more balmy for it seemed to carry some of your spirit along with it. I often thought that I would instantly return and take you along with me to some fertile island where we should live at peace for ever. As I returned my fervent hopes were dashed by so many fears; my impatience became in the highest degree painful. I dared not think that the sun should shine and the moon rise not on your living form but on your grave. But, no, it is not so; I have my Mathilda, my consolation, and my hope."—

My father was very little changed from what he described himself to be before his misfortunes. It is intercourse with civilized society; it is the disappointment of cherished hopes, the falsehood of friends, or the perpetual clash of mean passions that changes the heart and damps the ardour of youthful feelings; lonly wanderings in a wild country among people of simple or savage manners may inure the body but will not tame the soul, or extinguish the ardour and freshness of feeling incident to youth. The burning sun of India, and the freedom from all restraint had rather encreased the energy of his character: before he bowed under, now he was impatient of any censure except that of his own mind. He had seen so many customs and witnessed so great a variety of moral creeds that he had been obliged to form an independant one for himself which had no relation to the peculiar notions of any one country: his early prejudices of course influenced his judgement in the formation of his principles, and some raw colledge ideas were strangely mingled with the deepest deductions of his penetrating mind.

The vacuity his heart endured of any deep interest in life during his long absence from his native country had had a singular effect upon his ideas. There was a curious feeling of unreality attached by him to his foreign life in comparison with the years of his youth. All the time he had passed out of England was as a dream, and all the interest of his soul[,] all his affections belonged to events which had happened and persons who had existed sixteen years before. It was strange when you heard him talk to see how he passed over this lapse of time as a night of visions; while the remembrances of his youth standing seperate as they did from his after life had lost none of their vigour. He talked of my Mother as if she had lived but a few weeks before; not that he expressed poignant grief, but his discription of her person, and his relation of all anecdotes connected with her was thus fervent and vivid.

In all this there was a strangeness that attracted and enchanted me. He was, as it were, now awakened from his long, visionary sleep, and he felt some what like one of the seven sleepers, or like Nourjahad,[17] in that sweet imitation of an eastern tale: Diana was gone; his friends were changed or dead, and now on his awakening I was all that he had to love on earth.

How dear to me were the waters, and mountains, and woods of Loch Lomond now that I had so beloved a companion for my rambles. I visited with my father every delightful spot, either on the islands, or by the side of the tree-sheltered waterfalls; every shady path, or dingle entangled with underwood and fern. My ideas were enlarged by his conversation. I felt as if I were recreated and had about me all the freshness and life of a new being: I was, as it were, transported since his arrival from a narrow spot of earth into a universe boundless to the imagination and the understanding. My life had been before as a pleasing country rill, never destined to leave its native fields, but when its task was fulfilled quietly to be absorbed, and leave no trace. Now it seemed to me to be as a various river flowing through a fertile and lovely lanscape, ever changing and ever beautiful. Alas! I knew not the desart it was about to reach; the rocks that would tear its waters, and the hideous scene that would be reflected in a more distorted manner in its waves. Life was then brilliant; I began to learn to hope and what brings a more bitter despair to the heart than hope destroyed?

Is it not strange[18] that grief should quickly follow so divine a happiness? I drank of an enchanted cup but gall was at the bottom of its long drawn sweetness. My heart was full of deep affection, but it was calm from its very depth and fulness. I had no idea that misery could arise from love, and this lesson that all at last must learn was taught me in a manner few are obliged to receive it. I lament now, I must ever lament, those few short months of Paradisaical bliss; I disobeyed no command, I ate no apple, and yet I was ruthlessly driven from it. Alas! my companion did, and I was precipitated in his fall.[19] But I wander from my relation—let woe come at its appointed time; I may at this stage of my story still talk of happiness.

Three months passed away in this delightful intercourse, when my aunt fell ill. I passed a whole month in her chamber nursing her, but her disease was mortal and she died, leaving me for some time inconsolable, Death is so dreadful to the living;[20] the chains of habit are so strong even when affection does not link them that the heart must be agonized when they break. But my father was beside me to console me and to drive away bitter memories by bright hopes: methought that it was sweet to grieve that he might dry my tears.

Then again he distracted my thoughts from my sorrow by comparing it with his despair when he lost my mother. Even at that time I shuddered at the picture he drew of his passions: he had the imagination of a poet, and when he described the whirlwind that then tore his feelings he gave his words the impress of life so vividly that I believed while I trembled. I wondered how he could ever again have entered into the offices of life after his wild thoughts seemed to have given him affinity with the unearthly; while he spoke so tremendous were the ideas which he conveyed that it appeared as if the human heart were far too bounded for their conception. His feelings seemed better fitted for a spirit whose habitation is the earthquake and the volcano than for one confined to a mortal body and human lineaments. But these were merely memories; he was changed since then. He was now all love, all softness; and when I raised my eyes in wonder at him as he spoke the smile on his lips told me that his heart was possessed by the gentlest passions.

Two months after my aunt's death we removed to London where I was led by my father to attend to deeper studies than had before occupied me. My improvement was his delight; he was with me during all my studies and assisted or joined with me in every lesson. We saw a great deal of society, and no day passed that my father did not endeavour to embellish by some new enjoyment. The tender attachment that he bore me, and the love and veneration with which I returned it cast a charm over every moment. The hours were slow for each minute was employed; we lived more in one week than many do in the course of several months and the variety and novelty of our pleasures gave zest to each.

We perpetually made excursions together. And whether it were to visit beautiful scenery, or to see fine pictures, or sometimes for no object but to seek amusement as it might chance to arise, I was always happy when near my father. It was a subject of regret to me whenever we were joined by a third person, yet if I turned with a disturbed look towards my father, his eyes fixed on me and beaming with tenderness instantly restored joy to my heart. O, hours of intense delight! Short as ye were ye are made as long to me as a whole life when looked back upon through the mist of grief that rose immediately after as if to shut ye from my view. Alas! ye were the last of happiness that I ever enjoyed; a few, a very few weeks and all was destroyed. Like Psyche[21] I lived for awhile in an enchanted palace, amidst odours, and music, and every luxurious delight; when suddenly I was left on a barren rock; a wide ocean of despair rolled around me: above all was black, and my eyes closed while I still inhabited a universal death. Still I would not hurry on; I would pause for ever on the recollections of these happy weeks; I would repeat every word, and how many do I remember, record every enchantment of the faery habitation. But, no, my tale must not pause; it must be as rapid as was my fate,—I can only describe in short although strong expressions my precipitate and irremediable change from happiness to despair.[22]

CHAPTER IV

Among our most assiduous visitors was a young man of rank, well informed, and agreable in his person. After we had spent a few weeks in London his attentions towards me became marked and his visits more frequent. I was too much taken up by my own occupations and feelings to attend much to this, and then indeed I hardly noticed more than the bare surface of events as they passed around me; but I now remember that my father was restless and uneasy whenever this person visited us, and when we talked together watched us with the greatest apparent anxiety although he himself maintained a profound silence. At length these obnoxious visits suddenly ceased altogether, but from that moment I must date the change of my father: a change that to remember makes me shudder and then filled me with the deepest grief. There were no degrees which could break my fall from happiness to misery; it was as the stroke of lightning—sudden and entire.[23] Alas! I now met frowns where before I had been welcomed only with smiles: he, my beloved father, shunned me, and either treated me with harshness or a more heart-breaking coldness. We took no more sweet counsel together; and when I tried to win him again to me, his anger, and the terrible emotions that he exhibited drove me to silence and tears.

And this was sudden. The day before we had passed alone together in the country; I remember we had talked of future travels that we should undertake together—. There was an eager delight in our tones and gestures that could only spring from deep & mutual love joined to the most unrestrained confidence[;] and now the next day, the next hour, I saw his brows contracted, his eyes fixed in sullen fierceness on the ground, and his voice so gentle and so dear made me shiver when he addressed me. Often, when my wandering fancy brought by its various images now consolation and now aggravation of grief to my heart,[24] I have compared myself to Proserpine who was gaily and heedlessly gathering flowers on the sweet plain of Enna, when the King of Hell snatched her away to the abodes of death and misery. Alas! I who so lately knew of nought but the joy of life; who had slept only to dream sweet dreams and awoke to incomparable happiness, I now passed my days and nights in tears. I who sought and had found joy in the love-breathing countenance of my father now when I dared fix on him a supplicating look it was ever answered by an angry frown. I dared not speak to him; and when sometimes I had worked up courage to meet him and to ask an explanation one glance at his face where a chaos of mighty passion seemed for ever struggling made me tremble and shrink to silence. I was dashed down from heaven to earth as a silly sparrow when pounced on by a hawk; my eyes swam and my head was bewildered by the sudden apparition of grief. Day after day[25] passed marked only by my complaints and my tears; often I lifted my soul in vain prayer for a softer descent from joy to woe, or if that were denied me that I might be allowed to die, and fade for ever under the cruel blast that swept over me,

>—for what should I do here,
> Like a decaying flower, still withering
> Under his bitter words, whose kindly heat
> Should give my poor heart life?[c]

Sometimes I said to myself, this is an enchantment, and I must strive against it. My father is blinded by some malignant vision which I must remove. And then, like David, I would try music to win the evil spirit from him; and once while singing I lifted my eyes towards him and saw his fixed on me and filled with tears; all his muscles seemed relaxed to softness. I sprung towards him with a cry of joy and would have thrown myself into his arms, but he pushed me roughly from him and left me. And even from this slight incident he contracted fresh gloom and an additional severity of manner.

There are many incidents that I might relate which shewed the diseased yet incomprehensible state of his mind; but I will mention one that occurred while we were in company with several other persons. On this occasion I chanced to say that I thought Myrrha the best of Alfieri's tragedies; as I said this I chanced to cast my eyes on my father and met his: for the first time the expression of those beloved eyes displeased me, and I saw with affright that his whole frame shook with some concealed emotion that in spite of his efforts half conquered him: as this tempest faded from his soul he became melancholy and silent. Every day some new scene occured and displayed in him a mind working as [it] were with an unknown horror that now he could master but which at times threatened to overturn his reason, and to throw the bright seat of his intelligence into a perpetual chaos.

I will not dwell longer than I need on these disastrous circumstances.[26] I might waste days in describing how anxiously I watched every change of fleeting circumstance that promised better days, and with what despair I found that each effort of mine aggravated his seeming madness. To tell all my grief I might as well attempt to count the tears that have fallen from these eyes, or every sign that has torn my heart. I will be brief for there is in all this a horror that will not bear many words, and I sink almost a second time to death while I recall these sad scenes to my memory. Oh, my beloved father! Indeed you made me miserable beyond all words, but how truly did I even then forgive you, and how entirely did you possess my whole heart while I endeavoured, as a rainbow gleams upon a cataract,[D27] to soften thy tremendous sorrows.

Thus did this change come about. I seem perhaps to have dashed too suddenly into the description, but thus suddenly did it happen. In one sentence I have passed from the idea of unspeakable happiness to that of unspeakable grief but they were thus closely linked together. We had remained five months in London three of joy and two of sorrow. My father and I were now seldom alone or if we were he generally kept silence with his eyes fixed on the ground—the dark full orbs in which before I delighted to read all sweet and gentle feeling shadowed from my sight by their lids and the long lashes that fringed them. When we were in company he affected gaiety but I wept to hear his hollow laugh—begun by an empty smile and often ending in a bitter sneer such as never before this fatal period had wrinkled his lips. When others were there he often spoke to me and his eyes perpetually followed my slightest motion. His accents whenever he addressed me were cold and constrained although his voice would tremble when he perceived that my full heart choked the answer to words proffered with a mien yet new to me.

But days of peaceful melancholy were of rare occurence[:] they were often broken in upon by gusts of passion that drove me as a weak boat on a stormy sea to seek a cove for shelter; but the winds blew from my native harbour and I was cast far, far out untill shattered I perished when the tempest had passed and the sea was apparently calm. I do not know that I can describe his emotions: sometimes he only betrayed them by a word or gesture, and then retired to his chamber and I crept as near it as I dared and listened with fear to every sound, yet still more dreading a sudden silence—dreading I knew not what, but ever full of fear.

It was after one tremendous day when his eyes had glared on me like lightning—and his voice sharp and broken seemed unable to express the extent of his emotion that in the evening when I was alone he joined me with a calm countenance, and not noticing my tears which I quickly dried when he approached, told me that in three days that he intended to remove with me to his estate in Yorkshire, and bidding me prepare left me hastily as if afraid of being questioned.

This determination on his part indeed surprised me. This estate was that which he had inhabited in childhood and near which my mother resided while a girl; this was the scene of their youthful loves and where they had lived after their marriage; in happier days my father had often told me that however he might appear weaned from his widow sorrow, and free from bitter recollections elsewhere, yet he would never dare visit the spot where he had enjoyed her society or trust himself to see the rooms that so many years ago they had inhabited together; her favourite walks and the gardens the flowers of which she had delighted to cultivate. And now while he suffered intense misery he determined to plunge into still more intense, and strove for greater emotion than that which already tore him. I was perplexed, and most anxious to know what this portended; ah, what could it po[r]tend but ruin!

I saw little of my father during this interval, but he appeared calmer although not less unhappy than before. On the morning of the third day he informed me that he had determined to go to Yorkshire first alone, and that I should follow him in a fortnight unless I heard any thing from him in the mean time that should contradict this command. He departed the same day, and four days afterwards I received a letter from his steward telling me in his name to join him with as little delay as possible. After travelling day and night I arrived with an anxious, yet a hoping heart, for why should he send for me if it were only to avoid me and to treat me with the apparent aversion that he had in London. I met him at the distance of thirty miles from our mansion. His demeanour was sad; for a moment he appeared glad to see me and then he checked himself as if unwilling to betray his feelings. He was silent during our ride, yet his manner was kinder than before and I thought I beheld a softness in his eyes that gave me hope.

When we arrived, after a little rest, he led me over the house and pointed out to me the rooms which my mother had inhabited. Although more than sixteen years had passed since her death nothing had been changed; her work box, her writing desk were still there and in her room a book lay open on the table as she had left it. My father pointed out these circumstances with a serious and unaltered mien, only now and then fixing his deep and liquid eyes upon me; there was something strange and awful in his look that overcame me, and in spite of myself I wept, nor did he attempt to console me, but I saw his lips quiver and the muscles of his countenance seemed convulsed.

We walked together in the gardens and in the evening when I would have retired he asked me to stay and read to him; and first said, "When I was last here your mother read Dante to me; you shall go on where she left off." And then in a moment he said, "No, that must not be; you must not read Dante. Do you choose a book." I took up Spencer and read the descent of Sir Guyon to the halls of Avarice;[28] while he listened his eyes fixed on me in sad profound silence.

I heard the next morning from the steward that upon his arrival he had been in a most terrible state of mind: he had passed the first night in the garden lying on the damp grass; he did not sleep but groaned perpetually. "Alas!" said the old man[,] who gave me this account with tears in his eyes, "it wrings my heart to see my lord in this state: when I heard that he was coming down here with you, my young lady, I thought we should have the happy days over again that we enjoyed during the short life of my lady your mother—But that would be too much happiness for us poor creatures born to tears—and that was why she was taken from us so soon; [s]he was too beautiful and good for us[.] It was a happy day as we all thought it when my lord married her: I knew her when she was a child and many a good turn has she done for me in my old lady's time—You are like her although there is more of my lord in you—But has he been thus ever since his return? All my joy turned to sorrow when I first beheld him with that melancholy countenance enter these doors as it were the day after my lady's funeral—He seemed to recover himself a little after he had bidden me write to you—but still it is a woful thing to see him so unhappy."[29] These were the feelings of an old, faithful servant: what must be those of an affectionate daughter. Alas! Even then my heart was almost broken.

We spent two months together in this house. My father spent the greater part of his time with me; he accompanied me in my walks, listened to my music, and leant over me as I read or painted. When he conversed with me his manner was cold and constrained; his eyes only seemed to speak, and as he turned their black, full lustre towards me they expressed a living sadness. There was somthing in those dark deep orbs so liquid, and intense that even in happiness I could never meet their full gaze that mine did not overflow. Yet it was with sweet tears; now there was a depth of affliction in their gentle appeal that rent my heart with sympathy; they seemed to desire peace for me; for himself a heart patient to suffer; a craving for sympathy, yet a perpetual self denial. It was only when he was absent from me that his passion subdued him,—that he clinched his hands—knit his brows—and with haggard looks called for death to his despair, raving wildly, untill exhausted he sank down nor was revived untill I joined him.

While we were in London there was a harshness and sulleness in his sorrow which had now entirely disappeared. There I shrunk and fled from him, now I only wished to be with him that I might soothe him to peace. When he was silent I tried to divert him, and when sometimes I stole to him during the energy of his passion I wept but did not desire to leave him. Yet he suffered fearful agony; during the day he was more calm, but at night when I could not be with him he seemed to give the reins to his grief: he often passed his nights either on the floor in my mother's room, or in the garden; and when in the morning he saw me view with poignant grief his exhausted frame, and his person languid almost to death with watching he wept; but during all this time he spoke no word by which I might guess the cause of his unhappiness[.] If I ventured to enquire he would either leave me or press his finger on his lips, and with a deprecating look that I could not resist, turn away. If I wept he would gaze on me in silence but he was no longer harsh and although he repulsed every caress yet it was with gentleness.

He seemed to cherish a mild grief and softer emotions although sad as a relief from despair—He contrived in many ways to nurse his melancholy as an antidote to wilder passion[.] He perpetually frequented the walks that had been favourites with him when he and my mother wandered together talking of love and happiness; he collected every relick that remained of her and always sat opposite her picture which hung in the room fixing on it a look of sad despair—and all this was done in a mystic and awful silence. If his passion subdued him he locked himself in his room; and at night when he wandered restlessly about the house, it was when every other creature slept.

It may easily be imagined that I wearied myself with conjecture to guess the cause of his sorrow. The solution that seemed to me the most probable was that during his residence in London he had fallen in love with some unworthy person, and that his passion mastered him although he would not gratify it: he loved me too well to sacrifise me to this inclination, and that he had now visited this house that by reviving the memory of my mother whom he so passionately adored he might weaken the present impression. This was possible; but it was a mere conjecture unfounded on any fact. Could there be guilt in it? He was too upright and noble to *do* aught that his conscience would not approve; I did not yet know of the crime there may be in involuntary feeling and therefore ascribed his tumultuous starts and gloomy looks wholly to the struggles of his mind and not any as they were partly due to the worst fiend of all—Remorse.[30]

But still do I flatter myself that this would have passed away. His paroxisms of passion were terrific but his soul bore him through them triumphant, though almost destroyed by victory; but the day would finally have been won had not I, foolish and presumtuous wretch! hurried him on untill there was no recall, no hope. My rashness gave the victory in this dreadful fight to the enemy who triumphed over him as he lay fallen and vanquished. I! I alone was the cause of his defeat and justly did I pay the fearful penalty. I said to myself, let him receive sympathy and these struggles will cease. Let him confide his misery to another heart and half the weight of it will be lightened. I will win him to me; he shall not deny his grief to me and when I know his secret then will I pour a balm into his soul and again I shall enjoy the ravishing delight of beholding his smile, and of again seeing his eyes beam if not with pleasure at least with gentle love and thankfulness. This will I do, I said. Half I accomplished; I gained his secret and we were both lost for ever.

CHAPTER V

Nearly a year had past since my father's return, and the seasons had almost finished their round—It was now the end of May; the woods were clothed in their freshest verdure, and the sweet smell of the new mown grass was in the fields. I thought that the balmy air and the lovely face of Nature might aid me in inspiring him with mild sensations, and give him gentle feelings of peace and love preparatory to the confidence I determined to win from him.

I chose therefore the evening of one of these days for my attempt. I invited him to walk with me, and led him to a neighbouring wood of beech trees whose light shade shielded us from the slant and dazzling beams of the descending sun—After walking for some time in silence I seated my self with him on a mossy hillock—It is strange but even now I seem to see the spot—the slim and smooth trunks were many of them wound round by ivy whose shining leaves of the darkest green contrasted with the white bark and the light leaves of the young sprouts of beech that grew from their parent trunks—the short grass was mingled with moss and was partly covered by the dead leaves of the last autumn that driven by the winds had here and there collected in little hillocks—there were a few moss grown stumps about—The leaves were gently moved by the breeze and through their green canopy you could see the bright blue sky—As evening came on the distant trunks were reddened by the sun and the wind died entirely away while a few birds flew past us to their evening rest.

Well it was here we sat together, and when you hear all that past—all that of terrible tore our souls even in this placid spot, which but for strange passions might have been a paradise to us, you will not wonder that I remember it as I looked on it that its calm might give me calm, and inspire me not only with courage but with persuasive words. I saw all these things and in a vacant manner noted them in my mind[31] while I endeavoured to arrange my thoughts in fitting order for my attempt. My heart beat fast as I worked myself up to speak to him, for I was determined not to be repulsed but I trembled to imagine what effect my words might have on him; at length, with much hesitation I began:[32]

"Your kindness to me, my dearest father, and the affection—the excessive affection—that you had for me when you first returned will I hope excuse me in your eyes that I dare speak to you, although with the tender affection of a daughter, yet also with the freedom of a friend and equal. But pardon me, I entreat you and listen to me: do not turn away from me; do not be impatient; you may easily intimidate me into silence, but my heart is bursting, nor can I willingly consent to endure for one moment longer the agony of uncertitude which for the last four months has been my portion.

"Listen to me, dearest friend, and permit me to gain your confidence. Are the happy days of mutual love which have passed to be to me as a dream never to return? Alas! You have a secret grief that destroys us both: but you must permit me to win this secret from you. Tell me, can I do nothing? You well know that on the whole earth there is no sacrifise that I would not make, no labour that I would not undergo with the mere hope that I might bring you ease. But if no endeavour on my part can contribute to your happiness, let me at least know your sorrow, and surely my earnest love and deep sympathy must soothe your despair.

"I fear that I speak in a constrained manner: my heart is overflowing with the ardent desire I have of bringing calm once more to your thoughts and looks; but I fear to aggravate your grief, or to raise that in you which is death to me, anger and distaste. Do not then continue to fix your eyes on the earth; raise them on me for I can read your soul in them: speak to me to me , and pardon my presumption. Alas! I am a most unhappy creature!"

I was breathless with emotion, and I paused fixing my earnest eyes on my father, after I had dashed away the intrusive tears that dimmed them. He did not raise his, but after a short silence he replied to me in a low voice: "You are indeed presumptuous, Mathilda, presumptuous and very rash. In the heart of one like me there are secret thoughts working, and secret tortures which you ought not to seek to discover. I cannot tell you how it adds to my grief to know that I am the cause of uneasiness to you; but this will pass away, and I hope that soon we shall be as we were a few months ago. Restrain your impatience or you may mar what you attempt to alleviate. Do not again speak to me in this strain; but wait in submissive patience the event of what is passing around you."

"Oh, yes!" I passionately replied, "I will be very patient; I will not be rash or presumptuous: I will see the agonies, and tears, and despair of my father, my only friend, my hope, my shelter, I will see it all with folded arms and downcast eyes. You do not treat me with candour; it is not true what you say; this will not soon pass away, it will last forever if you deign not to speak to me; to admit my consolations.

"Dearest, dearest father, pity me and pardon me: I entreat you do not drive me to despair; indeed I must not be repulsed; there is one thing that which although it may torture me to know, yet that you must tell me. I demand, and most solemnly I demand if in any way I am the cause of your unhappiness. Do you not see my tears which I in vain strive against—You hear unmoved my voice broken by sobs—Feel how my hand trembles: my whole heart is in the words I speak and you must not endeavour to silence me by mere words barren of meaning: the agony of my doubt hurries me on, and you must reply. I beseech you; by your former love for me now lost, I adjure you to answer that one question. Am I the cause of your grief?"

He raised his eyes from the ground, but still turning them away from me, said: "Besought by that plea I will answer your rash question. Yes, you are the sole, the agonizing cause of all I suffer, of all I must suffer untill I die. Now, beware! Be silent! Do not urge me to your destruction. I am struck by the storm, rooted up, laid waste: but you can stand against it; you are young and your passions are at peace. One word I might speak and then you would be implicated in my destruction; yet that word is hovering on my lips. Oh! There is a fearful chasm; but I adjure you to beware!"

"Ah, dearest friend!" I cried, "do not fear! Speak that word; it will bring peace, not death. If there is a chasm our mutual love will give us wings to pass it, and we shall find flowers, and verdure, and delight on the other side." I threw myself at his feet, and took his hand, "Yes, speak, and we shall be happy; there will no longer be doubt, no dreadful uncertainty; trust me, my affection will soothe your sorrow; speak that word and all danger will be past, and we shall love each other as before, and for ever."

He snatched his hand from me, and rose in violent disorder: "What do you mean? You know not what you mean. Why do you bring me out, and torture me, and tempt me, and kill me—Much happier would [it] be for you and for me if in your frantic curiosity you tore my heart from my breast and tried to read its secrets in it as its life's blood was dropping from it. Thus you may console me by reducing me to nothing—but your words I cannot bear; soon they will make me mad, quite mad, and then I shall utter strange words, and you will believe them, and we shall be both lost for ever. I tell you I am on the very verge of insanity; why, cruel girl, do you drive me on: you will repent and I shall die."

When I repeat his words I wonder at my pertinacious folly; I hardly know what feelings resis[t]lessly impelled me. I believe it was that coming out with a determination not to be repulsed I went right forward to my object without well weighing his replies: I was led by passion and drew him with frantic heedlessness into the abyss that he so fearfully avoided—I replied to his terrific words: "You fill me with affright it is true, dearest father, but you only confirm my resolution to put an end to this state of doubt. I will not be put off thus: do you think that I can live thus fearfully from day to day—the sword in my bosom yet kept from its mortal wound by a hair—a word!—I demand that dreadful word; though it be as a flash of lightning to destroy me, speak it.

"Alas! Alas! What am I become? But a few months have elapsed since I believed that I was all the world to you; and that there was no happiness or grief for you on earth unshared by your Mathilda—your child: that happy time is no longer, and what I most dreaded in this world is come upon me. In the despair of my heart I see what you cannot conceal: you no longer love me. I adjure you, my father, has not an unnatural passion seized upon your heart? Am I not the most miserable worm that crawls? Do I not embrace your knees, and you most cruelly repulse me? I know it—I see it—you hate me!"

I was transported by violent emotion, and rising from his feet, at which I had thrown myself, I leant against a tree, wildly raising my eyes to heaven. He began to answer with violence: "Yes, yes, I hate you! You are my bane, my poison, my disgust! Oh! No[!]" And then his manner changed, and fixing his eyes on me with an expression that convulsed every nerve and member of my frame—"you are none of all these; you are my light, my only one, my life.—My daughter, I love you!" The last words died away in a hoarse whisper, but I heard them and sunk on the ground, covering my face and almost dead with excess of sickness and fear: a cold perspiration covered my forehead and I shivered in every limb—But he continued, clasping his hands with a frantic gesture:

"Now I have dashed from the top of the rock to the bottom! Now I have precipitated myself down the fearful chasm! The danger is over; she is alive! Oh, Mathilda, lift up those dear eyes in the light of which I live. Let me hear the sweet tones of your beloved voice in peace and calm. Monster as I am, you are still, as you ever were, lovely, beautiful beyond expression. What I have become since this last moment I know not; perhaps I am changed in mien as the fallen archangel. I do believe I am for I have surely a new soul within me, and my blood riots through my veins: I am burnt up with fever. But these are precious moments; devil as I am become, yet that is my Mathilda before me whom I love as one was never before loved: and she knows it now; she listens to these words which I thought, fool as I was, would blast her to death. Come, come, the worst is past: no more grief, tears or despair; were not those the words you uttered?—We have leapt the chasm I told you of, and now, mark me, Mathilda, we are to find flowers, and verdure and delight, or is it hell, and fire, and tortures? Oh! Beloved One, I am borne away; I can no longer sustain myself; surely this is death that is coming. Let me lay my head near your heart; let me die in your arms!"—He sunk to the earth fainting, while I, nearly as lifeless, gazed on him in despair.

Yes it was despair I felt; for the first time that phantom seized me; the first and only time for it has never since left me—After the first moments of speechless agony I felt her fangs on my heart: I tore my hair; I raved aloud; at one moment in pity for his sufferings I would have clasped my father in my arms; and then starting back with horror I spurned him with my foot; I felt as if stung by a serpent, as if scourged by a whip of scorpions which drove me—Ah! Whither—Whither?

Well, this could not last. One idea rushed on my mind; never, never may I speak to him again. As this terrible conviction came upon *him* [*me*?] it melted my soul to tenderness and love—I gazed on him as to take my last farewell—he lay insensible—his eyes closed as [*and*?] his cheeks deathly pale. Above, the leaves of the beech wood cast a flickering shadow on his face, and waved in mournful melody over him—I saw all these things and said, "Aye, this is his grave!" And then I wept aloud, and raised my eyes to heaven to entreat for a respite to my despair and an alleviation for his unnatural suffering—the tears that gushed in a warm & healing stream from my eyes relieved the burthen that oppressed my heart almost to madness. I wept for a long time untill I saw him about to revive, when horror and misery again recurred, and the tide of my sensations rolled back to their former channel: with a terror I could not restrain—I sprung up and fled, with winged speed, along the paths of the wood and across the fields untill nearly dead I reached our house and just ordering the servants to seek my father at the spot I indicated, I shut myself up in my own room[.]³³

CHAPTER VI

My chamber was in a retired part of the house, and looked upon the garden so that no sound of the other inhabitants could reach it; and here in perfect solitude I wept for several hours. When a servant came to ask me if I would take food I learnt from him that my father had returned, and was apparently well and this relieved me from a load of anxiety, yet I did not cease to weep bitterly. As [At] first, as the memory of former happiness contrasted to my present despair came across me, I gave relief to the oppression of heart that I felt by words, and groans, and heart rending sighs: but nature became wearied, and this more violent grief gave place to a passionate but mute flood of tears: my whole soul seemed to dissolve [in] them. I did not wring my hands, or tear my hair, or utter wild exclamations, but as Boccacio describes the intense and quiet grief [of] Sigismunda over the heart of Guiscardo,[34] I sat with my hands folded, silently letting fall a perpetual stream from my eyes. Such was the depth of my emotion that I had no feeling of what caused my distress, my thoughts even wandered to many indifferent objects; but still neither moving limb or feature my tears fell untill, as if the fountains were exhausted, they gradually subsided, and I awoke to life as from a dream.

When I had ceased to weep reason and memory returned upon me, and I began to reflect with greater calmness on what had happened, and how it became me to act—A few hours only had passed but a mighty revolution had taken place with regard to me—the natural work of years had been transacted since the morning: my father was as dead to me, and I felt for a moment as if he with white hairs were laid in his coffin and I—youth vanished in approaching age, were weeping at his timely dissolution. But it was not so, I was yet young, Oh! far too young, nor was he dead to others; but I, most miserable, must never see or speak to him again. I must fly from him with more earnestness than from my greatest enemy: in solitude or in cities I must never more behold him. That consideration made me breathless with anguish, and impressing itself on my imagination I was unable for a time to follow up any train of ideas. Ever after this, I thought, I would live in the most dreary seclusion. I would retire to the Continent and become a nun; not for religion's sake, for I was not a Catholic, but that I might be for ever shut out from the world. I should there find solitude where I might weep, and the voices of life might never reach me.

But my father; my beloved and most wretched father? Would he die? Would he never overcome the fierce passion that now held pityless dominion over him? Might he not many, many years hence, when age had quenched the burning sensations that he now experienced, might he not then be again a father to me? This reflection unwrinkled my brow, and I could feel (and I wept to feel it) a half melancholy smile draw from my lips their expression of suffering: I dared indulge better hopes for my future life; years must pass but they would speed lightly away winged by hope, or if they passed heavily, still they would pass and I had not lost my father for ever. Let him spend another sixteen years of desolate wandering: let him once more utter his wild complaints to the vast woods and the tremendous cataracts of another clime: let him again undergo fearful danger and soul-quelling hardships: let the hot sun of the south again burn his passion worn cheeks and the cold night rains fall on him and chill his blood.

To this life, miserable father, I devote thee!—Go!—Be thy days passed with savages, and thy nights under the cope of heaven! Be thy limbs worn and thy heart chilled, and all youth be dead within thee! Let thy hairs be as snow; thy walk trembling and thy voice have lost its mellow tones! Let the liquid lustre of thine eyes be quenched; and then return to me, return to thy Mathilda, thy child, who may then be clasped in thy loved arms, while thy heart beats with sinless emotion. Go, Devoted One, and return thus!—This is my curse, a daughter's curse: go, and return pure to thy child, who will never love aught but thee.

These were my thoughts; and with trembling hands I prepared to begin a letter to my unhappy parent. I had now spent many hours in tears and mournful meditation; it was past twelve o'clock; all was at peace in the house, and the gentle air that stole in at my window did not rustle the leaves of the twining plants that shadowed it. I felt the entire tranquillity of the hour when my own breath and involuntary sobs were all the sounds that struck upon the air. On a sudden I heard a gentle step ascending the stairs; I paused breathless, and as it approached glided into an obscure corner of the room; the steps paused at my door, but after a few moments they again receeded[,] descended the stairs and I heard no more.

This slight incident gave rise in me to the most painful reflections; nor do I now dare express the emotions I felt. That he should be restless I understood; that he should wander as an unlaid ghost and find no quiet from the burning hell that consumed his heart. But why approach my chamber? Was not that sacred? I felt almost ready to faint while he had stood there, but I had not betrayed my wakefulness by the slightest motion, although I had heard my own heart beat with violent fear. He had withdrawn. Oh, never, never, may I see him again! Tomorrow night the same roof may not cover us; he or I must depart. The mutual link of our destinies is broken; we must be divided by seas—by land. The stars and the sun must not rise at the same period to us: he must not say, looking at the setting crescent of the moon, "Mathilda now watches its fall."—No, all must be changed. Be it light with him when it is darkness with me! Let him feel the sun of summer while I am chilled by the snows of winter! Let there be the distance of the antipodes between us!

At length the east began to brighten, and the comfortable light of morning streamed into my room. I was weary with watching and for some time I had combated with the heavy sleep that weighed down my eyelids: but now, no longer fearful, I threw myself on my bed. I sought for repose although I did not hope for forgetfulness; I knew I should be pursued by dreams, but did not dread the frightful one that I really had. I thought that I had risen and went to seek my father to inform him of my determination to seperate myself from him. I sought him in the house, in the park, and then in the fields and the woods, but I could not find him. At length I saw him at some distance, seated under a tree, and when he perceived me he waved his hand several times, beckoning me to approach; there was something unearthly in his mien that awed and chilled me, but I drew near. When at [a] short distance from him I saw that he was deadlily pale, and clothed in flowing garments of white. Suddenly he started up and fled from me; I pursued him: we sped over the fields, and by the skirts of woods, and on the banks of rivers; he flew fast and I followed. We came at last, methought, to the brow of a huge cliff that over hung the sea which, troubled by the winds, dashed against its base at a distance. I heard the roar of the waters: he held his course right on towards the brink and I became breathless with fear lest he should plunge down the dreadful precipice; I tried to augment my speed, but my knees failed beneath me, yet I had just reached him; just caught a part of his flowing robe, when he leapt down and I awoke with a violent scream. I was trembling and my pillow was wet with my tears; for a few moments my heart beat hard, but the bright beams of the sun and the chirping of the birds quickly restored me to myself, and I rose with a languid spirit, yet wondering what events the day would bring forth. Some time passed before I summoned courage to ring the bell for my servant, and when she came I still dared not utter my father's name. I ordered her to bring my breakfast to my room, and was again left alone—yet still I could make no resolve, but only thought that I might write a note to my father to beg his permission to pay a visit to a relation who lived about thirty miles off, and who had before invited me to her house, but I had refused for then I could not quit my suffering father. When the servant came back she gave me a letter.

"From whom is this letter[?]" I asked trembling.

"Your father left it, madam, with his servant, to be given to you when you should rise."

"My father left it! Where is he? Is he not here?"

"No; he quitted the house before four this morning."

"Good God! He is gone! But tell how this was; speak quick!"

Her relation was short. He had gone in the carriage to the nearest town where he took a post chaise and horses with orders for the London road. He dismissed his servants there, only telling them that he had a sudden call of business and that they were to obey me as their mistress untill his return.

CHAPTER VII

With a beating heart and fearful, I knew not why, I dismissed the servant and locking my door, sat down to read my father's letter. These are the words that it contained.

"My dear Child

"I have betrayed your confidence; I have endeavoured to pollute your mind, and have made your innocent heart acquainted with the looks and language of unlawful and monstrous passion. I must expiate these crimes, and must endeavour in some degree to proportionate my punishment to my guilt. You are I doubt not prepared for what I am about to announce; we must seperate and be divided for ever.

"I deprive you of your parent and only friend. You are cast out shelterless on the world: your hopes are blasted; the peace and security of your pure mind destroyed; memory will bring to you frightful images of guilt, and the anguish of innocent love betrayed. Yet I who draw down all this misery upon you; I who cast you forth and remorselessly have set the seal of distrust and agony on the heart and brow of my own child, who with devilish levity have endeavoured to steal away her loveliness to place in its stead the foul deformity of sin; I, in the overflowing anguish of my heart, supplicate you to forgive me.

"I do not ask your pity; you must and do abhor me: but pardon me, Mathilda, and let not your thoughts follow me in my banishment with unrelenting anger. I must never more behold you; never more hear your voice; but the soft whisperings of your forgiveness will reach me and cool the burning of my disordered brain and heart; I am sure I should feel it even in my grave. And I dare enforce this request by relating how miserably I was betrayed into this net of fiery anguish and all my struggles to release myself: indeed if your soul were less pure and bright I would not attempt to exculpate myself to you; I should fear that if I led you to regard me with less abhorrence you might hate vice less: but in addressing you I feel as if I appealed to an angelic judge. I cannot depart without your forgiveness and I must endeavour to gain it, or I must despair.[35] I conjure you therefore to listen to my words, and if with the good guilt may be in any degree extenuated by sharp agony, and remorse that rends the brain as madness perhaps you may think, though I dare not, that I have some claim to your compassion.

"I entreat you to call to your remembrance our first happy life on the shores of Loch Lomond. I had arrived from a weary wandering of sixteen years, during which, although I had gone through many dangers and misfortunes, my affections had been an entire blank. If I grieved it was for your mother, if I loved it was your image; these sole emotions filled my heart in quietness. The human creatures around me excited in me no sympathy and I thought that the mighty change that the death of your mother had wrought within me had rendered me callous to any future impression. I saw the lovely and I did not love, I imagined therefore that all warmth was extinguished in my heart except that which led me ever to dwell on your then infantine image.

"It is a strange link in my fate that without having seen you I should passionately love you. During my wanderings I never slept without first calling down gentle dreams on your head. If I saw a lovely woman, I thought, does my Mathilda resemble her? All delightful things, sublime scenery, soft breezes, exquisite music seemed to me associated with you and only through you to be pleasant to me. At length I saw you. You appeared as the deity of a lovely region, the ministering Angel of a Paradise to which of all human kind you admitted only me. I dared hardly consider you as my daughter; your beauty, artlessness and untaught wisdom seemed to belong to a higher order of beings; your voice breathed forth only words of love: if there was aught of earthly in you it was only what you derived from the beauty of the world; you seemed to have gained a grace from the mountain breezes—the waterfalls and the lake; and this was all of earthly except your affections that you had; there was no dross, no bad feeling in the composition. You yet even have not seen enough[36] of the world to know the stupendous difference that exists between the women we meet in dayly life and a nymph of the woods such as you were, in whose eyes alone mankind may study for centuries & grow wiser & purer. Those divine lights which shone on me as did those of Beatrice upon Dante, and well might I say with him yet with what different feelings

E quasi mi perdei gli occhi chini.

Can you wonder, Mathilda, that I dwelt on your looks, your words, your motions, & drank in unmixed delight?

["]But I am afraid that I wander from my purpose. I must be more brief for night draws on apace and all my hours in this house are counted. Well, we removed to London, and still I felt only the peace of sinless passion. You were ever with me, and I desired no more than to gaze on your countenance, and to know that I was all the world to you; I was lapped in a fool's paradise of enjoyment and security. Was my love blamable? If it was I was ignorant of it; I desired only that which I possessed, and if I enjoyed from your looks, and words, and most innocent caresses a rapture usually excluded from the feelings of a parent towards his child, yet no uneasiness, no wish, no casual idea awoke me to a sense of guilt. I loved you as a human father might be supposed to love a daughter borne to him by a heavenly mother; as Anchises might have regarded the child of Venus if the sex had been changed; love mingled with respect and adoration. Perhaps also my passion was lulled to content by the deep and exclusive affection you felt for me.

"But when I saw you become the object of another's love; when I imagined that you might be loved otherwise than as a sacred type and image of loveliness and excellence; or that you might love another with a more ardent affection than that which you bore to me, then the fiend awoke within me; I dismissed your lover; and from that moment I have known no peace. I have sought in vain for sleep and rest; my lids refused to close, and my blood was for ever in a tumult. I awoke to a new life as one who dies in hope might wake in Hell. I will not sully your imagination by recounting my combats, my self-anger and my despair. Let a veil be drawn over the unimaginable sensations of a guilty father; the secrets of so agonized a heart may not be made vulgar. All was uproar, crime, remorse and hate, yet still the tenderest love; and what first awoke me to the firm resolve of conquering my passion and of restoring her father to my child was the sight of your bitter and sympathizing sorrows. It was this that led me here: I thought that if I could again awaken in my heart the grief I had felt at the loss of your mother, and the many associations with her memory which had been laid to sleep for seventeen years, that all love for her child would become extinct. In a fit of heroism I determined to go alone; to quit you, the life of my life, and not to see you again untill I might guiltlessly. But it would not do: I rated my fortitude too high, or my love too low. I should certainly have died if you had not hastened to me. Would that I had been indeed extinguished!

"And now, Mathilda I must make you my last confession. I have been miserably mistaken in imagining that I could conquer my love for you; I never can. The sight of this house, these fields and woods which my first love inhabited seems to have encreased it: in my madness I dared say to myself—Diana died to give her birth; her mother's spirit was transferred into her frame, and she ought to be as Diana to me.[37] With every effort to cast it off, this love clings closer, this guilty love more unnatural than hate, that withers your hopes and destroys me for ever.

Better have loved despair, & safer kissed her.

No time or space can tear from my soul that which makes a part of it. Since my arrival here I have not for a moment ceased to feel the hell of passion which has been implanted in me to burn untill all be cold, and stiff, and dead. Yet I will not die; alas! how dare I go where I may meet Diana, when I have disobeyed her last request; her last words said in a faint voice when all feeling but love, which survives all things else was already dead, she then bade me make her child happy: that thought alone gives a double sting to death. I will wander away from you, away from all life—in the solitude I shall seek I alone shall breathe of human kind. I must endure life; and as it is my duty so I shall untill the grave dreaded yet desired, receive me free from pain: for while I feel it will be pain that must make up the whole sum of my sensations. Is not this a fearful curse that I labour under? Do I not look forward to a miserable future? My child, if after this life I am permitted to see you again, if pain can purify the heart, mine will be pure: if remorse may expiate guilt, I shall be guiltless.

* * * * *

["]I have been at the door of your chamber: every thing is silent. You sleep. Do you indeed sleep, Mathilda? Spirits of Good, behold the tears of my earnest prayer! Bless my child! Protect her from the selfish among her fellow creatures: protect her from the agonies of passion, and the despair of disappointment! Peace, Hope and Love be thy guardians, oh, thou soul of my soul: thou in whom I breathe!

* * * * *

["]I dare not read my letter over for I have no time to write another, and yet I fear that some expressions in it might displease me. Since I last saw you I have been constantly employed in writing letters, and have several more to write; for I do not intend that any one shall hear of me after I depart. I need not conjure you to look upon me as one of whom all links that once existed between us are broken. Your own delicacy will not allow you, I am convinced, to attempt to trace me. It is far better for your peace that you should be ignorant of my destination. You will not follow me, for when I bannish myself would you nourish guilt by obtruding yourself upon me? You will not do this, I know you will not. You must forget me and all the evil that I have taught you. Cast off the only gift that I have bestowed upon you, your grief, and rise from under my blighting influence as no flower so sweet ever did rise from beneath so much evil.

"You will never hear from me again: receive these then as the last words of mine that will ever reach you; and although I have forfeited your filial love, yet regard them I conjure you as a father's command. Resolutely shake of[f] the wretchedness that this first misfortune in early life must occasion you. Bear boldly up against the storm: continue wise and mild, but believe it, and indeed it is, your duty to be happy. You are very young; let not this check for more than a moment retard your glorious course; hold on, beloved one. The sun of youth is not set for you; it will restore vigour and life to you; do not resist with obstinate grief its beneficent influence, oh, my child! bless me with the hope that I have not utterly destroyed you.

"Farewell, Mathilda. I go with the belief that I have your pardon. Your gentle nature would not permit you to hate your greatest enemy and though I be he, although I have rent happiness from your grasp;[38] though I have passed over your young love and hopes as the angel of destruction, finding beauty and joy, and leaving blight and despair, yet you will forgive me, and with eyes overflowing with tears I thank you; my beloved one, I accept your pardon with a gratitude that will never die, and that will, indeed it will, outlive guilt and remorse.

"Farewell for ever!"

The moment I finished this letter I ordered the carriage and prepared to follow my father. The words of his letter by which he had dissuaded me from this step were those that determined me. Why did he write them? He must know that if I believed that his intention was merely to absent himself from me that instead of opposing him it would be that which I should myself require—or if he thought that any lurking feeling, yet he could not think that, should lead me to him would he endeavour to overthrow the only hope he could have of ever seeing me again; a lover, there was madness in the thought, yet he was my lover, would not act thus. No, he had determined to die, and he wished to spare me the misery of knowing it. The few ineffectual words he had said concerning his duty were to me a further proof—and the more I studied the letter the more did I perceive a thousand slight expressions that could only indicate a knowledge that life was now over for him. He was about to die! My blood froze at the thought: a sickening feeling of horror came over me that allowed not of tears. As I waited for the carriage I walked up and down with a quick pace; then kneeling and passionately clasping my hands I tried to pray but my voice was choked by convulsive sobs—Oh the sun shone[,] the air was balmy—he must yet live for if he were dead all would surely be black as night to me![39]

The motion of the carriage knowing that it carried me towards him and that I might perhaps find him alive somewhat revived my courage: yet I had a dreadful ride. Hope only supported me, the hope that I should not be too late[.] I did not weep, but I wiped the perspiration from my brow, and tried to still my brain and heart beating almost to madness. Oh! I must not be mad when I see him; or perhaps it were as well that I should be, my distraction might calm his, and recall him to the endurance of life. Yet untill I find him I must force reason to keep her seat, and I pressed my forehead hard with my hands—Oh do not leave me; or I shall forget what I am about—instead of driving on as we ought with the speed of lightning they will attend to me, and we shall be too late. Oh! God help me! Let him be alive! It is all dark; in my abject misery I demand no more: no hope, no good: only passion, and guilt, and horror; but alive! Alive! My sensations choked me—No tears fell yet I sobbed, and breathed short and hard; one only thought possessed me, and I could only utter one word, that half screaming was perpetually on my lips; Alive! Alive!—

I had taken the steward[40] with me for he, much better than I[,] could make the requisite enquiries—the poor old man could not restrain his tears as he saw my deep distress and knew the cause—he sometimes uttered a few broken words of consolation: in moments like these the mistress and servant become in a manner equals and when I saw his old dim eyes wet with sympathizing tears; his gray hair thinly scattered on an age-wrinkled brow I thought oh if my father were as he is—decrepid & hoary—then I should be spared this pain—

When I had arrived at the nearest town I took post horses and followed the road my father had taken. At every inn where we changed horses we heard of him, and I was possessed by alternate hope and fear. A length I found that he had altered his route; at first he had followed the London road; but now he changed it, and upon enquiry I found that the one which he now pursued led *towards the sea*. My dream recurred to my thoughts; I was not usually superstitious but in wretchedness every one is so. The sea was fifty miles off, yet it was towards it that he fled. The idea was terrible to my half crazed imagination, and almost over-turned the little self possession that still remained to me. I journied all day; every moment my misery encreased and the fever of my blood became intolerable. The summer sun shone in an unclouded sky; the air was close but all was cool to me except my own scorching skin. Towards evening dark thunder clouds arose above the horrizon and I heard its distant roll—after sunset they darkened the whole sky and it began to rain[,] the lightning lighted up the whole country and the thunder drowned the noise of our carriage. At the next inn my father had not taken horses; he had left a box there saying he would return, and had walked over the fields to the town of—a seacost town eight miles off.

For a moment I was almost paralized by fear; but my energy returned and I demanded a guide to accompany me in following his steps. The night was tempestuous but my bribe was high and I easily procured a countryman. We passed through many lanes and over fields and wild downs; the rain poured down in torrents; and the loud thunder broke in terrible crashes over our heads. Oh! What a night it was! And I passed on with quick steps among the high, dank grass amid the rain and tempest. My dream was for ever in my thoughts, and with a kind of half insanity that often possesses the mind in despair, I said aloud; "Courage! We are not near the sea; we are yet several miles from the ocean"—Yet it was towards the sea that our direction lay and that heightened the confusion of my ideas. Once, overcome by fatigue, I sunk on the wet earth; about two hundred yards distant, alone in a large meadow stood a magnificent oak; the lightnings shewed its myriad boughs torn by the storm. A strange idea seized me; a person must have felt all the agonies of doubt concerning the life and death of one who is the whole world to them before they can enter into my feelings—for in that state, the mind working unrestrained by the will makes strange and fanciful combinations with outward circumstances and weaves the chances and changes of nature into an immediate connexion with the event they dread. It was with this feeling that I turned to the old Steward who stood pale and trembling beside me; "Mark, Gaspar, if the next flash of lightning rend not that oak my father will be alive."

I had scarcely uttered these words than a flash instantly followed by a tremendous peal of thunder descended on it; and when my eyes recovered their sight after the dazzling light, the oak no longer stood in the meadow—The old man uttered a wild exclamation of horror when he saw so sudden an interpretation given to my prophesy. I started up, my strength returned; with my terror; I cried, "Oh, God! Is this thy decree? Yet perhaps I shall not be too late."

Although still several miles distant we continued to approach the sea. We came at last to the road that led to the town of—and at an inn there we heard that my father had passed by somewhat before sunset; he had observed the approaching storm and had hired a horse for the next town which was situated a mile from the sea that he might arrive there before it should commence: this town was five miles off. We hired a chaise here, and with four horses drove with speed through the storm. My garments were wet and clung around me, and my hair hung in straight locks on my neck when not blown aside by the wind. I shivered, yet my pulse was high with fever. Great God! What agony I endured. I shed no tears but my eyes wild and inflamed were starting from my head; I could hardly support the weight that pressed upon my brain. We arrived at the town of—in a little more than half an hour. When my father had arrived the storm had already begun, but he had refused to stop and leaving his horse there he walked on—*towards the sea*. Alas! it was double cruelty in him to have chosen the sea for his fatal resolve; it was adding madness to my despair.[41]

The poor old servant who was with me endeavoured to persuade me to remain here and to let him go alone—I shook my head silently and sadly; sick almost to death I leant upon his arm, and as there was no road for a chaise dragged my weary steps across the desolate downs to meet my fate, now too certain for the agony of doubt. Almost fainting I slowly approached the fatal waters; when we had quitted the town we heard their roaring[.] I whispered to myself in a muttering voice—"The sound is the same as that which I heard in my dream. It is the knell of my father which I hear."[42]

The rain had ceased; there was no more thunder and lightning; the wind had paused. My heart no longer beat wildly; I did not feel any fever: but I was chilled; my knees sunk under me—I almost slept as I walked with excess of weariness; every limb trembled. I was silent: all was silent except the roaring of the sea which became louder and more dreadful. Yet we advanced slowly: sometimes I thought that we should never arrive; that the sound of waves would still allure us, and that we should walk on for ever and ever: field succeeding field, never would our weary journey cease, nor night nor day; but still we should hear the dashing of the sea, and to all this there would be no end. Wild beyond the imagination of the happy are the thoughts bred by misery and despair.

At length we reached the overhanging beach; a cottage stood beside the path; we knocked at the door and it was opened: the bed within instantly caught my eye; something stiff and straight lay on it, covered by a sheet; the cottagers looked aghast. The first words that they uttered confirmed what I before knew. I did not feel shocked or overcome: I believe that I asked one or two questions and listened to the answers. I har[d]ly know, but in a few moments I sank lifeless to the ground; and so would that then all had been at an end!

CHAPTER VIII

I was carried to the next town: fever succeeded to convulsions and faintings, & for some weeks my unhappy spirit hovered on the very verge of death. But life was yet strong within me; I recovered: nor did it a little aid my returning health that my recollections were at first vague, and that I was too weak to feel any violent emotion. I often said to myself, my father is dead. He loved me with a guilty passion, and stung by remorse and despair he killed himself. Why is it that I feel no horror? Are these circumstances not dreadful? Is it not enough that I shall never more meet the eyes of my beloved father; never more hear his voice; no caress, no look? All cold, and stiff, and dead! Alas! I am quite callous: the night I was out in was fearful and the cold rain that fell about my heart has acted like the waters of the cavern of Antiparos[43] and has changed it to stone. I do not weep or sigh; but I must reason with myself, and force myself to feel sorrow and despair. This is not resignation that I feel, for I am dead to all regret.

*I communed in this manner with myself, but I was silent to all around me. I hardly replied to the slightest question, and was uneasy when I saw a human creature near me. I was surrounded by my female relations, but they were all of them nearly strangers to me: I did not listen to their consolations; and so little did they work their designed effect that they seemed to me to be spoken in an unknown tongue. I found if sorrow was dead within me, so was love and desire of sympathy. Yet sorrow only slept to revive more fierce, but love never woke again—its ghost, ever hovering over my father's grave, alone survived—since his death all the world was to me a blank except where woe had stampt its burning words telling me to smile no more—the living were not fit companions for me, and I was ever meditating by what means I might shake them all off, and never be heard of again.

My convalescence rapidly advanced, yet this was the thought that haunted me, and I was for ever forming plans how I might hereafter contrive to escape the tortures that were prepared for me when I should mix in society, and to find that solitude which alone could suit one whom an untold grief seperated from her fellow creatures. Who can be more solitary even in a crowd than one whose history and the never ending feelings and remembrances arising from it is known to no living soul. There was too deep a horror in my tale for confidence; I was on earth the sole depository of my own secret. I might tell it to the winds and to the desert heaths but I must never among my fellow creatures, either by word or look give allowance to the smallest conjecture of the dread reality: I must shrink before the eye of man lest he should read my father's guilt in my glazed eyes: I must be silent lest my faltering voice should betray unimagined horrors. Over the deep grave of my secret I must heap an impenetrable heap of false smiles and words: cunning frauds, treacherous laughter and a mixture of all light deceits would form a mist to blind others and be as the poisonous simoon to me.[44] I, the offspring of love, the child of the woods, the nursling of Nature's bright self was to submit to this? I dared not.

How must I escape? I was rich and young, and had a guardian appointed for me; and all about me would act as if I were one of their great society, while I must keep the secret that I really was cut off from them for ever. If I fled I should be pursued; in life there was no escape for me: why then I must die. I shuddered; I dared not die even though the cold grave held all I loved; although I might say with Job

> Where is now my hope? For my hope who shall see it?
> They shall go down together to the bars of the pit, when our rest
>   together is in the dust—[45]

Yes my hope was corruption and dust and all to which death brings us.—Or after life—No, no, I will not persuade myself to die, I may not, dare not. And then I wept; yes, warm tears once more struggled into my eyes soothing yet bitter; and after I had wept much and called with unavailing anguish, with outstretched arms, for my cruel father; after my weak frame was exhausted by all variety of plaint I sank once more into reverie, and once more reflected on how I might find that which I most desired; dear to me if aught were dear, a death-like solitude.

I dared not die, but I might feign death, and thus escape from my comforters: they will believe me united to my father, and so indeed I shall be. For alone, when no voice can disturb my dream, and no cold eye meet mine to check its fire, then I may commune with his spirit; on a lone heath, at noon or at midnight, still I should be near him. His last injunction to me was that I should be happy; perhaps he did not mean the shadowy happiness that I promised myself, yet it was that alone which I could taste. He did not conceive that ever [qu. *never?*] again I could make one of the smiling hunters that go coursing after bubles that break to nothing when caught, and then after a new one with brighter colours; my hope also had proved a buble, but it had been so lovely, so adorned that I saw none that could attract me after it; besides I was wearied with the pursuit, nearly dead with weariness.

I would feign to die; my contented heirs would seize upon my wealth, and I should purchase freedom. But then my plan must be laid with art; I would not be left destitute, I must secure some money. Alas! to what loathsome shifts must I be driven? Yet a whole life of falsehood was otherwise my portion: and when remorse at being the contriver of any cheat made me shrink from my design I was irresistably led back and confirmed in it by the visit of some aunt or cousin, who would tell me that death was the end of all men. And then say that my father had surely lost his wits ever since my mother's death; that he was mad and that I was fortunate, for in one of his fits he might have killed me instead of destroying his own crazed being. And all this, to be sure, was delicately put; not in broad words for my feelings might be hurt but

> Whispered so and so
> In dark hint soft and low[E46]

with downcast eyes, and sympathizing smiles or whimpers; and I listened with quiet countenance while every nerve trembled; I that dared not utter aye or no to all this blasphemy. Oh, this was a delicious life quite void of guile! I with my dove's look and fox's heart: for indeed I felt only the degradation of falsehood, and not any sacred sentiment of conscious innocence that might redeem it. I who had before clothed myself in the bright garb of sincerity must now borrow one of divers colours: it might sit awkwardly at first, but use would enable me to place it in elegant folds, to lie with grace. Aye, I might die my soul with falsehood untill I had quite hid its native colour. Oh, beloved father! Accept the pure heart of your unhappy daughter; permit me to join you unspotted as I was or you will not recognize my altered semblance. As grief might change Constance[47] so would deceit change me untill in heaven you would say, "This is not my child"—My father, to be happy both now and when again we meet I must fly from all this life which is mockery to one like me. In solitude only shall I be myself; in solitude I shall be thine.

Alas! I even now look back with disgust at my artifices and contrivances by which, after many painful struggles, I effected my retreat. I might enter into a long detail of the means I used, first to secure myself a slight maintenance for the remainder of my life, and afterwards to ensure the conviction of my death: I might, but I will not. I even now blush at the falsehoods I uttered; my heart sickens: I will leave this complication of what I hope I may in a manner call innocent deceit to be imagined by the reader. The remembrance haunts me like a crime—I know that if I were to endeavour to relate it my tale would at length remain unfinished.[48] I was led to London, and had to endure for some weeks cold looks, cold words and colder consolations: but I escaped; they tried to bind me with fetters that they thought silken, yet which weighed on me like iron, although I broke them more easily than a girth formed of a single straw and fled to freedom.

 The few weeks that I spent in London were the most miserable of my life: a great city is a frightful habitation to one sorrowing. The sunset and the gentle moon, the blessed motion of the leaves and the murmuring of waters are all sweet physicians to a distempered mind. The soul is expanded and drinks in quiet, a lulling medecine—to me it was as the sight of the lovely water snakes to the bewitched mariner—in loving and blessing Nature I unawares, called down a blessing on my own soul. But in a city all is closed shut like a prison, a wiry prison from which you can peep at the sky only. I can not describe to you what were the frantic nature of my sensations while I resided there; I was often on the verge of madness. Nay, when I look back on many of my wild thoughts, thoughts with which actions sometimes endeavoured to keep pace; when I tossed my hands high calling down the cope of heaven to fall on me and bury me; when I tore my hair and throwing it to the winds cried, "Ye are free, go seek my father!" And then, like the unfortunate Constance, catching at them again and tying them up, that nought might find him if I might not. How, on my knees I have fancied myself close to my father's grave and struck the ground in anger that it should cover him from me. Oft when I have listened with gasping attention for the sound of the ocean mingled with my father's groans; and then wept untill my strength was gone and I was calm and faint, when I have recollected all this I have asked myself if this were not madness. While in London these and many other dreadful thoughts too harrowing for words were my portion: I lost all this suffering when I was free; when I saw the wild heath around me, and the evening star in the west, then I could weep, gently weep, and be at peace.

 Do not mistake me; I never was really mad. I was always conscious of my state when my wild thoughts seemed to drive me to insanity, and never betrayed them to aught but silence and solitude. The people around me saw nothing of all this. They only saw a poor girl broken in spirit, who spoke in a low and gentle voice, and from underneath whose downcast lids tears would sometimes steal which she strove to hide. One who loved to be alone, and shrunk from observation; who never smiled; oh, no! I never smiled—and that was all.

Well, I escaped. I left my guardian's house and I was never heard of again; it was believed from the letters that I left and other circumstances that I planned that I had destroyed myself. I was sought after therefore with less care than would otherwise have been the case; and soon all trace and memory of me was lost. I left London in a small vessel bound for a port in the north of England. And now having succeeded in my attempt, and being quite alone peace returned to me. The sea was calm and the vessel moved gently onwards, I sat upon deck under the open canopy of heaven and methought I was an altered creature. Not the wild, raving & most miserable Mathilda but a youthful Hermitess dedicated to seclusion and whose bosom she must strive to keep free from all tumult and unholy despair—The fanciful nunlike dress that I had adopted;[49] the knowledge that my very existence was a secret known only to myself; the solitude to which I was for ever hereafter destined nursed gentle thoughts in my wounded heart. The breeze that played in my hair revived me, and I watched with quiet eyes the sunbeams that glittered on the waves, and the birds that coursed each other over the waters just brushing them with their plumes. I slept too undisturbed by dreams; and awoke refreshed to again enjoy my tranquil freedom.

In four days we arrived at the harbour to which we were bound. I would not remain on the sea coast, but proceeded immediately inland. I had already planned the situation where I would live. It should be a solitary house on a wide plain near no other habitation: where I could behold the whole horizon, and wander far without molestation from the sight of my fellow creatures. I was not mysanthropic, but I felt that the gentle current of my feelings depended upon my being alone. I fixed myself on a wide solitude. On a dreary heath bestrewen with stones, among which short grass grew; and here and there a few rushes beside a little pool. Not far from my cottage was a small cluster of pines the only trees to be seen for many miles: I had a path cut through the furze from my door to this little wood, from whose topmost branches the birds saluted the rising sun and awoke me to my daily meditation. My view was bounded only by the horizon except on one side where a distant wood made a black spot on the heath, that every where else stretched out its faint hues as far as the eye could reach, wide and very desolate. Here I could mark the net work of the clouds as they wove themselves into thick masses: I could watch the slow rise of the heavy thunder clouds and could see the rack as it was driven across the heavens, or under the pine trees I could enjoy the stillness of the azure sky.

My life was very peaceful. I had one female servant who spent the greater part of the day at a village two miles off. My amusements were simple and very innocent; I fed the birds who built on the pines or among the ivy that covered the wall of my little garden, and they soon knew me: the bolder ones pecked the crumbs from my hands and perched on my fingers to sing their thankfulness. When I had lived here some time other animals visited me and a fox came every day for a portion of food appropriated for him & would suffer me to pat his head. I had besides many books and a harp with which when despairing I could soothe my spirits, and raise myself to sympathy and love.

Love! What had I to love? Oh many things: there was the moonshine, and the bright stars; the breezes and the refreshing rains; there was the whole earth and the sky that covers it: all lovely forms that visited my imagination[,] all memories of heroism and virtue. Yet this was very unlike my early life although as then I was confined to Nature and books. Then I bounded across the fields; my spirit often seemed to ride upon the winds, and to mingle in joyful sympathy with the ambient air. Then if I wandered slowly I cheered myself with a sweet song or sweeter day dreams. I felt a holy rapture spring from all I saw. I drank in joy with life;

my steps were light; my eyes, clear from the love that animated them, sought the heavens, and with my long hair loosened to the winds I gave my body and my mind to sympathy and delight. But now my walk was slow—My eyes were seldom raised and often filled with tears; no song; no smiles; no careless motion that might bespeak a mind intent on what surrounded it—I was gathered up into myself—a selfish solitary creature ever pondering on my regrets and faded hopes.

Mine was an idle, useless life; it was so; but say not to the lily laid prostrate by the storm arise, and bloom as before. My heart was bleeding from its death's wound; I could live no otherwise—Often amid apparent calm I was visited by despair and melancholy; gloom that nought could dissipate or overcome; a hatred of life; a carelessness of beauty; all these would by fits hold me nearly annihilated by their powers. Never for one moment when most placid did I cease to pray for death. I could be found in no state of mind which I would not willingly have exchanged for nothingness. And morning and evening my tearful eyes raised to heaven, my hands clasped tight in the energy of prayer, I have repeated with the poet—

> Before I see another day
> Oh, let this body die away!

Let me not be reproached then with inutility; I believed that by suicide I should violate a divine law of nature, and I thought that I sufficiently fulfilled my part in submitting to the hard task of enduring the crawling hours & minutes[50]—in bearing the load of time that weighed miserably upon me and that in abstaining from what I in my calm moments considered a crime, I deserved the reward of virtue. There were periods, dreadful ones, during which I despaired—& doubted the existence of all duty & the reality of crime—but I shudder, and turn from the rememberance.

CHAPTER IX

Thus I passed two years. Day after day so many hundreds wore on; they brought no outward changes with them, but some few slowly operated on my mind as I glided on towards death. I began to study more; to sympathize more in the thoughts of others as expressed in books; to read history, and to lose my individuallity among the crowd that had existed before me. Thus perhaps as the sensation of immediate suffering wore off, I became more human. Solitude also lost to me some of its charms: I began again to wish for sympathy; not that I was ever tempted to seek the crowd, but I wished for one friend to love me. You will say perhaps that I gradually became fitted to return to society. I do not think so. For the sympathy that I desired must be so pure, so divested of influence from outward circumstances that in the world I could not fail of being balked by the gross materials that perpetually mingle even with its best feelings. Believe me, I was then less fitted for any communion with my fellow creatures than before. When I left them they had tormented me but it was in the same way as pain and sickness may torment; somthing extraneous to the mind that galled it, and that I wished to cast aside. But now I should have desired sympathy; I should wish to knit my soul to some one of theirs, and should have prepared for myself plentiful draughts of disappointment and suffering; for I was tender as the sensitive plant, all nerve. I did not desire sympathy and aid in ambition or wisdom, but sweet and mutual affection; smiles to cheer me and gentle words of comfort. I wished for one heart in which I could pour unrestrained my plaints, and by the heavenly nature of the soil blessed fruit might spring from such bad seed. Yet how could I find this? The love that is the soul of friendship is a soft spirit seldom found except when two amiable creatures are knit from early youth, or when bound by mutual suffering and pursuits; it comes to some of the elect unsought and unaware; it descends as gentle dew on chosen spots which however barren they were before become under its benign influence fertile in all sweet plants; but when desired it flies; it scoffs at the prayers of its votaries; it will bestow, but not be sought.

I knew all this and did not go to seek sympathy; but there on my solitary heath, under my lowly roof where all around was desart, it came to me as a sun beam in winter to adorn while it helps to dissolve the drifted snow.—Alas the sun shone on blighted fruit; I did not revive under its radiance for I was too utterly undone to feel its kindly power. My father had been and his memory was the life of my life. I might feel gratitude to another but I never more could love or hope as I had done; it was all suffering; even my pleasures were endured, not enjoyed. I was as a solitary spot among mountains shut in on all sides by steep black precipices; where no ray of heat could penetrate; and from which there was no outlet to sunnier fields. And thus it was that although the spirit of friendship soothed me for a while it could not restore me. It came as some gentle visitation; it went and I hardly felt the loss. The spirit of existence was dead within me; be not surprised therefore that when it came I welcomed not more gladly, or when it departed I lamented not more bitterly the best gift of heaven—a friend.

The name of my friend was Woodville.[51] I will briefly relate his history that you may judge how cold my heart must have been not to be warmed by his eloquent words and tender sympathy; and how he also being most unhappy we were well fitted to be a mutual consolation to each other, if I had not been hardened to stone by the Medusa head of Misery. The misfortunes of Woodville were not of the hearts core like mine; his was a natural grief, not to destroy but to purify the heart and from which he might, when its shadow had passed from over him, shine forth brighter and happier than before.

Woodville was the son of a poor clergyman and had received a classical education. He was one of those very few whom fortune favours from their birth; on whom she bestows all gifts of intellect and person with a profusion that knew no bounds, and whom under her peculiar protection, no imperfection however slight, or disappointment however transitory has leave to touch. She seemed to have formed his mind of that excellence which no dross can tarnish, and his understanding was such that no error could pervert. His genius was transcendant, and when it rose as a bright star in the east all eyes were turned towards it in admiration. He was a Poet. That name has so often been degraded that it will not convey the idea of all that he was. He was like a poet of old whom the muses had crowned in his cradle, and on whose lips bees had fed. As he walked among other men he seemed encompassed with a heavenly halo that divided him from and lifted him above them. It was his surpassing beauty, the dazzling fire of his eyes, and his words whose rich accents wrapt the listener in mute and extatic wonder, that made him transcend all others so that before him they appeared only formed to minister to his superior excellence.

He was glorious from his youth. Every one loved him; no shadow of envy or hate cast even from the meanest mind ever fell upon him. He was, as one the peculiar delight of the Gods, railed and fenced in by his own divinity, so that nought but love and admiration could approach him. His heart was simple like a child, unstained by arrogance or vanity. He mingled in society unknowing of his superiority over his companions, not because he undervalued himself but because he did not perceive the inferiority of others. He seemed incapable of conceiving of the full extent of the power that selfishness & vice possesses in the world: when I knew him, although he had suffered disappointment in his dearest hopes, he had not experienced any that arose from the meaness and self love of men: his station was too high to allow of his suffering through their hardheartedness; and too low for him to have experienced ingratitude and encroaching selfishness: it is one of the blessings of a moderate fortune, that by preventing the possessor from confering pecuniary favours it prevents him also from diving into the arcana of human weakness or malice—To bestow on your fellow men is a Godlike attribute—So indeed it is and as such not one fit for mortality;—the giver like Adam and Prometheus, must pay the penalty of rising above his nature by being the martyr to his own excellence. Woodville was free from all these evils; and if slight examples did come across him[52] he did not notice them but passed on in his course as an angel with winged feet might glide along the earth unimpeded by all those little obstacles over which we of earthly origin stumble. He was a believer in the divinity of genius and always opposed a stern disbelief to the objections of those petty cavillers and minor critics who wish to reduce all men to their own miserable level—"I will make a scientific simile" he would say, "[i]n the manner, if you will, of Dr. Darwin—I consider the alledged errors of a man of genius as the aberrations of the fixed stars. It is our distance from them and our imperfect means of communication that makes them appear to move; in truth they always remain stationary, a glorious centre, giving us a fine lesson of modesty if we would thus receive it."[53]

I have said that he was a poet: when he was three and twenty years of age he first published a poem, and it was hailed by the whole nation with enthusiasm and delight. His good star perpetually shone upon him; a reputation had never before been made so rapidly: it was universal. The multitude extolled the same poems that formed the wonder of the sage in his closet: there was not one dissentient voice.[54]

It was at this time, in the height of his glory, that he became acquainted with Elinor. She was a young heiress of exquisite beauty who lived under the care of her guardian: from the moment they were seen together they appeared formed for each other. Elinor had not the genius of Woodville but she was generous and noble, and exalted by her youth and the love that she every where excited above the knowledge of aught but virtue and excellence. She was lovely; her manners were frank and simple; her deep blue eyes swam in a lustre which could only be given by sensibility joined to wisdom.

They were formed for one another and they soon loved. Woodville for the first time felt the delight of love; and Elinor was enraptured in possessing the heart of one so beautiful and glorious among his fellow men. Could any thing but unmixed joy flow from such a union?

Woodville was a Poet—he was sought for by every society and all eyes were turned on him alone when he appeared; but he was the son of a poor clergyman and Elinor was a rich heiress. Her guardian was not displeased with their mutual affection: the merit of Woodville was too eminent to admit of cavil on account of his inferior wealth; but the dying will of her father did not allow her to marry before she was of age and her fortune depended upon her obeying this injunction. She had just entered her twentieth year, and she and her lover were obliged to submit to this delay. But they were ever together and their happiness seemed that of Paradise: they studied together: formed plans of future occupations, and drinking in love and joy from each other's eyes and words they hardly repined at the delay to their entire union. Woodville for ever rose in glory; and Elinor become more lovely and wise under the lessons of her accomplished lover.

In two months Elinor would be twenty one: every thing was prepared for their union. How shall I relate the catastrophe to so much joy; but the earth would not be the earth it is covered with blight and sorrow if one such pair as these angelic creatures had been suffered to exist for one another: search through the world and you will not find the perfect happiness which their marriage would have caused them to enjoy; there must have been a revolution in the order of things as established among us miserable earth-dwellers to have admitted of such consummate joy. The chain of necessity ever bringing misery must have been broken and the malignant fate that presides over it would not permit this breach of her eternal laws. But why should I repine at this? Misery was my element, and nothing but what was miserable could approach me; if Woodville had been happy I should never have known him. And can I who for many years was fed by tears, and nourished under the dew of grief, can I pause to relate a tale of woe and death?[55]

Woodville was obliged to make a journey into the country and was detained from day to day in irksome absence from his lovely bride. He received a letter from her to say that she was slightly ill, but telling him to hasten to her, that from his eyes she would receive health and that his company would be her surest medecine. He was detained three days longer and then he hastened to her. His heart, he knew not why prognosticated misfortune; he had not heard from her again; he feared she might be worse and this fear made him impatient and restless for the moment of beholding her once more stand before him arrayed in health and beauty; for a sinister voice seemed always to whisper to him, "You will never more behold her as she was."

When he arrived at her habitation all was silent in it: he made his way through several rooms; in one he saw a servant weeping bitterly: he was faint with fear and could hardly ask, "Is she dead?" and just listened to the dreadful answer, "Not yet." These astounding words came on him as of less fearful import than those which he had expected; and to learn that she was still in being, and that he might still hope was an alleviation to him. He remembered the words of her letter and he indulged the wild idea that his kisses breathing warm love and life would infuse new spirit into her, and that with him near her she could not die; that his presence was the talisman of her life.

He hastened to her sick room; she lay, her cheeks burning with fever, yet her eyes were closed and she was seemingly senseless. He wrapt her in his arms; he imprinted breathless kisses on her burning lips; he called to her in a voice of subdued anguish by the tenderest names; "Return Elinor; I am with you; your life, your love. Return; dearest one, you promised me this boon, that I should bring you health. Let your sweet spirit revive; you cannot die near me: What is death? To see you no more? To part with what is a part of myself; without whom I have no memory and no futurity? Elinor die! This is frenzy and the most miserable despair: you cannot die while I am near."

And again he kissed her eyes and lips, and hung over her inanimate form in agony, gazing on her countenance still lovely although changed, watching every slight convulsion, and varying colour which denoted life still lingering although about to depart. Once for a moment she revived and recognized his voice; a smile, a last lovely smile, played upon her lips. He watched beside her for twelve hours and then she died.[56]

CHAPTER X

It was six months after this miserable conclusion to his long nursed hopes that I first saw him. He had retired to a part of the country where he was not known that he might peacefully indulge his grief. All the world, by the death of his beloved Elinor, was changed to him, and he could no longer remain in any spot where he had seen her or where her image mingled with the most rapturous hopes had brightened all around with a light of joy which would now be transformed to a darkness blacker than midnight since she, the sun of his life, was set for ever.

He lived for some time never looking on the light of heaven but shrouding his eyes in a perpetual darkness far from all that could remind him of what he had been; but as time softened his grief[57] like a true child of Nature he sought in the enjoyment of her beauties for a consolation in his unhappiness. He came to a part of the country where he was entirely unknown and where in the deepest solitude he could converse only with his own heart. He found a relief to his impatient grief in the breezes of heaven and in the sound of waters and woods. He became fond of riding; this exercise distracted his mind and elevated his spirits; on a swift horse he could for a moment gain respite from the image that else for ever followed him; Elinor on her death bed, her sweet features changed, and the soft spirit that animated her gradually waning into extinction. For many months Woodville had in vain endeavoured to cast off this terrible remembrance; it still hung on him untill memory was too great a burthen for his loaded soul, but when on horseback the spell that seemingly held him to this idea was snapt; then if he thought of his lost bride he pictured her radiant in beauty; he could hear her voice, and fancy her "a sylvan Huntress by his side," while his eyes brightened as he thought he gazed on her cherished form. I had several times seen him ride across the heath and felt angry that my solitude should be disturbed. It was so long [since] I had spoken to any but peasants that I felt a disagreable sensation at being gazed on by one of superior rank. I feared also that it might be some one who had seen me before: I might be recognized, my impostures discovered and I dragged back to a life of worse torture than that I had before endured. These were dreadful fears and they even haunted my dreams.[58]

I was one day seated on the verge of the clump of pines when Woodville rode past. As soon as I perceived him I suddenly rose to escape from his observation by entering among the trees. My rising startled his horse; he reared and plunged and the Rider was at length thrown. The horse then galopped swiftly across the heath and the stranger remained on the ground stunned by his fall. He was not materially hurt, a little fresh water soon recovered him. I was struck by his exceeding beauty, and as he spoke to thank me the sweet but melancholy cadence of his voice brought tears into my eyes.

A short conversation passed between us, but the next day he again stopped at my cottage and by degrees an intimacy grew between us. It was strange to him to see a female in extreme youth, I was not yet twenty, evidently belonging to the first classes of society & possessing every accomplishment an excellent education could bestow, living alone on a desolate health —One on whose forehead the impress of grief was strongly marked, and whose words and motions betrayed that her thoughts did not follow them but were intent on far other ideas; bitter and overwhelming miseries. I was dressed also in a whimsical nunlike habit which denoted that I did not retire to solitude from necessity, but that I might indulge in a luxury of grief, and fanciful seclusion.

He soon took great interest in me, and sometimes forgot his own grief to sit beside me and endeavour to cheer me. He could not fail to interest even one who had shut herself from the whole world, whose hope was death, and who lived only with the departed. His personal beauty; his conversation which glowed with imagination and sensibility; the poetry that seemed to hang upon his lips and to make the very air mute to listen to him were charms that no one could resist. He was younger, less worn, more passionless than my father and in no degree reminded me of him: he suffered under immediate grief yet its gentle influence instead of calling feelings otherwise dormant into action, seemed only to veil that which otherwise would have been too dazzling for me. When we were together I spoke little yet my selfish mind was sometimes borne away by the rapid course of his ideas; I would lift my eyes with momentary brilliancy until memories that never died and seldom slept would recur, and a tear would dim them.

Woodville for ever tried to lead me to the contemplation of what is beautiful and happy in the world.[59] His own mind was constitunially bent to a former belief in good [rather] than in evil and this feeling which must even exhilirate the hopeless ever shone forth in his words. He would talk of the wonderful powers of man, of their present state and of their hopes: of what they had been and what they were, and when reason could no longer guide him, his imagination as if inspired shed light on the obscurity that veils the past and the future. He loved to dwell on what might have been the state of the earth before man lived on it, and how he first arose and gradually became the strange, complicated, but as he said, the glorious creature he now is. Covering the earth with their creations and forming by the power of their minds another world more lovely than the visible frame of things, even all the world that we find in their writings. A beautiful creation, he would say, which may claim this superiority to its model, that good and evil is more easily seperated[:] the good rewarded in the way they themselves desire; the evil punished as all things evil ought to be punished, not by pain which is revolting to all philanthropy to consider but by quiet obscurity, which simply deprives them of their harmful qualities; why kill the serpent when you have extracted his fangs?

The poetry of his language and ideas which my words ill convey held me enchained to his discourses. It was a melancholy pleasure to me to listen to his inspired words; to catch for a moment the light of his eyes[;] to feel a transient sympathy and then to awaken from the delusion, again to know that all this was nothing,—a dream—a shadow for that there was no reallity for me; my father had for ever deserted me, leaving me only memories which set an eternal barrier between me and my fellow creatures. I was indeed fellow to none. He—Woodville, mourned the loss of his bride: others wept the various forms of misery as they visited them: but infamy and guilt was mingled with my portion; unlawful and detestable passion had poured its poison into my ears and changed all my blood, so that it was no longer the kindly stream that supports life but a cold fountain of bitterness corrupted in its very source.[60] It must be the excess of madness that could make me imagine that I could ever be aught but one alone; struck off from humanity; bearing no affinity to man or woman; a wretch on whom Nature had set her ban.

Sometimes Woodville talked to me of himself. He related his history brief in happiness and woe and dwelt with passion on his and Elinor's mutual love. "She was["], he said, "the brightest vision that ever came upon the earth: there was somthing in her frank countenance, in her voice, and in every motion of her graceful form that overpowered me, as if it were a celestial creature that deigned to mingle with me in intercourse more sweet than man had ever before enjoyed. Sorrow fled before her; and her smile seemed to possess an influence like light to irradiate all mental darkness. It was not like a human loveliness that these gentle smiles went and came; but as a sunbeam on a lake, now light and now obscure, flitting before as you strove to catch them, and fold them for ever to your heart. I saw this smile fade for ever. Alas! I could never have believed that it was indeed Elinor that died if once when I spoke she had not lifted her almost benighted eyes, and for one moment like nought beside on earth, more lovely than a sunbeam, slighter, quicker than the waving plumage of a bird, dazzling as lightning and like it giving day to night, yet mild and faint, that smile came; it went, and then there was an end of all joy to me."

Thus his own sorrows, or the shapes copied from nature that dwelt in his mind with beauty greater than their own, occupied our talk while I railed in my own griefs with cautious secresy. If for a moment he shewed curiosity, my eyes fell, my voice died away and my evident suffering made him quickly endeavour to banish the ideas he had awakened; yet he for ever mingled consolation in his talk, and tried to soften my despair by demonstrations of deep sympathy and compassion. "We are both unhappy—" he would say to me; "I have told you my melancholy tale and we have wept together the loss of that lovely spirit that has so cruelly deserted me; but you hide your griefs: I do not ask you to disclose them, but tell me if I may not console you. It seems to me a wild adventure to find in this desart one like you quite solitary: you are young and lovely; your manners are refined and attractive; yet there is in your settled melancholy, and something, I know not what, in your expressive eyes that seems to seperate you from your kind: you shudder; pardon me, I entreat you but I cannot help expressing this once at least the lively interest I feel in your destiny.

"You never smile: your voice is low, and you utter your words as if you were afraid of the slight sound they would produce: the expression of awful and intense sorrow never for a moment fades from your countenance. I have lost for ever the loveliest companion that any man could ever have possessed, one who rather appears to have been a superior spirit who by some strange accident wandered among us earthly creatures, than as belonging to our kind. Yet I smile, and sometimes I speak almost forgetful of the change I have endured. But your sad mien never alters; your pulses beat and you breathe, yet you seem already to belong to another world; and sometimes, pray pardon my wild thoughts, when you touch my hand I am surprised to find your hand warm when all the fire of life seems extinct within you.

"When I look upon you, the tears you shed, the soft deprecating look with which you withstand enquiry; the deep sympathy your voice expresses when I speak of my lesser sorrows add to my interest for you. You stand here shelterless[.] You have cast yourself from among us and you wither on this wild plain fo[r]lorn and helpless: some dreadful calamity must have befallen you. Do not turn from me; I do not ask you to reveal it: I only entreat you to listen to me and to become familiar with the voice of consolation and kindness. If pity, and admiration, and gentle affection can wean you from despair let me attempt the task. I cannot see your look of deep grief without endeavouring to restore you to happier feelings. Unbend your brow; relax the stern melancholy of your regard; permit a friend, a sincere, affectionate friend, I will be one, to convey some relief, some momentary pause to your sufferings.

"Do not think that I would intrude upon your confidence: I only ask your patience. Do not for ever look sorrow and never speak it; utter one word of bitter complaint and I will reprove it with gentle exhortation and pour on you the balm of compassion. You must not shut me from all communion with you: do not tell me why you grieve but only say the words, "I am unhappy," and you will feel relieved as if for some time excluded from all intercourse by some magic spell you should suddenly enter again the pale of human sympathy. I entreat you to believe in my most sincere professions and to treat me as an old and tried friend: promise me never to forget me, never causelessly to banish me; but try to love me as one who would devote all his energies to make you happy. Give me the name of friend; I will fulfill its duties; and if for a moment complaint and sorrow would shape themselves into words let me be near to speak peace to your vext soul."

I repeat his persuasions in faint terms and cannot give you at the same time the tone and gesture that animated them. Like a refreshing shower on an arid soil they revived me, and although I still kept their cause secret he led me to pour forth my bitter complaints and to clothe my woe in words of gall and fire. With all the energy of desperate grief

I told him how I had fallen at once from bliss to misery; how that for me there was no joy, no hope; that death however bitter would be the welcome seal to all my pangs; death the skeleton was to be beautiful as love. I know not why but I found it sweet to utter these words to human ears; and though I derided all consolation yet I was pleased to see it offered me with gentleness and kindness. I listened quietly, and when he paused would again pour out my misery in expressions that shewed how far too deep my wounds were for any cure.

But now also I began to reap the fruits of my perfect solitude. I had become unfit for any intercourse, even with Woodville the most gentle and sympathizing creature that existed. I had become captious and unreasonable: my temper was utterly spoilt. I called him my friend but I viewed all he did with jealous eyes. If he did not visit me at the appointed hour I was angry, very angry, and told him that if indeed he did feel interest in me it was cold, and could not be fitted for me, a poor worn creature, whose deep unhappiness demanded much more than his worldly heart could give. When for a moment I imagined that his manner was cold I would fretfully say to him—"I was at peace before you came; why have you disturbed me? You have given me new wants and now your trifle with me as if my heart were as whole as yours, as if I were not in truth a shorn lamb thrust out on the bleak hill side, tortured by every blast. I wished for no friend, no sympathy[.] I avoided you, you know I did, but you forced yourself upon me and gave me those wants which you see with triump[h] give you power over me. Oh the brave power of the bitter north wind which freezes the tears it has caused to shed! But I will not bear this; go: the sun will rise and set as before you came, and I shall sit among the pines or wander on the heath weeping and complaining without wishing for you to listen. You are cruel, very cruel, to treat me who bleed at every pore in this rough manner."[61]

And then, when in answer to my peevish words, I saw his countenance bent with living pity on me[,] when I saw him

Gli occhi drizzo ver me con quel sembiante
Che madre fa sopra figlioul deliro

                              P[a]radiso. C 1.[62]

I wept and said, "Oh, pardon me! You are good and kind but I am not fit for life. Why am I obliged to live? To drag hour after hour, to see the trees wave their branches restlessly, to feel the air, & to suffer in all I feel keenest agony. My frame is strong, but my soul sinks beneath this endurance of living anguish. Death is the goal that I would attain, but, alas! I do not even see the end of the course. Do you, my compassionate friend,[63] tell me how to die peacefully and innocently and I will bless you: all that I, poor wretch, can desire is a painless death."

But Woodville's words had magic in them, when beginning with the sweetest pity, he would raise me by degrees out of myself and my sorrows until I wondered at my own selfishness: but he left me and despair returned; the work of consolation was ever to begin anew. I often desired his entire absence; for I found that I was grown out of the ways of life and that by long seclusion, although I could support my accustomed grief, and drink the bitter daily draught with some degree of patience, yet I had become unfit for the slightest novelty of feeling. Expectation, and hopes, and affection were all too much for me. I knew this, but at other times I was unreasonable and laid the blame upon him, who was most blameless, and pevishly thought that if his gentle soul were more gentle, if his intense sympathy were more intense, he could drive the fiend from my soul and make me more human. I am, I thought, a tragedy; a character that he comes to see act: now and then he gives me my cue[64] that I may make a speech more to his purpose: perhaps he is already planning a poem in which I am to figure. I am a farce and play to him, but to me this is all dreary reality: he takes all the profit and I bear all the burthen.

CHAPTER XI

It is a strange circumstance but it often occurs that blessings by their use turn to curses; and that I who in solitude had desired sympathy as the only relief I could enjoy should now find it an additional torture to me. During my father's life time I had always been of an affectionate and forbearing disposition, but since those days of joy alas! I was much changed. I had become arrogant, peevish, and above all suspicious. Although the real interest of my narration is now ended and I ought quickly to wind up its melancholy catastrophe, yet I will relate one instance of my sad suspicion and despair and how Woodville with the goodness and almost the power of an angel, softened my rugged feelings and led me back to gentleness.[65]

He had promised to spend some hours with me one afternoon but a violent and continual rain[66] prevented him. I was alone the whole evening. I had passed two whole years alone unrepining, but now I was miserable. He could not really care for me, I thought, for if he did the storm would rather have made him come even if I had not expected him, than, as it did, prevent a promised visit. He would well know that this drear sky and gloomy rain would load my spirit almost to madness: if the weather had been fine I should not have regretted his absence as heavily as I necessarily must shut up in this miserable cottage with no companions but my own wretched thoughts. If he were truly my friend he would have calculated all this; and let me now calculate this boasted friendship, and discover its real worth. He got over his grief for Elinor, and the country became dull to him, so he was glad to find even me for amusement; and when he does not know what else to do he passes his lazy hours here, and calls this friendship—It is true that his presence is a consolation to me, and that his words are sweet, and, when he will he can pour forth thoughts that win me from despair. His words are sweet,—and so, truly, is the honey of the bee, but the bee has a sting, and unkindness is a worse smart that that received from an insect's venom. I will[67] put him to the proof. He says all hope is dead to him, and I know that it is dead to me, so we are both equally fitted for death. Let me try if he will die with me; and as I fear to die alone, if he will accompany [me] to cheer me, and thus he can shew himself my friend in the only manner my misery will permit.[68]

It was madness I believe, but I so worked myself up to this idea that I could think of nothing else. If he dies with me it is well, and there will be an end of two miserable beings; and if he will not, then will I scoff at his friendship and drink the poison before him to shame his cowardice. I planned the whole scene with an earnest heart and franticly set my soul on this project. I procured Laudanum and placing it in two glasses on the table, filled my room with flowers and decorated the last scene of my tragedy with the nicest care. As the hour for his coming approached my heart softened and I wept; not that I gave up my plan, but even when resolved the mind must undergo several revolutions of feeling before it can drink its death.

Now all was ready and Woodville came. I received him at the door of my cottage and leading him solemnly into the room, I said: "My friend, I wish to die. I am quite weary of enduring the misery which hourly I do endure, and I will throw it off. What slave will not, if he may, escape from his chains? Look, I weep: for more than two years I have never enjoyed one moment free from anguish. I have often desired to die; but I am a very coward. It is hard for one so young who was once so happy as I was; voluntarily to divest themselves of all sensation and to go alone to the dreary grave; I dare not. I must die, yet my fear chills me; I pause and shudder and then for months I endure my excess of wretchedness. But now the time is come when I may quit life, I have a friend who will not refuse to accompany me in this dark journey; such is my request:[69] earnestly do I entreat and implore you to die with me. Then we shall find Elinor and what I have lost. Look, I am prepared; there is the death draught, let us drink it together and willingly & joyfully quit this hated round of daily life[.]

"You turn from me; yet before you deny me reflect, Woodville, how sweet it were to cast off the load of tears and misery under which we now labour: and surely we shall find light after we have passed the dark valley. That drink will plunge us in a sweet slumber, and when we awaken what joy will be ours to find all our sorrows and fears past. *A little patience, and all will be over*; aye, a very little patience; for, look, there is the key of our prison; we hold it in our own hands, and are we more debased than slaves to cast it away and give ourselves up to voluntary bondage? Even now if we had courage we might be free. Behold, my cheek is flushed with pleasure at the imagination of death; all that we love are dead. Come, give me your hand, one look of joyous sympathy and we will go together and seek them; a lulling journey; where our arrival will bring bliss and our waking be that of angels. Do you delay? Are you a coward, Woodville? Oh fie! Cast off this blank look of human melancholy. Oh! that I had words to express the luxury of death that I might win you. I tell you we are no longer miserable mortals; we are about to become Gods; spirits free and happy as gods. What fool on a bleak shore, seeing a flowery isle on the other side with his lost love beckoning to him from it would pause because the wave is dark and turbid?

> "What if some little payne the passage have
> That makes frayle flesh to fear the bitter wave?
> Is not short payne well borne that brings long ease,
> And lays the soul to sleep in quiet grave?[F]

"Do you mark my words; I have learned the language of despair: I have it all by heart, for I am Despair; and a strange being am I, joyous, triumphant Despair. But those words are false, for the wave may be dark but it is not bitter. We lie down, and close our eyes with a gentle good night, and when we wake, we are free. Come then, no more delay, thou tardy one! Behold the pleasant potion! Look, I am a spirit of good, and not a human maid that invites thee, and with winning accents, (oh, that they would win thee!) says, Come and drink."[70]

As I spoke I fixed my eyes upon his countenance, and his exquisite beauty, the heavenly compassion that beamed from his eyes, his gentle yet earnest look of deprecation and wonder even before he spoke wrought a change in my high strained feelings taking from me all the sternness of despair and filling me only with the softest grief. I saw his eyes humid also as he took both my hands in his; and sitting down near me, he said:[71]

"This is a sad deed to which you would lead me, dearest friend, and your woe must indeed be deep that could fill you with these unhappy thoughts. You long for death and yet you fear it and wish me to be your companion. But I have less courage than you and even thus accompanied I dare not die. Listen to me, and then reflect if you ought to win me to your project, even if with the over-bearing eloquence of despair you could make black death so inviting that the fair heaven should appear darkness. Listen I entreat you to the words of one who has himself nurtured desperate thoughts, and longed with impatient desire for death, but who has at length trampled the phantom under foot, and crushed his sting. Come, as you have played Despair with me I will play the part of Una with you and bring you hurtless from his dark cavern. Listen to me, and let yourself be softened by words in which no selfish passion lingers.

"We know not what all this wide world means; its strange mixture of good and evil. But we have been placed here and bid live and hope. I know not what we are to hope; but there is some good beyond us that we must seek; and that is our earthly task. If misfortune come against us we must fight with her; we must cast her aside, and still go on to find out that which it is our nature to desire. Whether this prospect of future good be the preparation for another existence I know not; or whether that it is merely that we, as workmen in God's vineyard, must lend a hand to smooth the way for our posterity. If it indeed be that; if the efforts of the virtuous now, are to make the future inhabitants of this fair world more happy; if the labours of those who cast aside selfishness, and try to know the truth of things, are to free the men of ages, now far distant but which will one day come, from the burthen under which those who now live groan, and like you weep bitterly; if they free them but from one of what are now the necessary evils of life, truly I will not fail but will with my whole soul aid the work. From my youth I have said, I will be virtuous; I will dedicate my life for the good of others; I will do my best to extirpate evil and if the spirit who protects ill should so influence circumstances that I should suffer through my endeavour, yet while there is hope and hope there ever must be, of success, cheerfully do I gird myself to my task.

"I have powers; my countrymen think well of them. Do you think I sow my seed in the barren air, & have no end in what I do? Believe me, I will never desert life untill this last hope is torn from my bosom, that in some way my labours may form a link in the chain of gold with which we ought all to strive to drag Happiness from where she sits enthroned above the clouds, now far beyond our reach, to inhabit the earth with us. Let us suppose that Socrates, or Shakespear, or Rousseau had been seized with despair and died in youth when they were as young as I am; do you think that we and all the world should not have lost incalculable improvement in our good feelings and our happiness thro' their destruction. I am not like one of these; they influenced millions: but if I can influence but a hundred, but ten, but one solitary individual, so as in any way to lead him from ill to good, that will be a joy to repay me for all my sufferings, though they were a million times multiplied; and that hope will support me to bear them[.]

"And those who do not work for posterity; or working, as may be my case, will not be known by it; yet they, believe me, have also their duties.

You grieve because you are unhappy[;] it is happiness you seek but you despair of obtaining it. But if you can bestow happiness on another; if you can give one other person only one hour of joy ought you not to live to do it? And every one has it in their power to do that. The inhabitants of this world suffer so much pain. In crowded cities, among cultivated plains, or on the desert mountains, pain is thickly sown, and if we can tear up but one of these noxious weeds, or more, if in its stead we can sow one seed of corn, or plant one fair flower, let that be motive sufficient against suicide. Let us not desert our task while there is the slightest hope that we may in a future day do this.

"Indeed I dare not die. I have a mother whose support and hope I am. I have a friend who loves me as his life, and in whose breast I should infix a mortal sting if I ungratefully left him. So I will not die. Nor shall you, my friend; cheer up; cease to weep, I entreat you. Are you not young, and fair, and good? Why should you despair? Or if you must for yourself, why for others? If you can never be happy, can you never bestow happiness[?] Oh! believe me, if you beheld on lips pale with grief one smile of joy and gratitude, and knew that you were parent of that smile, and that without you it had never been, you would feel so pure and warm a happiness that you would wish to live for ever again and again to enjoy the same pleasure[.]

"Come, I see that you have already cast aside the sad thoughts you before franticly indulged. Look in that mirror; when I came your brow was contracted, your eyes deep sunk in your head, your lips quivering; your hands trembled violently when I took them; but now all is tranquil and soft. You are grieved and there is grief in the expression of your countenance but it is gentle and sweet. You allow me to throw away this cursed drink; you smile; oh, Congratulate me, hope is triumphant, and I have done some good."

These words are shadowy as I repeat them but they were indeed words of fire and produced a warm hope in me (I, miserable wretch, to hope!) that tingled like pleasure in my veins. He did not leave me for many hours; not until he had improved the spark that he had kindled, and with an angelic hand fostered the return of somthing that seemed like joy. He left me but I still was calm, and after I had saluted the starry sky and dewy earth with eyes of love and a contented good night, I slept sweetly, visited by dreams, the first of pleasure I had had for many long months.

But this was only a momentary relief and my old habits of feeling returned; for I was doomed while in life to grieve, and to the natural sorrow of my father's death and its most terrific cause, immagination added a tenfold weight of woe. I believed myself to be polluted by the unnatural love I had inspired, and that I was a creature cursed and set apart by nature. I thought that like another Cain, I had a mark set on my forehead to shew mankind that there was a barrier between me and they .[72] Woodville had told me that there was in my countenance an expression as if I belonged to another world; so he had seen that sign: and there it lay a gloomy mark to tell the world that there was that within my soul that no silence could render sufficiently obscure. Why when fate drove me to become this outcast from human feeling; this monster with whom none might mingle in converse and love; why had she not from that fatal and most accursed moment, shrouded me in thick mists and placed real darkness between me and my fellows so that I might never more be seen?, and as I passed, like a murky cloud loaded with blight, they might only perceive me by the cold chill I should cast upon them; telling them, how truly, that something unholy was near? Then I should have lived upon this dreary heath unvisited, and blasting none by my unhallowed gaze. Alas! I verily believe that if the near prospect of death did not dull and soften my bitter [fe]elings, if for a few months longer I had continued to live as I then lived, strong in body, but my soul corrupted to its core by a deadly cancer[,] if day after day I had dwelt on these dreadful sentiments I should have become mad, and should have fancied myself a living pestilence: so horrible to my own solitary thoughts did this form, this voice, and all this wretched self appear; for had it not been the source of guilt that wants a name?[73]

This was superstition. I did not feel thus franticly when first I knew that the holy name of father was become a curse to me: but my lonely life inspired me with wild thoughts; and then when I saw Woodville & day after day he tried to win my confidence and I never dared give words to my dark tale, I was impressed more strongly with the withering fear that I was in truth a marked creature, a pariah, only fit for death.

CHAPTER XII

As I was perpetually haunted by these ideas, you may imagine that the influence of Woodville's words was very temporary; and that although I did not again accuse him of unkindness, yet I soon became as unhappy as before. Soon after this incident we parted. He heard that his mother was ill, and he hastened to her. He came to take leave of me, and we walked together on the heath for the last time. He promised that he would come and see me again; and bade me take cheer, and to encourage what happy thoughts I could, untill time and fortitude should overcome my misery, and I could again mingle in society.

"Above all other admonition on my part," he said, "cherish and follow this one: do not despair. That is the most dangerous gulph on which you perpetually totter; but you must reassure your steps, and take hope to guide you.[74] Hope, and your wounds will be already half healed: but if you obstinately despair, there never more will be comfort for you. Believe me, my dearest friend, that there is a joy that the sun and earth and all its beauties can bestow that you will one day feel. The refreshing bliss of Love will again visit your heart, and undo the spell that binds you to woe, untill you wonder how your eyes could be closed in the long night that burthens you. I dare not hope that I have inspired you with sufficient interest that the thought of me, and the affection that I shall ever bear you, will soften your melancholy and decrease the bitterness of your tears. But if my friendship can make you look on life with less disgust, beware how you injure it with suspicion. Love is a delicate sprite[75] and easily hurt by rough jealousy. Guard, I entreat you, a firm persuasion of my sincerity in the inmost recesses of your heart out of the reach of the casual winds that may disturb its surface. Your temper is made unequal by suffering, and the tenor of your mind is, I fear, sometimes shaken by unworthy causes; but let your confidence in my sympathy and love be deeper far, and incapable of being reached by these agitations that come and go, and if they touch not your affections leave you uninjured."

These were some of Woodville's last lessons. I wept as I listened to him; and after we had taken an affectionate farewell, I followed him far with my eyes until they saw the last of my earthly comforter. I had insisted on accompanying him across the heath towards the town where he dwelt: the sun was yet high when he left me, and I turned my steps towards my cottage. It was at the latter end of the month of September when the nights have become chill. But the weather was serene, and as I walked on I fell into no unpleasing reveries. I thought of Woodville with gratitude and kindness and did not, I know not why, regret his departure with any bitterness. It seemed that after one great shock all other change was trivial to me; and I walked on wondering when the time would come when we should all four, my dearest father restored to me, meet in some sweet Paradise[.] I pictured to myself a lovely river such as that on whose banks Dante describes Mathilda gathering flowers, which ever flows

—bruna, bruna,
Sotto l'ombra perpetua, che mai
Raggiar non lascia sole ivi, nè Luna.[76]

And then I repeated to myself all that lovely passage that relates the entrance of Dante into the terrestrial Paradise; and thought it would be sweet when I wandered on those lovely banks to see the car of light descend with my long lost parent to be restored to me. As I waited there in expectation of that moment, I thought how, of the lovely flowers that grew there, I would wind myself a chaplet and crown myself for joy: I would sing *sul margine d'un rio*,[77] my father's favourite song, and that my voice gliding through the windless air would announce to him in whatever bower he sat expecting the moment of our union, that his daughter was come. Then the mark of misery would have faded from my brow, and I should raise my eyes fearlessly to meet his, which ever beamed with the soft lustre of innocent love. When I reflected on the magic look of those deep eyes I wept, but gently, lest my sobs should disturb the fairy scene.

I was so entirely wrapt in this reverie that I wandered on, taking no heed of my steps until I actually stooped down to gather a flower for my wreath on that bleak plain where no flower grew, when I awoke from my day dream and found myself I knew not where.

The sun had set and the roseate hue which the clouds had caught from him in his descent had nearly died away. A wind swept across the plain, I looked around me and saw no object that told me where I was; I had lost myself, and in vain attempted to find my path. I wandered on, and the coming darkness made every trace indistinct by which I might be guided. At length all was veiled in the deep obscurity of blackest night; I became weary and knowing that my servant was to sleep that night at the neighbouring village, so that my absence would alarm no one; and that I was safe in this wild spot from every intruder, I resolved to spend the night where I was. Indeed I was too weary to walk further: the air was chill but I was careless of bodily inconvenience, and I thought that I was well inured to the weather during my two years of solitude, when no change of seasons prevented my perpetual wanderings.

I lay upon the grass surrounded by a darkness which not the slightest beam of light penetrated—There was no sound for the deep night had laid to sleep the insects, the only creatures that lived on the lone spot where no tree or shrub could afford shelter to aught else—There was a wondrous silence in the air that calmed my senses yet which enlivened my soul, my mind hurried from image to image and seemed to grasp an eternity. All in my heart was shadowy yet calm, untill my ideas became confused and at length died away in sleep.[78]

When I awoke it rained:[79] I was already quite wet, and my limbs were stiff and my head giddy with the chill of night. It was a drizzling, penetrating shower; as my dank hair clung to my neck and partly covered my face, I had hardly strength to part with my fingers, the long strait locks that fell before my eyes. The darkness was much dissipated and in the east where the clouds were least dense the moon was visible behind the thin grey cloud—

> The moon is behind, and at the full
> And yet she looks both small and dull.[80]

Its presence gave me a hope that by its means I might find my home. But I was languid and many hours passed before I could reach the cottage, dragging as I did my slow steps, and often resting on the wet earth unable to proceed.

I particularly mark this night, for it was that which has hurried on the last scene of my tragedy, which else might have dwindled on through long years of listless sorrow. I was very ill when I arrived and quite incapable of taking off my wet clothes that clung about me. In the morning, on her return, my servant found me almost lifeless, while possessed by a high fever I was lying on the floor of my room.

I was very ill for a long time, and when I recovered from the immediate danger of fever, every symptom of a rapid consumption declared itself. I was for some time ignorant of this and thought that my excessive weakness was the consequence of the fever; But my strength became less and less; as winter came on I had a cough; and my sunken cheek, before pale, burned with a hectic fever. One by one these symptoms struck me; & I became convinced that the moment I had so much desired was about to arrive and that I was dying. I was sitting by my fire, the physician who had attended me ever since my fever had just left me, and I looked over his prescription in which digitalis was the prominent medecine. "Yes," I said, "I see how this is, and it is strange that I should have deceived myself so long; I am about to die an innocent death, and it will be sweeter even than that which the opium promised."

I rose and walked slowly to the window; the wide heath was covered by snow which sparkled under the beams of the sun that shone brightly thro' the pure, frosty air: a few birds were pecking some crumbs under my window.[81] I smiled with quiet joy; and in my thoughts, which through long habit would for ever connect themselves into one train, as if I shaped them into words, I thus addressed the scene before me:

"I salute thee, beautiful Sun, and thou, white Earth, fair and cold! Perhaps I shall never see thee again covered with green, and the sweet flowers of the coming spring will blossom on my grave. I am about to leave thee; soon this living spirit which is ever busy among strange shapes and ideas, which belong not to thee, soon it will have flown to other regions and this emaciated body will rest insensate on thy bosom

"Rolled round in earth's diurnal course
With rocks, and stones, and trees.

"For it will be the same with thee, who art called our Universal Mother,[82] when I am gone. I have loved thee; and in my days both of happiness and sorrow I have peopled your solitudes with wild fancies of my own creation. The woods, and lakes, and mountains which I have loved, have for me a thousand associations; and thou, oh, Sun! hast smiled upon, and borne your part in many imaginations that sprung to life in my soul alone, and which will die with me. Your solitudes, sweet land, your trees and waters will still exist, moved by your winds, or still beneath the eye of noon, though[83] [w]hat I have felt about ye, and all my dreams which have often strangely deformed thee, will die with me. You will exist to reflect other images in other minds, and ever will remain the same, although your reflected semblance vary in a thousand ways, changeable as the hearts of those who view thee. One of these fragile mirrors, that ever doted on thine image, is about to be broken, crumbled to dust. But everteeming Nature will create another and another, and thou wilt loose nought by my destruction.[84]

"Thou wilt ever be the same. Recieve then the grateful farewell of a fleeting shadow who is about to disappear, who joyfully leaves thee, yet with a last look of affectionate thankfulness. Farewell! Sky, and fields and woods; the lovely flowers that grow on thee; thy mountains & thy rivers; to the balmy air and the strong wind of the north, to all, a last farewell. I shall shed no more tears for my task is almost fulfilled, and I am about to be rewarded for long and most burthensome suffering. Bless thy child even even in death, as I bless thee; and let me sleep at peace in my quiet grave."

I feel death to be near at hand and I am calm. I no longer despair, but look on all around me with placid affection. I find it sweet to watch the progressive decay of my strength, and to repeat to myself, another day and yet another, but again I shall not see the red leaves of autumn; before that time I shall be with my father. I am glad Woodville is not with me for perhaps he would grieve, and I desire to see smiles alone during the last scene of my life; when I last wrote to him I told him of my ill health but not of its mortal tendency, lest he should conceive it to be his duty to come to me for I fear lest the tears of friendship should destroy the blessed calm of my mind. I take pleasure in arranging all the little details which will occur when I shall no longer be. In truth I am in love with death; no maiden ever took more pleasure in the contemplation of her bridal attire than I in fancying my limbs already enwrapt in their shroud: is it not my marriage dress? Alone it will unite me to my father when in an eternal mental union we shall never part.

I will not dwell on the last changes that I feel in the final decay of nature. It is rapid but without pain: I feel a strange pleasure in it. For long years these are the first days of peace that have visited me. I no longer exhaust my miserable heart by bitter tears and frantic complaints; I no longer the reproach the sun, the earth, the air, for pain and wretchedness. I wait in quiet expectation for the closing hours of a life which has been to me most sweet & bitter. I do not die not having enjoyed life; for sixteen years I was happy: during the first months of my father's return

I had enjoyed ages of pleasure: now indeed I am grown old in grief; my steps are feeble like those of age; I have become peevish and unfit for life; so having passed little more than twenty years upon the earth I am more fit for my narrow grave than many are when they reach the natural term of their lives.

Again and again I have passed over in my remembrance the different scenes of my short life: if the world is a stage and I merely an actor on it my part has been strange, and, alas! tragical. Almost from infancy I was deprived of all the testimonies of affection which children generally receive; I was thrown entirely upon my own resources, and I enjoyed what I may almost call unnatural pleasures, for they were dreams and not realities. The earth was to me a magic lantern and I [a] gazer, and a listener but no actor; but then came the transporting and soul-reviving era of my existence: my father returned and I could pour my warm affections on a human heart; there was a new sun and a new earth created to me; the waters of existence sparkled: joy! joy! but, alas! what grief! My bliss was more rapid than the progress of a sunbeam on a mountain, which discloses its glades & woods, and then leaves it dark & blank; to my happiness followed madness and agony, closed by despair.

This was the drama of my life which I have now depicted upon paper. During three months I have been employed in this task. The memory of sorrow has brought tears; the memory of happiness a warm glow the lively shadow of that joy. Now my tears are dried; the glow has faded from my cheeks, and with a few words of farewell to you, Woodville, I close my work: the last that I shall perform.

Farewell, my only living friend; you are the sole tie that binds me to existence, and now I break it[.] It gives me no pain to leave you; nor can our seperation give you much. You never regarded me as one of this world, but rather as a being, who for some penance was sent from the Kingdom of Shadows; and she passed a few days weeping on the earth and longing to return to her native soil. You will weep but they will be tears of gentleness. I would, if I thought that it would lessen your regret, tell you to smile and congratulate me on my departure from the misery you beheld me endure. I would say; Woodville, rejoice with your friend, I triumph now and am most happy. But I check these expressions; these may not be the consolations of the living; they weep for their own misery, and not for that of the being they have lost. No; shed a few natural tears due to my memory: and if you ever visit my grave, pluck from thence a flower, and lay it to your heart; for your heart is the only tomb in which my memory will be enterred.

My death is rapidly approaching and you are not near to watch the flitting and vanishing of my spirit. Do no[t] regret this; for death is a too terrible an object for the living. It is one of those adversities which hurt instead of purifying the heart; for it is so intense a misery that it hardens & dulls the feelings. Dreadful as the time was when I pursued my father towards the ocean, & found their only his lifeless corpse; yet for my own sake I should prefer that to the watching one by one his senses fade; his pulse weaken—and sleeplessly as it were devour his life in gazing. To see life in his limbs & to know that soon life would no longer be there; to see the warm breath issue from his lips and to know they would soon be chill—I will not continue to trace this frightful picture; you suffered this torture once; I never did.[85] And the remembrance fills your heart sometimes with bitter despair when otherwise your feelings would have melted into soft sorrow.

So day by day I become weaker, and life flickers in my wasting form, as a lamp about to loose it vivifying oil. I now behold the glad sun of May. It was May, four years ago, that I first saw my beloved father; it was in May, three years ago that my folly destroyed the only being I was doomed to love. May is returned, and I die. Three days ago, the anniversary of our meeting; and, alas! of our eternal seperation, after a day of killing emotion, I caused myself to be led once more to behold the face of nature. I caused myself to be carried to some meadows some miles distant from my cottage; the grass was being mowed, and there was the scent of hay in the fields; all the earth look[ed] fresh and its inhabitants happy. Evening approached and I beheld the sun set. Three years ago and on that day and hour it shone through the branches and leaves of the beech wood and its beams flickered upon the countenance of him whom I then beheld for the last time.[86] I now saw that divine orb, gilding all the clouds with unwonted splendour, sink behind the horizon; it disappeared from a world where he whom I would seek exists not; it approached a world where he exists not[.] Why do I weep so bitterly? Why my does my heart heave with vain endeavour to cast aside the bitter anguish that covers it "as the waters cover the sea." I go from this world where he is no longer and soon I shall meet him in another.

Farewell, Woodville, the turf will soon be green on my grave; and the violets will bloom on it. *There* is my hope and my expectation; your's are in this world; may they be fulfilled.[87]

THE FIELDS OF FANCY[88]

It was in Rome—the Queen of the World that I suffered a misfortune that reduced me to misery & despair[89]—The bright sun & deep azure sky were oppressive but nought was so hateful as the voice of Man—I loved to walk by the shores of the Tiber which were solitary & if the sirocco blew to see the swift clouds pass over St. Peters and the many domes of Rome or if the sun shone I turned my eyes from the sky whose light was too dazzling & gay to be reflected in my tearful eyes I turned them to the river whose swift course was as the speedy departure of happiness and whose turbid colour was gloomy as grief—

Whether I slept I know not or whether it was in one of those many hours which I spent seated on the ground my mind a chaos of despair & my eyes for ever wet by tears but I was here visited by a lovely spirit whom I have ever worshiped & who tried to repay my adoration by diverting my mind from the hideous memories that racked it. At first indeed this wanton spirit played a false part & appearing with sable wings & gloomy countenance seemed to take a pleasure in exagerating all my miseries—and as small hopes arose to snatch them from me & give me in their place gigantic fears which under her fairy hand appeared close, impending & unavoidable—sometimes she would cruelly leave me while I was thus on the verge of madness and without consoling me leave me nought but heavy leaden sleep—but at other times she would wilily link less unpleasing thoughts to these most dreadful ones & before I was aware place hopes before me—futile but consoling[90]—

One day this lovely spirit—whose name as she told me was Fantasia came to me in one of her consolotary moods—her wings which seemed coloured by her tone of mind were not gay but beautiful like that of the partridge & her lovely eyes although they ever burned with an unquenshable fire were shaded & softened by her heavy lids & the black long fringe of her eye lashes—She thus addressed me—You mourn for the loss of those you love. They are gone for ever & great as my power is I cannot recall them to you—if indeed I wave my wand over you you will fancy that you feel their gentle spirits in the soft air that steals over your cheeks & the distant sound of winds & waters may image to you their voices which will bid you rejoice for that they live—This will not take away your grief but you will shed sweeter tears than those which full of anguish & hopelessness now start from your eyes—This I can do & also can I take you to see many of my provinces my fairy lands which you have not yet visited and whose beauty will while away the heavy time—I have many lovely spots under my command which poets of old have visited and have seen those sights the relation of which has been as a revelation to the world—many spots I have still in keeping of lovely fields or horrid rocks peopled by the beautiful or the tremendous which I keep in reserve for my future worshippers—to one of those whose grim terrors frightened sleep from the eye I formerly led you[91] but you now need more pleasing images & although I will not promise you to shew you any new scenes yet if I lead you to one often visited by my followers you will at least see new combinations that will sooth if they do not delight you—Follow me—

Alas! I replied—when have you found me slow to obey your voice—some times indeed I have called you & you have not come—but when before have I not followed your slightest sign and have left what was either of joy or sorrow in our world to dwell with you in yours till you have dismissed me ever unwilling to depart—But now the weight of grief that oppresses me takes from me that lightness which is necessary to follow your quick & winged motions alas in the midst of my course one thought would make me droop to the ground while you would outspeed me to your Kingdom of Glory & leave me here darkling

Ungrateful! replied the Spirit Do I not tell you that I will sustain & console you My wings shall aid your heavy steps & I will command my winds to disperse the mist that over casts you—I will lead you to a place where you will not hear laughter that disturbs you or see the sun that dazzles you—We will choose some of the most sombre walks of the Elysian fields—

The Elysian fields—I exclaimed with a quick scream—shall I then see? I gasped & could not ask that which I longed to know—the friendly spirit replied more gravely—I have told you that you will not see those whom you mourn—But I must away—follow me or I must leave you weeping deserted by the spirit that now checks your tears—

Go—I replied I cannot follow—I can only sit here & grieve—& long to see those who are gone for ever for to nought but what has relation to them can I listen—

The spirit left me to groan & weep to wish the sun quenched in eternal darkness—to accuse the air the waters all—all the universe of my utter & irremediable misery—Fantasia came again and ever when she came tempted me to follow her but as to follow her was to leave for a while the thought of those loved ones whose memories were my all although they were my torment I dared not go—Stay with me I cried & help me to clothe my bitter thoughts in lovelier colours give me hope although fallacious & images of what has been although it never will be again—diversion I cannot take cruel fairy do you leave me alas all my joy fades at thy departure but I may not follow thee—

One day after one of these combats when the spirit had left me I wandered on along the banks of the river to try to disperse the excessive misery that I felt untill overcome by fatigue—my eyes weighed down by tears—I lay down under the shade of trees & fell asleep—I slept long and when I awoke I knew not where I was—I did not see the river or the distant city—but I lay beside a lovely fountain shadowed over by willows & surrounded by blooming myrtles—at a short distance the air seemed pierced by the spiry pines & cypresses and the ground was covered by short moss & sweet smelling heath—the sky was blue but not dazzling like that of Rome and on every side I saw long allies—clusters of trees with intervening lawns & gently stealing rivers—Where am I? [I] exclaimed—& looking around me I beheld Fantasia—She smiled & as she smiled all the enchanting scene appeared lovelier—rainbows played in the fountain & the heath flowers at our feet appeared as if just refreshed by dew—I have seized you, said she—as you slept and will for some little time retain you as my prisoner—I will introduce you to some of the inhabitants of these peaceful Gardens—It shall not be to any whose exuberant happiness will form an u[n]pleasing contrast with your heavy grief but it shall be to those whose chief care here is to acquired knowledged & virtue—or to those who having just escaped from care & pain have not yet recovered full sense of enjoyment—This part of these Elysian Gardens is devoted to those who as before in your world wished to become wise & virtuous by study & action here endeavour after the same ends by contemplation—They are still unknowing of their final destination but they have a clear knowledge of what on earth is only supposed by some which is that their happiness now & hereafter depends upon their intellectual improvement—Nor do they only study the forms of this universe but search deeply in their own minds and love to meet & converse on all those high subjects of which the philosophers of Athens loved to treat—With deep feelings but with no outward circumstances to excite their passions you will perhaps imagine that their life is uniform & dull—but these sages are of that disposition fitted to find wisdom in every thing & in every lovely colour or form ideas that excite their love—Besides many years are consumed before they arrive here—When a soul longing for knowledge & pining at its narrow conceptions escapes from your earth many spirits wait to receive it and to open its eyes to the mysteries of the universe—many centuries are often consumed in these travels and they at last retire here to digest their knowledge & to become still wiser by thought and imagination working upon memory [92]—When the fitting period is accomplished they leave this garden to inhabit another world fitted for the reception of beings almost infinitely wise—but what this world is neither can you conceive or I teach you—some of the spirits whom you will see here are yet unknowing in the secrets of nature—They are those whom care & sorrow have consumed on earth & whose hearts although active in virtue have been shut through suffering from knowledge—These spend sometime here to recover their equanimity & to get a thirst of knowledge from converse with their wiser companions—They now securely hope to see again those whom they love & know that it is ignorance alone that detains them from them. As for those who in your world knew not the loveliness of benevolence & justice they are placed apart some claimed by the evil spirit & in vain sought for by the good but She whose delight is to reform the wicked takes all she can & delivers them to her ministers not to be punished but to be exercised & instructed untill acquiring a love of virtue they are fitted for these gardens where they will acquire a love of knowledge

As Fantasia talked I saw various groupes of figures as they walked among the allies of the gardens or were seated on the grassy plots either in contemplation or conversation several advanced together towards the fountain where I sat—As they approached I observed the principal figure to be that of a woman about 40 years of age her eyes burned with a deep fire and every line of her face expressed enthusiasm & wisdom—Poetry seemed seated on her lips which were beautifully formed & every motion of her limbs although not youthful was inexpressibly graceful—her black hair was bound in tresses round her head and her brows were encompassed by a fillet—her dress was that of a simple tunic bound at the waist by a broad girdle and a mantle which fell over her left arm she was encompassed by several youths of both sexes who appeared to hang on her words & to catch the inspiration as it flowed from her with looks either of eager wonder or stedfast attention with eyes all bent towards her eloquent countenance which beamed with the mind within—I am going said Fantasia but I leave my spirit with you without which this scene wd fade away—I leave you in good company—that female whose eyes like the loveliest planet in the heavens draw all to gaze on her is the Prophetess Diotima the instructress of Socrates[93]—The company about her are those just escaped from the world there they were unthinking or misconducted in the pursuit of knowledge. She leads them to truth & wisdom untill the time comes when they shall be fitted for the journey through the universe which all must one day undertake—farewell—

And now, gentlest reader—I must beg your indulgence—I am a being too weak to record the words of Diotima her matchless wisdom & heavenly eloquence[.] What I shall repeat will be as the faint shadow of a tree by moonlight—some what of the form will be preserved but there will be no life in it—Plato alone of Mortals could record the thoughts of Diotima hopeless therefore I shall not dwell so much on her words as on those of her pupils which being more earthly can better than hers be related by living lips[.]

Diotima approached the fountain & seated herself on a mossy mound near it and her disciples placed themselves on the grass near her—Without noticing me who sat close under her she continued her discourse addressing as it happened one or other of her listeners—but before I attempt to repeat her words I will describe the chief of these whom she appeared to wish principally to impress—One was a woman of about 23 years of age in the full enjoyment of the most exquisite beauty her golden hair floated in ringlets on her shoulders—her hazle eyes were shaded by heavy lids and her mouth the lips apart seemed to breathe sensibility[94]—But she appeared thoughtful & unhappy—her cheek was pale she seemed as if accustomed to suffer and as if the lessons she now heard were the only words of wisdom to which she had ever listened— The youth beside her had a far different aspect—his form was emaciated nearly to a shadow—his features were handsome but thin & worn—& his eyes glistened as if animating the visage of decay—his forehead was expansive but there was a doubt & perplexity in his looks that seemed to say that although he had sought wisdom he had got entangled in some mysterious mazes from which he in vain endeavoured to extricate himself—As Diotima spoke his colour went & came with quick changes & the flexible muscles of his countenance shewed every impression that his mind received—he seemed one who in life had studied hard but whose feeble frame sunk beneath the weight of the mere exertion of life—the spark of intelligence burned with uncommon strength within him but that of life seemed ever on the eve of fading[95]—At present I shall not describe any other of this groupe but with deep attention try to recall in my memory some of the words of Diotima—they were words of fire but their path is faintly marked on my recollection—[96]

It requires a just hand, said she continuing her discourse, to weigh & divide the good from evil—On the earth they are inextricably entangled and if you would cast away what there appears an evil a multitude of beneficial causes or effects cling to it & mock your labour—When I was on earth and have walked in a solitary country during the silence of night & have beheld the multitude of stars, the soft radiance of the moon reflected on the sea, which was studded by lovely islands—When I have felt the soft breeze steal across my cheek & as the words of love it has soothed & cherished me—then my mind seemed almost to quit the body that confined it to the earth & with a quick mental sense to mingle with the scene that I hardly saw—I felt—Then I have exclaimed, oh world how beautiful thou art!—Oh brightest universe behold thy worshiper!—spirit of beauty & of sympathy which pervades all things, & now lifts my soul as with wings, how have you animated the light & the breezes!—Deep & inexplicable spirit give me words to express my adoration; my mind is hurried away but with language I cannot tell how I feel thy loveliness! Silence or the song of the nightingale the momentary apparition of some bird that flies quietly past—all seems animated with thee & more than all the deep sky studded with worlds!"—If the winds roared & tore the sea and the dreadful lightnings seemed falling around me—still love was mingled with the sacred terror I felt; the majesty of loveliness was deeply impressed on me—So also I have felt when I have seen a lovely countenance—or heard solemn music or the eloquence of divine wisdom flowing from the lips of one of its worshippers—a lovely animal or even the graceful undulations of trees & inanimate objects have excited in me the same deep feeling of love & beauty; a feeling which while it made me alive & eager to seek the cause & animator of the scene, yet satisfied me by its very depth as if I had already found the solution to my enquires & as if in feeling myself a part of the great whole I had found the truth & secret of the universe—But when retired in my cell I have studied & contemplated the various motions and actions in the world the weight of evil has confounded me—If I thought of the creation I saw an eternal chain of evil linked one to the other—from the great whale who in the sea swallows & destroys multitudes & the smaller fish that live on him also & torment him to madness—to the cat whose pleasure it is to torment her prey I saw the whole creation filled with pain—each creature seems to exist through the misery of another & death & havoc is the watchword of the animated world—And Man also—even in Athens the most civilized spot on the earth what a multitude of mean passions—envy, malice—a restless desire to depreciate all that was great and good did I see—And in the dominions of the great being I saw man [reduced?][97] far below the animals of the field preying on one anothers hearts; happy in the downfall of others—themselves holding on with bent necks and cruel eyes to a wretch more a slave if possible than they to his miserable passions—And if I said these are the consequences of civilization & turned to the savage world I saw only ignorance unrepaid by any noble feeling—a mere animal, love of life joined to a low love of power & a fiendish love of destruction—I saw a creature drawn on by his senses & his selfish passions but untouched by aught noble or even Human—

And then when I sought for consolation in the various faculties man is possessed of & which I felt burning within me—I found that spirit of union with love & beauty which formed my happiness & pride degraded into superstition & turned from its natural growth which could bring forth only good fruit:—cruelty—& intolerance & hard tyranny was grafted on its trunk & from it sprung fruit suitable to such grafts—If I mingled with my fellow creatures was the voice I heard that of love & virtue or that of selfishness & vice, still misery was ever joined to it & the tears of mankind formed a vast sea ever blown on by its sighs & seldom illuminated by its smiles—Such taking only one side of the picture & shutting wisdom from the view is a just portraiture of the creation as seen on earth

But when I compared the good & evil of the world & wished to divide them into two seperate principles I found them inextricably intwined together & I was again cast into perplexity & doubt—I might have considered the earth as an imperfect formation where having bad materials to work on the Creator could only palliate the evil effects of his combinations but I saw a wanton malignity in many parts & particularly in the mind of man that baffled me a delight in mischief a love of evil for evils sake—a siding of the multitude—a dastardly applause which in their hearts the crowd gave to triumphant wick[ed]ness over lowly virtue that filled me with painful sensations. Meditation, painful & continual thought only encreased my doubts—I dared not commit the blasphemy of ascribing the slightest evil to a beneficent God—To whom then should I ascribe the creation? To two principles? Which was the upermost? They were certainly independant for neither could the good spirit allow the existence of evil or the evil one the existence of good—Tired of these doubts to which I could form no probable solution—Sick of forming theories which I destroyed as quickly as I built them I was one evening on the top of Hymettus beholding the lovely prospect as the sun set in the glowing sea—I looked towards Athens & in my heart I exclaimed—oh busy hive of men! What heroism & what meaness exists within thy walls! And alas! both to the good & to the wicked what incalculable misery—Freemen ye call yourselves yet every free man has ten slaves to build up his freedom—and these slaves are men as they are yet d[e]graded by their station to all that is mean & loathsome—Yet in how many hearts now beating in that city do high thoughts live & magnanimity that should methinks redeem the whole human race—What though the good man is unhappy has he not that in his heart to satisfy him? And will a contented conscience compensate for fallen hopes—a slandered name torn affections & all the miseries of civilized life?—

Oh Sun how beautiful thou art! And how glorious is the golden ocean that receives thee! My heart is at peace—I feel no sorrow—a holy love stills my senses—I feel as if my mind also partook of the inexpressible loveliness of surrounding nature—What shall I do? Shall I disturb this calm by mingling in the world?—shall I with an aching heart seek the spectacle of misery to discover its cause or shall I hopless leave the search of knowledge & devote myself to the pleasures they say this world affords?—Oh! no—I will become wise! I will study my own heart—and there discovering as I may the spring of the virtues I possess I will teach others how to look for them in their own souls—I will find whence arrises this unquenshable love of beauty I possess that seems the ruling star of my life—I will learn how I may direct it aright and by what loving I may become more like that beauty which I adore And when I have traced the steps of the godlike feeling which ennobles me & makes me that which I esteem myself to be then I will teach others & if I gain but one proselyte—if I can teach but one other mind what is the beauty which they ought to love—and what is the sympathy to which they ought to aspire what is the true end of their being—which must be the true end of that of all men then shall I be satisfied & think I have done enough—

Farewell doubts—painful meditation of evil—& the great, ever inexplicable cause of all that we see—I am content to be ignorant of all this happy that not resting my mind on any unstable theories I have come to the conclusion that of the great secret of the universe I *can know nothing*—There is a veil before it—my eyes are not piercing enough to see through it my arms not long enough to reach it to withdraw it—I will study the end of my being—oh thou universal love inspire me—oh thou beauty which I see glowing around me lift me to a fit understanding of thee! Such was the conclusion of my long wanderings I sought the end of my being & I found it to be knowledge of itself—Nor think this a confined study—Not only did it lead me to search the mazes of the human soul—but I found that there existed nought on earth which contained not a part of that universal beauty with which it [was] my aim & object to become acquainted—the motions of the stars of heaven the study of all that philosophers have unfolded of wondrous in nature became as it where the steps by which my soul rose to the full contemplation & enjoyment of the beautiful—Oh ye who have just escaped from the world ye know not what fountains of love will be opened in your hearts or what exquisite delight your minds will receive when the secrets of the world will be unfolded to you and ye shall become acquainted with the beauty of the universe—Your souls now growing eager for the acquirement of knowledge will then rest in its possession disengaged from every particle of evil and knowing all things ye will as it were be mingled in the universe & ye will become a part of that celestial beauty that you admire—[98]

Diotima ceased and a profound silence ensued—the youth with his cheeks flushed and his eyes burning with the fire communicated from hers still fixed them on her face which was lifted to heaven as in inspiration—The lovely female bent hers to the ground & after a deep sigh was the first to break the silence—

Oh divinest prophetess, said she—how new & to me how strange are your lessons—If such be the end of our being how wayward a course did I pursue on earth—Diotima you know not how torn affections & misery incalculable misery—withers up the soul. How petty do the actions of our earthly life appear when the whole universe is opened to our gaze—yet there our passions are deep & irrisisbable and as we are floating hopless yet clinging to hope down the impetuous stream can we perceive the beauty of its banks which alas my soul was too turbid to reflect—If knowledge is the end of our being why are passions & feelings implanted in us that hurries us from wisdom to selfconcentrated misery & narrow selfish feeling? Is it as a trial? On earth I thought that I had well fulfilled my trial & my last moments became peaceful with the reflection that I deserved no blame—but you take from me that feeling—My passions were there my all to me and the hopeless misery that possessed me shut all love & all images of beauty from my soul—Nature was to me as the blackest night & if rays of loveliness ever strayed into my darkness it was only to draw bitter tears of hopeless anguish from my eyes—Oh on earth what consolation is there to misery?

Your heart I fear, replied Diotima, was broken by your sufferings—but if you had struggled—if when you found all hope of earthly happiness wither within you while desire of it scorched your soul—if you had near you a friend to have raised you to the contemplation of beauty & the search of knowledge you would have found perhaps not new hopes spring within you but a new life distinct from that of passion by which you had before existed[99]—relate to me what this misery was that thus engroses you—tell me what were the vicissitudes of feeling that you endured on earth—after death our actions & worldly interest fade as nothing before us but the traces of our feelings exist & the memories of those are what furnish us here with eternal subject of meditation.

A blush spread over the cheek of the lovely girl—Alas, replied she what a tale must I relate what dark & phre[n]zied passions must I unfold—When you Diotima lived on earth your soul seemed to mingle in love only with its own essence & to be unknowing of the various tortures which that heart endures who if it has not sympathized with has been witness of the dreadful struggles of a soul enchained by dark deep passions which were its hell & yet from which it could not escape—Are there in the peaceful language used by the inhabitants of these regions—words burning enough to paint the tortures of the human heart—Can you understand them? or can you in any way sympathize with them—alas though dead I do and my tears flow as when I lived when my memory recalls the dreadful images of the past—

—As the lovely girl spoke my own eyes filled with bitter drops—the spirit of Fantasia seemed to fade from within me and when after placing my hand before my swimming eyes I withdrew it again I found myself under the trees on the banks of the Tiber—The sun was just setting & tinging with crimson the clouds that floated over St. Peters—all was still no human voice was heard—the very air was quiet I rose—& bewildered with the grief that I felt within me the recollection of what I had heard—I hastened to the city that I might see human beings not that I might forget my wandering recollections but that I might impress on my mind what was reality & what was either dream—or at least not of this earth—The Corso of Rome was filled with carriages and as I walked up the Trinita dei' Montes I became disgusted with the crowd that I saw about me & the vacancy & want of beauty not to say deformity of the many beings who meaninglessly buzzed about me—I hastened to my room which overlooked the whole city which as night came on became tranquil—Silent lovely Rome I now gaze on thee—thy domes are illuminated by the moon—and the ghosts of lovely memories float with the night breeze among thy ruins—contemplating thy loveliness which half soothes my miserable heart I record what I have seen—Tomorrow I will again woo Fantasia to lead me to the same walks & invite her to visit me with her visions which I before neglected—Oh let me learn this lesson while yet it may be useful to me that to a mind hopeless & unhappy as mine—a moment of forgetfullness a moment [in] which it can pass out of itself is worth a life of painful recollection.

CHAP. 2

The next morning while sitting on the steps of the temple of Aesculapius in the Borghese gardens Fantasia again visited me & smilingly beckoned to me to follow her—My flight was at first heavy but the breezes commanded by the spirit to convoy me grew stronger as I advanced—a pleasing languour seized my senses & when I recovered I found my self by the Elysian fountain near Diotima—The beautiful female who[m] I had left on the point of narrating her earthly history seemed to have waited for my return and as soon as I appeared she spoke thus—[100]

AUTHOR'S FOOTNOTES:

A   Wordsworth
B   Dante
C   Fletcher's comedy of the Captain.
D   Lord Byron
E   Coleridge's Fire, Famine and Slaughter.
F   Spencer's Faery Queen Book 1—Canto [9]

FOOTNOTES TO THE PREFACE:

i   They are listed in Nitchie, *Mary Shelley*, Appendix II, pp. 205-208. To them should be added an unfinished and unpublished novel, *Cecil*, in Lord Abinger's collection.

ii   On the basis of the Bodleian notebook and some information about the complete story kindly furnished me by Miss R. Glynn Grylls, I wrote an article, "Mary Shelley's *Mathilda*, an Unpublished Story and Its Biographical Significance," which appeared in *Studies in Philology*, XL (1943), 447-462. When the other manuscripts became available, I was able to use them for my book, *Mary Shelley*, and to draw conclusions more certain and well-founded than the conjectures I had made ten years earlier.

iii   A note, probably in Richard Garnett's hand, enclosed in a MS box with the two notebooks in Lord Abinger's collection describes them as of Italian make with "slanting head bands, inserted through the covers." Professor Lewis Patton's list of the contents of the microfilms in the Duke University Library (*Library Notes*, No. 27, April, 1953) describes them as vellum bound, the back cover of the *Mathilda* notebook being missing. Lord Abinger's notebooks are on Reel 11. The Bodleian notebook is catalogued as MSS. Shelley d. 1, the Shelley-Rolls fragments as MSS. Shelley adds c. 5.

iv   See note 83 to *Mathilda*, page 89.

v   See *Posthumous Works of the Author of a Vindication of the Rights of Woman* (4 vols., London, 1798), IV, 97-155.

vi   See *Maria Gisborne & Edward E. Williams... Their Journals and Letters*, ed. by Frederick L. Jones (Norman: University of Oklahoma Press, [1951]), p. 27.

vii   See Thomas Medwin, *The Life of Percy Bysshe Shelley*, revised, with introduction and notes by H. Buxton Forman (London, 1913), p. 252.

viii   *Journal*, pp. 159, 160.

ix   *Maria Gisborne, etc.*, pp. 43-44.

x   *Letters*, I, 182.

xi   *Ibid.*, I, 224.

xii   See White, *Shelley*, II, 40-56.

xiii   See *Letters*, II, 88, and note 23 to *Mathilda*.

xiv   See *Shelley and Mary* (4 vols. Privately printed [for Sir Percy and Lady Shelley], 1882), II, 338A.

xv   See Mrs. Julian Marshall, *The Life and Letters of Mary W. Shelley* (2 vols. London: Richard Bentley & Son, 1889), I, 255.

xvi   Julian *Works*, X, 69.

xvii   *Lives of the Most Eminent Literary and Scientific Men of Italy, Spain, and Portugal* (3 vols., Nos. 63, 71, and 96 of the Rev. Dionysius Lardner's *Cabinet Cyclopaedia*, London, 1835-1837), II, 291-292.

xviii   The most significant revisions are considered in detail in the notes. The text of the opening of *The Fields of Fancy*, containing the fanciful framework of the story, later discarded, is printed after the text of *Mathilda*.

NOTES TO *MATHILDA*

Abbreviations:
F of F—A The Fields of Fancy, in Lord Abinger's notebook
F of F—B The Fields of Fancy, in the notebook in the Bodleian Library
S-R fr fragments of *The Fields of Fancy* among the papers of the late Sir John Shelley-Rolls, now in the Bodleian Library

1. The name is spelled thus in the MSS of *Mathilda* and *The Fields of Fancy*, though in the printed *Journal* (taken from *Shelley and Mary*) and in the *Letters* it is spelled *Matilda*. In the MS of the journal, however, it is spelled first *Matilda*, later *Mathilda*.

2. Mary has here added detail and contrast to the description in *F of F—A*, in which the passage "save a few black patches ... on the plain ground" does not appear.

3. The addition of "I am alone ... withered me" motivates Mathilda's state of mind and her resolve to write her history.

4. Mathilda too is the unwitting victim in a story of incest. Like Oedipus, she has lost her parent-lover by suicide; like him she leaves the scene of the revelation overwhelmed by a sense of her own guilt, "a sacred horror"; like him, she finds a measure of peace as she is about to die.

5. The addition of "the precious memorials ... gratitude towards you," by its suggestion of the relationship between Mathilda and Woodville, serves to justify the detailed narration.

6. At this point two sheets have been removed from the notebook. There is no break in continuity, however.

7. The descriptions of Mathilda's father and mother and the account of their marriage in the next few pages are greatly expanded from *F of F—A*, where there is only one brief paragraph. The process of expansion can be followed in *S-R fr* and in *F of F—B*. The

development of the character of Diana (who represents Mary's own mother, Mary Wollstonecraft) gave Mary the most trouble. For the identifications with Mary's father and mother, see Nitchie, *Mary Shelley*, pp. 11, 90-93, 96-97.

8   The passage "There was a gentleman ... school & college vacations" is on a slip of paper pasted on page 11 of the MS. In the margin are two fragments, crossed out, evidently parts of what is supplanted by the substituted passage: "an angelic disposition and a quick, penetrating understanding" and "her visits ... to ... his house were long & frequent & there." In *F of F—B* Mary wrote of Diana's understanding "that often receives the name of masculine from its firmness and strength." This adjective had often been applied to Mary Wollstonecraft's mind. Mary Shelley's own understanding had been called masculine by Leigh Hunt in 1817 in the *Examiner*. The word was used also by a reviewer of her last published work, *Rambles in Germany and Italy, 1844*. (See Nitchie, *Mary Shelley*, p. 178.)

9   The account of Diana in *Mathilda* is much better ordered and more coherent than that in *F of F—B*.

10   The description of the effect of Diana's death on her husband is largely new in *Mathilda*. *F of F—B* is frankly incomplete; *F of F—A* contains some of this material; *Mathilda* puts it in order and fills in the gaps.

11   This paragraph is an elaboration of the description of her aunt's coldness as found in *F of F—B*. There is only one sentence in *F of F—A*.

12   The description of Mathilda's love of nature and of animals is elaborated from both rough drafts. The effect, like that of the preceding addition (see note 11), is to emphasize Mathilda's loneliness. For the theme of loneliness in Mary Shelley's work, see Nitchie, *Mary Shelley*, pp. 13-17.

13 This paragraph is a revision of *F of F—B*, which is fragmentary. There is nothing in *F of F—A* and only one scored-out sentence in *S-R fr*. None of the rough drafts tells of her plans to join her father.
14 The final paragraph in Chapter II is entirely new.
15 The account of the return of Mathilda's father is very slightly revised from that in *F of F—A*. *F of F—B* has only a few fragmentary sentences, scored out. It resumes with the paragraph beginning, "My father was very little changed."
16 Symbolic of Mathilda's subsequent life.
17 *Illusion, or the Trances of Nourjahad*, a melodrama, was performed at Drury Lane, November 25, 1813. It was anonymous, but it was attributed by some reviewers to Byron, a charge which he indignantly denied. See Byron, *Letters and Journals*, ed. by Rowland E. Prothero (6 vols. London: Murray, 1902-1904), II, 288.
18 This paragraph is in *F of F—B* but not in *F of F—A*. In the margin of the latter, however, is written: "It was not of the tree of knowledge that I ate for no evil followed—it must be of the tree of life that grows close beside it or—". Perhaps this was intended to go in the preceding paragraph after "My ideas were enlarged by his conversation." Then, when this paragraph was added, the figure, noticeably changed, was included here.
19 Here the MS of *F of F—B* breaks off to resume only with the meeting of Mathilda and Woodville.
20 At the end of the story (p. 79) Mathilda says, "Death is too terrible an object for the living." Mary was thinking of the deaths of her two children.
21 Mary had read the story of Cupid and Psyche in Apuleius in 1817 and she had made an Italian translation, the MS of which is now in the Library of Congress. See *Journal*, pp. 79, 85-86.
22 The end of this paragraph gave Mary much trouble. In *F of F—A* after the words, "my tale must," she develops an elaborate figure:

"go with the stream that hurries on—& now was this stream precipitated by an overwhelming fall from the pleasant vallies through which it wandered—down hideous precipieces to a desart black & hopeless—". This, the original ending of the chapter, was scored out, and a new, simplified version which, with some deletions and changes, became that used in *Mathilda* was written in the margins of two pages (ff. 57, 58). This revision is a good example of Mary's frequent improvement of her style by the omission of purple patches.

23 In *F of F—A* there follows a passage which has been scored out and which does not appear in *Mathilda*. "I have tried in somewhat feeble language to describe the excess of what I may almost call my adoration for my father—you may then in some faint manner imagine my despair when I found that he shunned [me] & that all the little arts I used to re-awaken his lost love made him"—. This is a good example of Mary's frequent revision for the better by the omission of the obvious and expository. But the passage also has intrinsic interest. Mathilda's "adoration" for her father may be compared to Mary's feeling for Godwin. In an unpublished letter (1822) to Jane Williams she wrote, "Until I met Shelley I [could?] justly say that he was my God—and I remember many childish instances of the [ex]cess of attachment I bore for him." See Nitchie, *Mary Shelley*, p. 89, and note 9.

24 Cf. the account of the services of Fantasia in the opening chapter of *F of F—A* (see pp. 90-102) together with note 3 to *The Fields of Fancy*.

25 This passage beginning "Day after day" and closing with the quotation is not in *F of F—A*, but it is in *S-R fr*. The quotation is from *The Captain* by John Fletcher and a collaborator, possibly Massinger. These lines from Act I, Sc. 3 are part of a speech by Lelia addressed to her lover. Later in the play Lelia attempts to seduce her father—possibly a reason for Mary's selection of the lines.

26   At this point (f. 56 of the notebook) begins a long passage, continuing through Chapter V, in which Mary's emotional disturbance in writing about the change in Mathilda's father (representing both Shelley and Godwin?) shows itself on the pages of the MS. They look more like the rough draft than the fair copy. There are numerous slips of the pen, corrections in phrasing and sentence structure, dashes instead of other marks of punctuation, a large blot of ink on f. 57, one major deletion (see note 32).

27   In the margin of *F of F—A* Mary wrote, "Lord B's Ch^{de} Harold." The reference is to stanzas 71 and 72 of Canto IV. Byron compares the rainbow on the cataract first to "Hope upon a death-bed" and finally

   Resembling, 'mid the torture of the scene,
   Love watching Madness with unalterable mien.

28   In *F of F—A* Mathilda "took up Ariosto & read the story of Isabella." Mary's reason for the change is not clear. Perhaps she thought that the fate of Isabella, a tale of love and lust and death (though not of incest), was too close to what was to be Mathilda's fate. She may have felt—and rightly—that the allusions to Lelia and to Myrrha were ample foreshadowings. The reasons for the choice of the seventh canto of Book II of the *Faerie Queene* may lie in the allegorical meaning of Guyon, or Temperance, and the "dread and horror" of his experience.

29   With this speech, which is not in *F of F—A*, Mary begins to develop the character of the Steward, who later accompanies Mathilda on her search for her father. Although he is to a very great extent the stereptyped faithful servant, he does serve to dramatize the situation both here and in the later scene.

30   This clause is substituted for a more conventional and less dramatic passage in *F of F—A*: "& besides there appeared more of struggle than remorse in his manner although sometimes I thought I saw

glim[p]ses of the latter feeling in his tumultuous starts & gloomy look."

31 These paragraphs beginning Chapter V are much expanded from *F of F—A*. Some of the details are in the *S-R fr*. This scene is recalled at the end of the story. (See page 80) Cf. what Mary says about places that are associated with former emotions in her *Rambles in Germany and Italy* (2 vols., London: Moxon, 1844), II, 78-79. She is writing of her approach to Venice, where, twenty-five years before, little Clara had died. "It is a strange, but to any person who has suffered, a familiar circumstance, that those who are enduring mental or corporeal agony are strangely alive to immediate external objects, and their imagination even exercises its wild power over them . . . Thus the banks of the Brenta presented to me a moving scene; not a palace, not a tree of which I did not recognize, as marked and recorded, at a moment when life and death hung upon our speedy arrival at Venice."

32 The remainder of this chapter, which describes the crucial scene between Mathilda and her father, is the result of much revision from *F of F—A*. Some of the revisions are in *S-R fr*. In general the text of *Mathilda* is improved in style. Mary adds concrete, specific words and phrases; e.g., at the end of the first paragraph of Mathilda's speech, the words "of incertitude" appear in *Mathilda* for the first time. She cancels, even in this final draft, an over-elaborate figure of speech after the words in the father's reply, "implicated in my destruction"; the cancelled passage is too flowery to be appropriate here: "as if when a vulture is carrying off some hare it is struck by an arrow his helpless victim entangled in the same fate is killed by the defeat of its enemy. One word would do all this." Furthermore the revised text shows greater understanding and penetration of the feelings of both speakers: the addition of "Am I the cause of your grief?" which brings out more dramatically what Mathilda has said in the first part of this paragraph; the analysis of the reasons

for her presistent questioning; the addition of the final paragraph of her plea, "Alas! Alas! . . . you hate me!" which prepares for the father's reply.

33 Almost all the final paragraph of the chapter is added to *F of F—A*. Three brief *S-R fr* are much revised and simplified.

34 *Decameron*, 4th day, 1st story. Mary had read the *Decameron* in May, 1819. See *Journal*, p. 121.

35 The passage "I should fear . . . I must despair" is in *S-R fr* but not in *F of F—A*. There, in the margin, is the following: "Is it not the prerogative of superior virtue to pardon the erring and to weigh with mercy their offenses?" This sentence does not appear in *Mathilda*. Also in the margin of *F of F—A* is the number (9), the number of the *S-R fr*.

36 The passage "enough of the world . . . in unmixed delight" is on a slip pasted over the middle of the page. Some of the obscured text is visible in the margin, heavily scored out. Also in the margin is "Canto IV Vers Ult," referring to the quotation from Dante's *Paradiso*. This quotation, with the preceding passage beginning "in whose eyes," appears in *Mathilda* only.

37 The reference to Diana, with the father's rationalization of his love for Mathilda, is in *S-R fr* but not in *F of F—A*.

38 In *F of F—A* this is followed by a series of other gloomy concessive clauses which have been scored out to the advantage of the text.

39 This paragraph has been greatly improved by the omission of elaborate over-statement; e.g., "to pray for mercy & respite from my fear" (*F of F—A*) becomes merely "to pray."

40 This paragraph about the Steward is added in *Mathilda*. In *F of F—A* he is called a servant and his name is Harry. See note 29.

41 This sentence, not in *F of F—A*, recalls Mathilda's dream.

42 This passage is somewhat more dramatic than that in *F of F—A*, putting what is there merely a descriptive statement into quotation marks.

43   A stalactite grotto on the island of Antiparos in the Aegean Sea.
44   A good description of Mary's own behavior in England after Shelley's death, of the surface placidity which concealed stormy emotion. See Nitchie, *Mary Shelley*, pp. 8-10.
45   *Job*, 17: 15-16, slightly misquoted.
46   Not in *F of F—A*. The quotation should read:

   Fam. Whisper it, sister! so and so!
      In a dark hint, soft and slow.

47   The mother of Prince Arthur in Shakespeare's *King John*. In the MS the words "the little Arthur" are written in pencil above the name of Constance.
48   In *F of F—A* this account of her plans is addressed to Diotima, and Mathilda's excuse for not detailing them is that they are too trivial to interest spirits no longer on earth; this is the only intrusion of the framework into Mathilda's narrative in *The Fields of Fancy*. Mathilda's refusal to recount her stratagems, though the omission is a welcome one to the reader, may represent the flagging of Mary's invention. Similarly in *Frankenstein* she offers excuses for not explaining how the Monster was brought to life. The entire passage, "Alas! I even now ... remain unfinished. I was," is on a slip of paper pasted on the page.
49   The comparison to a Hermitess and the wearing of the "fanciful nunlike dress" are appropriate though melodramatic. They appear only in *Mathilda*. Mathilda refers to her "whimsical nunlike habit" again after she meets Woodville (see page 60) and tells us in a deleted passage that it was "a close nunlike gown of black silk."
50   Cf. Shelley, *Prometheus Unbound*, I, 48: "the wingless, crawling hours." This phrase ("my part in submitting ... minutes") and the remainder of the paragraph are an elaboration of the simple phrase in *F of F—A*, "my part in enduring it—," with its ambiguous pronoun. The last page

of Chapter VIII shows many corrections, even in the MS of *Mathilda*. It is another passage that Mary seems to have written in some agitation of spirit. Cf. note 26.

51   In *F of F—A* there are several false starts before this sentence. The name there is Welford; on the next page it becomes Lovel, which is thereafter used throughout *The Fields of Fancy* and appears twice, probably inadvertently, in *Mathilda*, where it is crossed out. In a few of the *S-R fr* it is Herbert. In *Mathilda* it is at first Herbert, which is used until after the rewritten conclusion (see note 83) but is corrected throughout to Woodville. On the final pages Woodville alone is used. (It is interesting, though not particularly significant, that one of the minor characters in Lamb's *John Woodvil* is named Lovel. Such mellifluous names rolled easily from the pens of all the romantic writers.) This, her first portrait of Shelley in fiction, gave Mary considerable trouble: revisions from the rough drafts are numerous. The passage on Woodville's endowment by fortune, for example, is much more concise and effective than that in *S-R fr*. Also Mary curbed somewhat the extravagance of her praise of Woodville, omitting such hyperboles as "When he appeared a new sun seemed to rise on the day & he had all the benignity of the dispensor of light," and "he seemed to come as the God of the world."

52   This passage beginning "his station was too high" is not in *F of F—A*.

53   This passage beginning "He was a believer in the divinity of genius" is not in *F of F—A*. Cf. the discussion of genius in "Giovanni Villani" (Mary Shelley's essay in *The Liberal*, No. IV, 1823), including the sentence: "The fixed stars appear to abberate; but it is we that move, not they." It is tempting to conclude that this is a quotation or echo of something which Shelley said, perhaps in conversation with Byron. I have not found it in any of his published writings.

54 Is this wishful thinking about Shelley's poetry? It is well known that a year later Mary remonstrated with Shelley about *The Witch of Atlas*, desiring, as she said in her 1839 note, "that Shelley should increase his popularity ... It was not only that I wished him to acquire popularity as redounding to his fame; but I believed that he would obtain a greater mastery over his own powers, and greater happiness in his mind, if public applause crowned his endeavours ... Even now I believe that I was in the right." Shelley's response is in the six introductory stanzas of the poem.

55 The preceding paragraphs about Elinor and Woodville are the result of considerable revision for the better of *F of F—A* and *S-R fr*. Mary scored out a paragraph describing Elinor, thus getting rid of several clichés ("fortune had smiled on her," "a favourite of fortune," "turning tears of misery to those of joy"); she omitted a clause which offered a weak motivation of Elinor's father's will (the possibility of her marrying, while hardly more than a child, one of her guardian's sons); she curtailed the extravagance of a rhapsody on the perfect happiness which Woodville and Elinor would have enjoyed.

56 The death scene is elaborated from *F of F—A* and made more melodramatic by the addition of Woodville's plea and of his vigil by the death-bed.

57 *F of F—A* ends here and *F of F—B* resumes.

58 A similar passage about Mathilda's fears is cancelled in *F of F—B* but it appears in revised form in *S-R fr*. There is also among these fragments a long passage, not used in *Mathilda*, identifying Woodville as someone she had met in London. Mary was wise to discard it for the sake of her story. But the first part of it is interesting for its correspondence with fact: "I knew him when I first went to London with my father he was in the height of his glory & happiness—Elinor was living & in her life he lived—I did not know her but he had been introduced to my father & had once

or twice visited us—I had then gazed with wonder on his beauty & listened to him with delight—" Shelley had visited Godwin more than "once or twice" while Harriet was still living, and Mary had seen him. Of course she had seen Harriet too, in 1812, when she came with Shelley to call on Godwin. Elinor and Harriet, however, are completely unlike.

59 Here and on many succeeding pages, where Mathilda records the words and opinions of Woodville, it is possible to hear the voice of Shelley. This paragraph, which is much expanded from *F of F—B*, may be compared with the discussion of good and evil in *Julian and Maddalo* and with *Prometheus Unbound* and *A Defence of Poetry*.

60 In the revision of this passage Mathilda's sense of her pollution is intensified; for example, by addition of "infamy and guilt was mingled with my portion."

61 Some phrases of self-criticism are added in this paragraph.

62 In *F of F—B* this quotation is used in the laudanum scene, just before Level's (Woodville's) long speech of dissuasion.

63 The passage "air, & to suffer . . . my compassionate friend" is on a slip of paper pasted across the page.

64 This phrase sustains the metaphor better than that in *F of F—B*: "puts in a word."

65 This entire paragraph is added to *F of F—B*; it is in rough draft in *S-R fr*.

66 This is changed in the MS of *Mathilda* from "a violent thunderstorm." Evidently Mary decided to avoid using another thunderstorm at a crisis in the story.

67 The passage "It is true . . . I will" is on a slip of paper pasted across the page.

68 In the revision from *F of F—B* the style of this whole episode becomes more concise and specific.

69 An improvement over the awkward phrasing in *F of F—B*: "a friend who will not repulse my request that he would accompany me."

70 These two paragraphs are not in *F of F—B*; portions of them are in *S-R fr*.

71 This speech is greatly improved in style over that in *F of F—B*, more concise in expression (though somewhat expanded), more specific. There are no corresponding *S-R fr* to show the process of revision. With the ideas expressed here cf. Shelley, *Julian and Maddalo*, ll. 182-187, 494-499, and his letter to Claire in November, 1820 (Julian *Works*, X, 226). See also White, *Shelley*, II, 378.

72 This solecism, copied from *F of F—B*, is not characteristic of Mary Shelley.

73 This paragraph prepares for the eventual softening of Mathilda's feeling. The idea is somewhat elaborated from *F of F—B*. Other changes are necessitated by the change in the mode of presenting the story. In *The Fields of Fancy* Mathilda speaks as one who has already died.

74 Cf. Shelley's emphasis on hope and its association with love in all his work. When Mary wrote *Mathilda* she knew *Queen Mab* (see Part VIII, ll. 50-57, and Part IX, ll. 207-208), the *Hymn to Intellectual Beauty*, and the first three acts of *Prometheus Unbound*. The fourth act was written in the winter of 1819, but Demogorgon's words may already have been at least adumbrated before the beginning of November:

> To love and bear, to hope till hope creates
> From its own wreck the thing it contemplates.

75 Shelley had written, "Desolation is a delicate thing" (*Prometheus Unbound*, Act I, l. 772) and called the Spirit of the Earth "a delicate spirit" (*Ibid.*, Act III, Sc. iv, l. 6).

76 *Purgatorio*, Canto 28, ll. 31-33. Perhaps by this time Shelley had translated ll. 1-51 of this canto. He had read the *Purgatorio* in April, 1818, and again with Mary in August, 1819, just as she was beginning

to write *Mathilda*. Shelley showed his translation to Medwin in 1820, but there seems to be no record of the date of composition.

77   An air with this title was published about 1800 in London by Robert Birchall. See *Catalogue of Printed Music Published between 1487 and 1800 and now in the British Museum,* by W. Barclay Squire, 1912. Neither author nor composer is listed in the *Catalogue*.

78   This paragraph is materially changed from *F of F—B*. Clouds and darkness are substituted for starlight, silence for the sound of the wind. The weather here matches Mathilda's mood. Four and a half lines of verse (which I have not been able to identify, though they sound Shelleyan—are they Mary's own?) are omitted: of the stars she says,

      the wind is in the tree
But they are silent;—still they roll along
Immeasurably distant; & the vault
Built round by those white clouds, enormous clouds
Still deepens its unfathomable depth.

79   If Mary quotes Coleridge's *Ancient Mariner* intentionally here, she is ironic, for this is no merciful rain, except for the fact that it brings on the illness which leads to Mathilda's death, for which she longs.

80   This quotation from *Christabel* (which suggests that the preceding echo is intentional) is not in *F of F—B*.

81   Cf. the description which opens *Mathilda*.

82   Among Lord Abinger's papers, in Mary's hand, are some comparable (but very bad) fragmentary verses addressed to Mother Earth.

83   At this point four sheets are cut out of the notebook. They are evidently those with pages numbered 217 to 223 which are among the *S-R fr*. They contain the conclusion of the story, ending, as does *F of F—B* with Mathilda's words spoken to Diotima in the

Elysian Fields: "I am here, not with my father, but listening to lessons of wisdom, which will one day bring me to him when we shall never part. THE END." Some passages are scored out, but not this final sentence. Tenses are changed from past to future. The name *Herbert* is changed to *Woodville*. The explanation must be that Mary was hurrying to finish the revision (quite drastic on these final pages) and the transcription of her story before her confinement, and that in her haste she copied the pages from *F of F—B* as they stood. Then, realizing that they did not fit *Mathilda*, she began to revise them; but to keep her MS neat, she cut out these pages and wrote the fair copy. There is no break in *Mathilda* in story or in pagination. This fair copy also shows signs of haste: slips of the pen, repetition of words, a number of unimportant revisions.

84   Here in *F of F—B* there is an index number which evidently points to a note at the bottom of the next page. The note is omitted in *Mathilda*. It reads:

"Dante in his Purgatorio describes a grifon as remaining unchanged but his reflection in the eyes of Beatrice as perpetually varying (Purg. Cant. 31) So nature is ever the same but seen differently by almost every spectator and even by the same at various times. All minds, as mirrors, receive her forms—yet in each mirror the shapes apparently reflected vary & are perpetually changing—"

85   See note 20. Mary Shelley had suffered this torture when Clara and William died.
86   See the end of Chapter V.
87   This sentence is not in *F of F—B* or in *S-R fr*.

NOTES TO *THE FIELDS OF FANCY*

88   Here is printed the opening of *F of F—A*, which contains the fanciful framework abandoned in *Mathilda*. It has some intrinsic interest, as it shows that Mary as well as Shelley had been reading Plato, and especially as it reveals the close connection of the writing of *Mathilda* with Mary's own grief and depression. The first chapter is a fairly good rough draft. Punctuation, to be sure, consists largely of dashes or is non-existent, and there are some corrections. But there are not as many changes as there are in the remainder of this MS or in *F of F—B*.

89   It was in Rome that Mary's oldest child, William, died on June 7, 1819.

90   Cf. two entries in Mary Shelley's journal. An unpublished entry for October 27, 1822, reads: "Before when I wrote Mathilda, miserable as I was, the inspiration was sufficient to quell my wretchedness temporarily." Another entry, that for December 2, 1834, is quoted in abbreviated and somewhat garbled form by R. Glynn Grylls in *Mary Shelley* (London: Oxford University Press, 1938), p. 194, and reprinted by Professor Jones (*Journal*, p. 203). The full passage follows: "Little harm has my imagination done to me & how much good!—My poor heart pierced through & through has found balm from it—it has been the aegis to my sensibility—Sometimes there have been periods when Misery has pushed it aside—& those indeed were periods I shudder to remember—but the fairy only stept aside, she watched her time—& at the first opportunity her . . . beaming face peeped in, & the weight of deadly woe was lightened."

91   An obvious reference to *Frankenstein*.

92   With the words of Fantasia (and those of Diotima), cf. the association of wisdom and virtue in Plato's *Phaedo*, the myth of Er in the *Republic*, and the doctrine of love and beauty in the *Symposium*.

233

93 See Plato's *Symposium*. According to Mary's note in her edition of Shelley's *Essays, Letters from Abroad, etc.* (1840), Shelley planned to use the name for the instructress of the Stranger in his unfinished prose tale, *The Coliseum*, which was written before *Mathilda*, in the winter of 1818-1819. Probably at this same time Mary was writing an unfinished (and unpublished) tale about Valerius, an ancient Roman brought back to life in modern Rome. Valerius, like Shelley's Stranger, was instructed by a woman whom he met in the Coliseum. Mary's story is indebted to Shelley's in other ways as well.

94 Mathilda.

95 I cannot find a prototype for this young man, though in some ways he resembles Shelley.

96 Following this paragraph is an incomplete one which is scored out in the MS. The comment on the intricacy of modern life is interesting. Mary wrote: "The world you have just quitted she said is one of doubt & perplexity often of pain & misery—The modes of suffering seem to me to be much multiplied there since I made one of the throng & modern feelings seem to have acquired an intracacy then unknown but now the veil is torn aside—the events that you felt deeply on earth have passed away & you see them in their nakedness all but your knowledge & affections have passed away as a dream you now wonder at the effect trifles had on you and that the events of so passing a scene should have interested you so deeply—You complain, my friends of the"

97 The word is blotted and virtually illegible.

98 With Diotima's conclusion here cf. her words in the *Symposium*: "When any one ascending from a correct system of Love, begins to contemplate this supreme beauty, he already touches the consummation of his labour. For such as discipline themselves upon this system, or are conducted by another beginning to ascend through these transitory objects which are beautiful, towards that which is beauty itself, proceeding as on steps from the love of one

form to that of two, and from that of two, to that of all forms which are beautiful; and from beautiful forms to beautiful habits and institutions, and from institutions to beautiful doctrines; until, from the meditation of many doctrines, they arrive at that which is nothing else than the doctrine of the supreme beauty itself, in the knowledge and contemplation of which at length they repose." (Shelley's translation) Love, beauty, and self-knowledge are keywords not only in Plato but in Shelley's thought and poetry, and he was much concerned with the problem of the presence of good and evil. Some of these themes are discussed by Woodville in *Mathilda*. The repetition may have been one reason why Mary discarded the framework.

99   Mathilda did have such a friend, but, as she admits, she profited little from his teachings.

100 In *F of F—B* there is another, longer version (three and a half pages) of this incident, scored out, recounting the author's return to the Elysian gardens, Diotima's consolation of Mathilda, and her request for Mathilda's story. After wandering through the alleys and woods adjacent to the gardens, the author came upon Diotima seated beside Mathilda. "It is true indeed she said our affections outlive our earthly forms and I can well sympathize in your disappointment that you do not find what you loved in the life now ended to welcome you here[.] But one day you will all meet how soon entirely depends upon yourself—It is by the acquirement of wisdom and the loss of the selfishness that is now attached to the sole feeling that possesses you that you will at last mingle in that universal world of which we all now make a divided part." Diotima urges Mathilda to tell her story, and she, hoping that by doing so she will break the bonds that weigh heavily upon her, proceeds to "tell this history of strange woe."

PROSERPINE & MIDAS

Edited with Introduction by
A. KOSZUL

PREFATORY NOTE.

The editor came across the unpublished texts included in this volume as early as 1905. Perhaps he ought to apologize for delaying their appearance in print. The fact is he has long been afraid of overrating their intrinsic value. But as the great Shelley centenary year has come, perhaps this little monument of his wife's collaboration may take its modest place among the tributes which will be paid to his memory. For Mary Shelley's mythological dramas can at least claim to be the proper setting for some of the most beautiful lyrics of the poet, which so far have been read in undue isolation. And even as a literary sign of those times, as an example of that classical renaissance which the romantic period fostered, they may not be altogether negligible.

These biographical and literary points have been dealt with in an introduction for which the kindest help was long ago received from the late Dr. Garnett and the late Lord Abinger. Sir Walter Raleigh was also among the first to give both encouragement and guidance. My friends M. Emile Pons and Mr. Roger Ingpen have read the book in manuscript. The authorities of the Bodleian Library and of the Clarendon Press have been as generously helpful as is their well-known wont. To all the editor wishes to record his acknowledgements and thanks.

STRASBOURG.

INTRODUCTION.

I.

'The compositions published in Mrs. Shelley's lifetime afford but an inadequate conception of the intense sensibility and mental vigour of this extraordinary woman.'

Thus wrote Dr. Garnett, in 1862 (Preface to his Relics of Shelley). The words of praise may have sounded unexpectedly warm at that date. Perhaps the present volume will make the reader more willing to subscribe, or less inclined to demur.

Mary Godwin in her younger days certainly possessed a fair share of that nimbleness of invention which generally characterizes women of letters. Her favourite pastime as a child, she herself testifies,[1] had been to write stories. And a dearer pleasure had been—to use her own characteristic abstract and elongated way of putting it—'the following up trains of thought which had for their subject the formation of a succession of imaginary incidents'. All readers of Shelley's life remember how later on, as a girl of nineteen—and a two years' wife—she was present, 'a devout but nearly silent listener', at the long symposia held by her husband and Byron in Switzerland (June 1816), and how the pondering over 'German horrors', and a common resolve to perpetrate ghost stories of their own, led her to imagine that most unwomanly of all feminine romances, Frankenstein. The paradoxical effort was paradoxically successful, and, as publishers' lists aver to this day, Frankenstein's monster has turned out to be the hardest-lived specimen of the 'raw-head-and-bloody-bones' school of romantic tales. So much, no doubt, to the credit of Mary Shelley. But more creditable, surely, is the fact that she was not tempted, as 'Monk' Lewis had been, to persevere in those lugubrious themes.

Although her publishers—et pour cause—insisted on styling her 'the author of Frankenstein', an entirely different vein appears in her later productions. Indeed, a quiet reserve of tone, a slow, sober, and sedate bearing, are henceforth characteristic of all her literary attitudes. It is almost a case of running from one to the other extreme. The force of style which even adverse critics acknowledged in Frankenstein was sometimes perilously akin to the most disputable kinds of romantic rant. But in the historical or society novels which followed, in the contributions which graced the 'Keepsakes' of the thirties, and even—alas—in the various prefaces and commentaries which accompanied the publication of so many poems of Shelley, his wife succumbed to an increasing habit of almost Victorian reticence and dignity. And those later novels and tales, though they sold well in their days and were kindly reviewed, can hardly boast of any reputation now. Most of them are pervaded by a brooding spirit of melancholy of the 'moping' rather than the 'musical' sort, and consequently rather ineffective as an artistic motive. Students of Shelley occasionally scan those pages with a view to pick some obscure 'hints and indirections', some veiled reminiscences, in the stories of the adventures and misfortunes of The Last Man or Lodore. And the books may be good biography at times—they are never life.

Altogether there is a curious contrast between the two aspects, hitherto revealed, of Mary Shelley's literary activities. It is as if the pulse which had been beating so wildly, so frantically, in Frankenstein (1818), had lapsed, with Valperga (1823) and the rest, into an increasingly sluggish flow.

The following pages may be held to bridge the gap between those two extremes in a felicitous way. A more purely artistic mood, instinct with the serene joy and clear warmth of Italian skies, combining a good deal of youthful buoyancy with a sort of quiet and unpretending philosophy, is here represented. And it is submitted that the little classical fancies which Mrs. Shelley never ventured to publish are quite as worthy of consideration as her more ambitious prose works.

For one thing they give us the longest poetical effort of the writer. The moon of Epipsychidion never seems to have been thrilled with the music of the highest spheres. Yet there were times when Shelley's inspiration and example fired her into something more than her usual calm and cold brilliancy.

One of those periods—perhaps the happiest period in Mary's life—was during the early months in Italy of the English 'exiles'. 'She never was more strongly impelled to write than at this time; she felt her powers fresh and strong within her; all she wanted was some motive, some suggestion to guide her in the choice of a subject.'[2]

Shelley then expected her to try her hand at a drama, perhaps on the terrible story of the Cenci, or again on the catastrophes of Charles the First. Her Frankenstein was attracting more attention than had ever been granted to his own works. And Shelley, with that touching simplicity which characterized his loving moments, showed the greatest confidence in the literary career of his wife. He helped her and encouraged her in every way. He then translated for her Plato's Symposium. He led her on in her Latin and Italian studies. He wanted her—probably as a sort of preliminary exercise before her flight into tragedy—to translate Alfieri's Myrrha. 'Remember Charles the First, and do you be prepared to bring at least some of Myrrha translated,' he wrote; 'remember, remember Charles the First and Myrrha,' he insisted; and he quoted, for her benefit, the presumptuous aphorism of Godwin, in St. Leon, 'There is nothing which the human mind can conceive which it may not execute'.[3]

But in the year that followed these auspicious days, the strain and stress of her life proved more powerful on Mary Shelley than the inspiration of literature. The loss of her little girl Clara, at Venice, on the 24th of September 1818, was cruel enough. However, she tried hard not to show the 'pusillanimous disposition' which, Godwin assured his daughter, characterizes the persons 'that sink long under a calamity of this nature'.[4] But the death of her boy, William, at Rome, on the 4th of June 1819, reduced her to a 'kind of despair'. Whatever it could be to her husband, Italy no longer was for her a 'paradise of exiles'. The flush and excitement of the early months, the 'first fine careless rapture', were for ever gone. 'I shall never recover that blow,' Mary wrote on the 27th of June 1819; 'the thought never leaves me for a single moment; everything on earth has lost its interest for me,' This time her imperturbable father 'philosophized' in vain. With a more sympathetic and acuter intelligence of her case, Leigh Hunt insisted (July 1819) that she should try and give her paralysing sorrow some literary expression, 'strike her pen into some ... genial subject ... and bring up a fountain of gentle tears for us'. But the poor childless mother could only rehearse her complaint— 'to have won, and thus cruelly to have lost' (4 August 1819). In fact she had, on William's death, discontinued her diary.

Yet on the date just mentioned, as Shelley reached his twenty-seven years, she plucked up courage and resumed the task. Shelley, however absorbed by the creative ardour of his *Annus mirabilis*, could not but observe that his wife's 'spirits continued wretchedly depressed' (5 August 1819); and though masculine enough to resent the fact at times more than pity it, he was human enough to persevere in that habit of co-operative reading and writing which is one of the finest traits of his married life. 'I write in the morning,' his wife testifies, 'read Latin till 2, when we dine; then I read some English book, and two cantos of Dante with Shelley'[5]—a fair average, no doubt, of the homely aspect of the great days which produced The Cenci and Prometheus.

On the 12th November, in Florence, the birth of a second son, Percy Florence Shelley, helped Mary out of her sense of bereavement. Subsequent letters still occasionally admit 'low spirits'. But the entries in the Journal make it clear that the year 1819-20 was one of the most pleasantly industrious of her life. Not Dante only, but a motley series of books, great and small, ancient and modern, English and foreign, bespoke her attention. Not content with Latin, and the extemporized translations which Shelley could give her of Plato's Republic, she started Greek in 1820, and soon came to delight in it. And again she thought of original composition. 'Write', 'work,'—the words now occur daily in her Journal. These must mainly refer to the long historical novel, which she had planned, as early as 1819,[6] under the title of Castruccio, Prince of Lucca, and which was not published until 1823, as Valperga. It was indeed a laborious task. The novel 'illustrative of the manners of the Middle Ages in Italy' had to be 'raked out of fifty old books', as Shelley said.[7]

But heavy as the undertaking must have been, it certainly did not engross all the activities of Shelley's wife in this period. And it seems highly probable that the two little mythological dramas which we here publish belong to this same year 1820.

The evidence for this date is as follows. Shelley's lyrics, which these dramas include, were published by his wife (Posthumous Poems, 1824) among the 'poems written in 1820'. Another composition, in blank verse, curiously similar to Mary's own work, entitled Orpheus, has been allotted by Dr. Garnett (Relics of Shelley, 1862) to the same category.[8] Again, it may well be more than a coincidence, that the Proserpine motive occurs in that passage from Dante's Purgatorio, canto 28, on 'Matilda gathering flowers', which Shelley is known to have translated shortly before Medwin's visit in the late autumn of 1820.

> O come, that I may hear
> Thy song: like Proserpine, in Enna's glen,
> Thou seemest to my fancy,—singing here,
> And gathering flowers, as that fair maiden, when
> She lost the spring and Ceres her more dear.[9]

But we have a far more important, because a direct, testimony in a manuscript addition made by Thomas Medwin in the margin of a copy of his Life of Shelley (1847). [10] The passage is clearly intended—though chronology is no more than any other exact science the 'forte' of that most tantalizing of biographers—to refer to the year 1820.

'Mrs. Shelley had at this time been writing some little Dramas on classical subjects, one of which was the Rape of Proserpine, a very graceful composition which she has never published. Shelley contributed to this the exquisite fable of Arethusa and the Invocation to Ceres.—Among the Nymphs gathering flowers on Enna were two whom she called Ino and Uno, names which I remember in the Dialogue were irresistibly ludicrous. She also wrote one on Midas, into which were introduced by Shelley, in the Contest between Pan and Apollo, the Sublime Effusion of the latter, and Pan's characterised Ode.'

This statement of Medwin finally settles the question. The 'friend' at whose request, Mrs. Shelley says,[11] the lyrics were written by her husband, was herself. And she was the author of the dramas.[12]

The manuscript (Bodleian Library, MS. Shelley, d. 2) looks like a cheap exercise-book, originally of 40, now of 36 leaves, 8 1/4 x 6 inches, in boards. The contents are the dramas here presented, written in a clear legible hand—the equable hand of Mrs. Shelley.[13] There are very few words corrected or cancelled. It is obviously a fair copy. Mr. C. D. Locock, in his Examination of the Shelley Manuscripts in the Bodleian Library (Clarendon Press, Oxford, 1903, pp. 24-25), has already pointed out the valuable emendations of the 'received' text of Shelley's lyrics which are found here. In fact the only mystery is why neither Shelley, nor Mary in the course of her long widowed years, should have published these curious, and surely not contemptible, by-products of their co-operation in the fruitful year 1820.

Footnotes

1 Preface to the 1831 edition of Frankenstein.
2 Mrs. Marshall, The Life and Letters of Mary W. Shelley, i. 216.
3 Letter from Padua, 22 September 1818.
4 27 October 1818

5   Letter to Mrs. Hunt, 28 August 1819.

6   She had 'thought of it' at Marlow, as appears from her letter to Mrs. Gisborne, 30 June 1821 (in Mrs. Marshall, i. p. 291); but the materials for it were not found before the stay at Naples, and it was not actually begun 'till a year afterwards, at Pisa' (ibid.).

7   Letter to T. L. Peacock, November 1820.

8   Dr. Garnett, in his prefatory note, states that Orpheus 'exists only in a transcript by Mrs. Shelley, who has written in playful allusion to her toils as amanuensis Aspetto fin che il diluvio cala, ed allora cerco di posare argine alle sue parole'. The poem is thus supposed to have been Shelley's attempt at improvisation, if not indeed a translation from the Italian of the 'improvvisatore' Sgricci. The Shelleys do not seem to have come to know and hear Sgricci before the end of December 1820. The Italian note after all has no very clear import. And Dr. Garnett in 1905 inclined to the view that Orpheus was the work not of Shelley, but of his wife. A comparison of that fragment and the dramas here published seems to me to suggest the same conclusion, though in both cases Mary Shelley must have been helped by her husband.

9   As published by Medwin, 1834 and 1847.

10   The copy, 2 vols., was sold at Sotheby's on the 6th December 1906: Mr. H. Buxton Forman (who was, I think, the buyer) published the contents in The Life of Percy Bysshe Shelley, By Thomas Medwin, A New Edition printed from a copy copiously amended and extended by the Author... Milford, 1913. The passage here quoted appears on p. 27 of the 2nd vol. of the 1847 edition (Forman ed., p. 252)

11   The Hymns of Pan and Apollo were first published by Mrs. Shelley in the Posthumous Poems, 1824, with a note saying that they had been 'written at the request of a friend to be inserted in a drama on the subject of Midas'. Arethusa appeared in the same volume, dated 'Pisa, 1820'. Proserpine's song was not published before the first collected edition of 1839.

12   Not E. E. Williams (Buxton Forman, ed. 1882, vol. iv, p. 34). The manuscript of the poetical play composed about 1822 by the latter, 'The Promise', with Shelley's autograph poem ('Night! with all thine eyes look down'), was given to the Bodleian Library in 1914.

13   Shelley's lyrics are also in his wife's writing—Mr. Locock is surely mistaken in assuming two different hands to this manuscript (The Poems of Percy Bysshe Shelley, Methuen, 1909, vol. iii, p. xix).

II.

For indeed there is more than a personal interest attached to these writings of Mrs. Shelley's. The fact that the same mind which had revelled, a few years earlier, in the fantastical horrors of Frankenstein's abortive creation, could now dwell on the melancholy fate of Proserpine or the humorous disappointment of Midas, and delight in their subtle poetical or moral symbolism—this fact has its significance. It is one of the earliest indications of the revival, in the heart of Romanticism, of the old love of classical myths and classical beauty.

The subject is a wide one, and cannot be adequately dealt with in this place. But a few words may not be superfluous for a correct historical appreciation of Mrs. Shelley's attempt.

How deficient had been the sense of classical beauty in the so-called classical age of English literature, is a trite consideration of criticism. The treatment of mythology is particularly conclusive on this point. Throughout the 'Augustan' era, mythology was approached as a mere treasure-house of pleasant fancies, artificial decorations, 'motives', whether sumptuous or meretricious. Allusions to Jove and Venus, Mercury, Apollo, or Bacchus, are of course found in every other page of Dryden, Pope, Prior, Swift, Gay, and Parnell. But no fresh presentation, no loving interpretation, of the old myths occur anywhere. The immortal stories were then part and parcel of a sort of poetical curriculum through which the whole school must be taken by the stern masters Tradition and Propriety. There is little to be wondered at, if this matter of curriculum was treated by the more passive scholars as a matter of course, and by the sharper and less reverent disciples as a matter of fun. Indeed, if any personality is then evinced in the adaptation of these old world themes, it is generally connected with a more or less emphatic disparagement or grotesque distortion of their real meaning.

When Dryden, for example, makes use of the legend of Midas, in his Wife of Bath's Tale, he makes, not Midas's minister, but his queen, tell the mighty secret—and thus secures another hit at woman's loquacity.

Prior's Female Phaëton is a younger sister, who, jealous of her elder's success, thus pleads with her 'mamma':

> I'll have my earl as well as she
>   Or know the reason why.

And she wants to flaunt it accordingly.
Finally,

> Fondness prevailed; mamma gave way;
>   Kitty, at heart's desire,
> Obtained the chariot for a day,
>   And set the world on fire.

Pandora, in Parnell's Hesiod or the Rise of Woman, is only a

> 'shining vengeance . . .
> A pleasing bosom-cheat, a specious ill'

sent by the gods upon earth to punish the race of Prometheus.

The most poetical fables of Greece are desecrated by Gay into mere miniatures for the decoration of his Fan.

Similar instances abound later on. When Armstrong brings in an apostrophe to the Naiads, it is in the course of a Poetical Essay on the Art of Preserving Health. And again, when Cowper stirs himself to intone an Ode to Apollo, it is in the same mock-heroic vein:

> Patron of all those luckless brains,
>   That to the wrong side leaning
> Indite much metre with much pains
>   And little or no meaning . . .

Even in Gray's—'Pindaric Gray's'—treatment of classical themes, there is a sort of pervading ennui, or the forced appreciativeness of a gouty, disappointed man. The daughter of Jove to whom he dedicates his hymns too often is 'Adversity'. And classical reminiscences have, even with him, a dull musty tinge which recalls the antiquarian in his Cambridge college-rooms rather than the visitor to Florence and Rome. For one thing, his allusions are too many, and too transitory, to appear anything but artistic tricks and verse-making tools. The 'Aegean deep', and 'Delphi's steep', and 'Meander's amber waves', and the 'rosy-crowned Loves', are too cursorily summoned, and dismissed, to suggest that they have been brought in for their own sweet sakes.

It was thus with all the fine quintessences of ancient lore, with all the pearl-like accretions of the faiths and fancies of the old world: they were handled about freely as a kind of curious but not so very rare coins, which found no currency in the deeper thoughts of our modern humanity, and could therefore be used as a mere badge of the learning and taste of a literary 'coterie'.

The very names of the ancient gods and heroes were in fact assuming that abstract anaemic look which common nouns have in everyday language. Thus, when Garrick, in his verses Upon a Lady's Embroidery, mentions 'Arachne', it is obvious that he does not expect the reader to think of the daring challenger of Minerva's art, or the Princess of Lydia, but just of a plain spider. And again, when Falconer, in his early Monody on the death of the Prince of Wales, expresses a rhetorical wish

> 'to aid hoarse howling Boreas with his sighs,'

that particular son of Astræus, whose love for the nymph Orithyia was long unsuccessful, because he could not 'sigh', is surely far from the poet's mind; and 'to swell the wind', or 'the gale', would have served his turn quite as well, though less 'elegantly'.

Even Gibbon, with all his partiality for whatever was pre- or post-Christian, had indeed no better word than 'elegant' for the ancient mythologies of Greece and Rome, and he surely reflected no particularly advanced opinion when he praised and damned, in one breath, 'the pleasant and absurd system of Paganism.'[1] No wonder if in his days, and for a long time after, the passionate giants of the Ages of Fable had dwindled down to the pretty puppets with which the daughters of the gentry had to while away many a school hour.

But the days of this rhetorical—or satirical, didactic—or perfunctory, treatment of classical themes were doomed. It is the glory of Romanticism to have opened 'magic casements' not only on 'the foam of perilous seas' in the West, but also on

> the chambers of the East,
> The chambers of the Sun, that now
> From ancient melody had ceased.[2]

Romanticism, as a freshening up of all the sources of life, a general rejuvenescence of the soul, a ubiquitous visiting of the spirit of delight and wonder, could not confine itself to the fields of mediaeval romance. Even the records of the Greek and Roman thought assumed a new beauty; the classical sense was let free from its antiquarian trammels, and the perennial fanes resounded to the songs of a more impassioned worship.

The change, however, took some time. And it must be admitted that in England, especially, the Romantic movement was slow to go back to classical themes. Winckelmann and Goethe, and Chénier—the last, indeed, practically all unknown to his contemporaries—had long rediscovered

Antiquity, and felt its pulse anew, and praised its enduring power, when English poetry had little, if anything, to show in answer to the plaintive invocation of Blake to the Ancient Muses.

The first generation of English Romantics either shunned the subject altogether, or simply echoed Blake's isolated lines in isolated passages as regretful and almost as despondent. From Persia to Paraguay Southey could wander and seek after exotic themes; his days could be 'passed among the dead'—but neither the classic lands nor the classic heroes ever seem to have detained him. Walter Scott's 'sphere of sensation may be almost exactly limited by the growth of heather', as Ruskin says;[3] and when he came to Rome, his last illness prevented him from any attempt he might have wished to make to enlarge his field of vision. Wordsworth was even less far-travelled, and his home-made poetry never thought of the 'Pagan' and his 'creed outworn', but as a distinct pis-aller in the way of inspiration.[4] And again, though Coleridge has a few magnificent lines about them, he seems to have even less willingly than Wordsworth hearkened after

> The intelligible forms of ancient poets,
> The fair humanities of old religion.[5]

It was to be otherwise with the later English Romantic poets. They lived and worked at a time when the whole atmosphere and even the paraphernalia of literary composition had just undergone a considerable change. After a period of comparative seclusion and self-concentration, England at the Peace of Amiens once more found its way to Europe—and vice versa. And from our point of view this widening of prospects is especially noticeable. For the classical revival in Romanticism appears to be closely connected with it.

It is an alluring subject to investigate. How the progress of scholarship, the recent 'finds' of archaeology, the extension of travelling along Mediterranean shores, the political enthusiasms evoked by the stirrings of young Italy and young Greece, all combined to reawaken in the poetical imagination of the times the dormant memories of antiquity has not yet been told by the historians of literature.[6]

But—and this is sufficient for our purpose—every one knows what the Elgin Marbles have done for Keats and Shelley; and what inspirations were derived from their pilgrimages in classic lands by all the poets of this and the following generation, from Byron to Landor. Such experiences could not but react on the common conception of mythology. A knowledge of the great classical sculpture of Greece could not but invest with a new dignity and chastity the notions which so far had been nurtured on the Venus de' Medici and the Belvedere Apollo—even Shelley lived and possibly died under their spell. And 'returning to the nature which had inspired the ancient myths', the Romantic poets must have felt with a keener sense 'their exquisite vitality'.[7] The whole tenor of English Romanticism may be said to have been affected thereby.

For English Romanticism—and this is one of its most distinctive merits—had no exclusiveness about it. It was too spontaneous, one would almost say, too unconscious, ever to be clannish. It grew, untrammelled by codes, uncrystallized into formulas, a living thing always, not a subject-matter for grandiloquent manifestoes and more or less dignified squabbles. It could therefore absorb and turn to account elements which seemed antagonistic to it in the more sophisticated forms it assumed in other literatures. Thus, whilst French Romanticism—in spite of what it may or may not have owed to Chénier—became often distinctly, deliberately, wilfully anti-classical, whilst for example[8] Victor Hugo in that all-comprehending Légende des Siècles could find room for the Hegira and for Zim-Zizimi, but did not consecrate a single line to the departed glories of mythical Greece, the Romantic poets of England may claim to have restored in freshness and purity the religion of antiquity. Indeed their voice was so convincing that even the great Christian chorus that broke out afresh in the Victorian era could not entirely drown it, and

Elizabeth Barrett had an apologetic way of dismissing 'the dead Pan', and all the 'vain false gods of Hellas', with an acknowledgement of

> your beauty which confesses
> Some chief Beauty conquering you.

This may be taken to have been the average attitude, in the forties, towards classical mythology. That twenty years before, at least in the Shelley circle, it was far less grudging, we now have definite proof.

Not only was Shelley prepared to admit, with the liberal opinion of the time, that ancient mythology 'was a system of nature concealed under the veil of allegory', a system in which 'a thousand fanciful fables contained a secret and mystic meaning':[9] he was prepared to go a considerable step farther, and claim that there was no essential difference between ancient mythology and the theology of the Christians, that both were interpretations, in more or less figurative language, of the great mysteries of being, and indeed that the earlier interpretation, precisely because it was more frankly figurative and poetical than the later one, was better fitted to stimulate and to allay the sense of wonder which ought to accompany a reverent and high-souled man throughout his life-career.

In the earlier phase of Shelley's thought, this identification of the ancient and the modern faiths was derogatory to both. The letter which he had written in 1812 for ihe edification of Lord Ellenborough revelled in the contemplation of a time 'when the Christian religion shall have faded from the earth, when its memory like that of Polytheism now shall remain, but remain only as the subject of ridicule and wonder'. But as time went on, Shelley's views became less purely negative. Instead of ruling the adversaries back to back out of court, he bethought himself of venturing a plea in favour of the older and weaker one. It may have been in 1817 that he contemplated an 'Essay in favour of polytheism'.[10] He was then living on the fringe of a charmed circle of amateur and adventurous Hellenists who could have furthered the scheme. His great friend, Thomas

Love Peacock, 'Greeky Peaky', was a personal acquaintance of Thomas Taylor 'the Platonist', alias 'Pagan Taylor'. And Taylor's translations and commentaries of Plato had been favourites of Shelley in his college days. Something at least of Taylor's queer mixture of flaming enthusiasm and tortuous ingenuity may be said to appear in the unexpected document we have now to examine.

It is a little draft of an Essay, which occurs, in Mrs. Shelley's handwriting, as an insertion in her Journal for the Italian period. The fragment—for it is no more—must be quoted in full.[11]

> The necessity of a Belief in the
> Heathen Mythology
> to a Christian

If two facts are related not contradictory of equal probability & with equal evidence, if we believe one we must believe the other.

> 1st. There is as good proof of the Heathen Mythology as of the Christian Religion.
> 2ly. that they [do] not contradict one another.
> Con[clusion]. If a man believes in one he must believe in both.

Examination of the proofs of the Xtian religion—the Bible & its authors. The twelve stones that existed in the time of the writer prove the miraculous passage of the river Jordan.[12] The immoveability of the Island of Delos proves the accouchement of Latona[13]—the Bible of the Greek religion consists in Homer, Hesiod & the Fragments of Orpheus &c.—All that came afterwards to be considered apocryphal—Ovid = Josephus—of each of these writers we may believe just what we cho[o]se.

To seek in these Poets for the creed & proofs of mythology which are as follows—Examination of these—1st with regard to proof—2 in

255

contradiction or conformity to the Bible—various apparitions of God in that Book [—] Jupiter considered by himself—his attributes—disposition [—] acts—whether as God revealed himself as the Almighty to the Patriarchs & as Jehovah to the Jews he did not reveal himself as Jupiter to the Greeks—the possibility of various revelations—that he revealed himself to Cyrus.[14]

The inferior deities—the sons of God & the Angels—the difficulty of Jupiter's children explained away—the imagination of the poets—of the prophets—whether the circumstance of the sons of God living with women[15] being related in one sentence makes it more probable than the details of Greek—Various messages of the Angels—of the deities—Abraham, Lot or Tobit. Raphael [—]Mercury to Priam[16]—Calypso & Ulysses—the angel w^d then play the better part of the two whereas he now plays the worse. The ass of Balaam—Oracles—Prophets. The revelation of God as Jupiter to the Greeks—a more successful revelation than that as Jehovah to the Jews—Power, wisdom, beauty, & obedience of the Greeks—greater & of longer continuance—than those of the Jews. Jehovah's promises worse kept than Jupiter's—the Jews or Prophets had not a more consistent or decided notion concerning after life & the Judgements of God than the Greeks [—] Angels disappear at one time in the Bible & afterwards appear again. The revelation to the Greeks more complete than to the Jews—prophesies of Christ by the heathens more incontrovertible than those of the Jews. The coming of X. a confirmation of both religions. The cessation of oracles a proof of this. The Xtians better off than any but the Jews as blind as the Heathens—Much more conformable to an idea of [the] goodness of God that he should have revealed himself to the Greeks than that he left them in ignorance. Vergil & Ovid not truth of the heathen Mythology, but the interpretation of a heathen—as Milton's Paradise Lost is the interpretation of a Christian religion of the Bible. The interpretation of the mythology of Vergil & the interpretation of the Bible by Milton compared—whether one is more inconsistent than the other—In what they are contradictory. Prometheus desmotes quoted by Paul[17] [—] all religion false except that which is revealed—revelation depends upon a certain degree of civilization—writing necessary—no oral tradition to be a part of faith—the worship of the Sun no revelation—Having lost the books [of] the Egyptians we have no knowledge of their peculiar revelations. If the revelation of God to the Jews on Mt Sinai had been more peculiar & impressive than some of those to the Greeks they w^d not immediately after have worshiped a calf—A latitude in revelation—How to judge of prophets—the proof [of] the Jewish Prophets being prophets.

The only public revelation that Jehovah ever made of himself was on Mt Sinai—Every other depended upon the testimony of a very few & usually of a single individual—We will first therefore consider the revelation of Mount Sinai. Taking the fact plainly it happened thus. The Jews were told by a man whom they believed to have supernatural powers that they were to prepare for that God w^d reveal himself in three days on the mountain at the sound of a trumpet. On the 3rd day there was a cloud & lightning on the mountain & the voice of a trumpet extremely loud. The people were ordered to stand round the foot of the mountain & not on pain of death to infringe upon the bounds—The man in whom they confided went up the mountain & came down again bringing them word

The draft unfortunately leaves off here, and we are unable to know for certain whether this Shelleyan paradox, greatly daring, meant to minimize the importance of the 'only public revelation' granted to the chosen people. But we have enough to understand the general trend of the argument. It did not actually intend to sap the foundations of Scriptural authority. But it was bold enough to risk a little shaking in order to prove that the Sacred Books of the Greeks and Romans did not, after all, present us with a much more rickety structure. This was a task of conciliation rather than destruction. And yet even this conservative view of the Shelleys' exegesis cannot—and will not—detract from the value of the above document. Surely, this curious theory of the equal 'inspiration' of Polytheism and the Jewish or Christian religions, whether it was invented or simply espoused by Mrs. Shelley, evinces in her—for the time being at least—a very considerable share of that adventurous if somewhat uncritical alacrity of mind which carried the poet through so many religious and political problems. It certainly vindicates her, more completely perhaps than anything hitherto published, against the strictures of those who knew her chiefly or exclusively in later years, and could speak of her as a 'most conventional slave', who 'even affected the pious dodge', and 'was not a suitable companion for the poet'.[18] Mrs. Shelley—at twenty-three years of age—had not yet run the full 'career of her humour'; and her enthusiasm for classical mythology may well have, later on, gone the way of her admiration for Spinoza, whom she read with Shelley that winter (1820-1), as Medwin notes,[19] and 'whose arguments she then thought irrefutable—tempora mutantur!'

However that may be, the two little mythological dramas on Proserpine and Midas assume, in the light of that enthusiasm, a special interest. They stand—or fall—both as a literary, and to a certain extent as an intellectual effort. They are more than an attitude, and not much less than an avowal. Not only do they claim our attention as the single poetical work of any length which seems to have been undertaken by Mrs. Shelley; they are a unique and touching monument of that intimate co-operation which at times, especially in the early years in Italy, could make the union of 'the May' and 'the Elf' almost unreservedly delightful. It would undoubtedly be fatuous exaggeration to ascribe a very high place in literature to these little Ovidian fancies of Mrs. Shelley. The scenes, after all, are little better than adaptations—fairly close adaptations—of the Latin poet's well-known tales.

Even Proserpine, though clearly the more successful of the two, both more strongly knit as drama, and less uneven in style and versification, cannot for a moment compare with the far more original interpretations of Tennyson, Swinburne, or Meredith.[20] But it is hardly fair to draw in the great names of the latter part of the century. The parallel would be more illuminating—and the final award passed on Mrs. Shelley's attempt more favourable—if we were to think of a contemporary production like 'Barry Cornwall's' Rape of Proserpine, which, being published in 1820, it is just possible that the Shelleys should have known. B. W. Procter's poem is also a dramatic 'scene', written 'in imitation of the mode originated by the Greek Tragic Writers'. In fact those hallowed models seem to have left far fewer traces in Barry Cornwall's verse than the Alexandrian—or pseudo-Alexandrian—tradition of meretricious graces and coquettish fancies, which the eighteenth century had already run to death.[21] And, more damnable still, the poetical essence of the legend, the identification of Proserpine's twofold existence with the grand alternation of nature's seasons, has been entirely neglected by the author. Surely his work, though published, is quite as deservedly obscure as Mrs. Shelley's derelict manuscript. Midas has the privilege, if it be one, of not challenging any obvious comparison. The subject, since Lyly's and Dryden's days, has hardly attracted the attention of the poets. It was so eminently fit for the lighter kinds of presentation that the agile bibliographer who aimed at completeness would have to go through a fairly long list of masques,[22] comic operas, or 'burlettas', all dealing with the ludicrous misfortunes of the Phrygian king. But an examination of these would be sheer pedantry in this place. Here again Mrs. Shelley has stuck to her Latin source as closely as she could.[23] She has made a gallant attempt to connect the two stories with which Midas has ever since Ovid's days been associated, and a distinct—indeed a too perceptible—effort to press out a moral meaning in this, as she had easily extricated a cosmological meaning in the other tale.

Perhaps we have said too much to introduce these two little unpretending poetical dramas. They might indeed have been allowed to speak for themselves. A new frame often makes a new face; and some of the best known and most exquisite of Shelley's lyrics, when restored to the surroundings for which the poet intended them, needed no other set-off to appeal to the reader with a fresh charm of quiet classical grace and beauty. But the charm will operate all the more unfailingly, if we remember that this clear classical mood was by no means such a common element in the literary atmosphere of the times—not even a permanent element in the authors' lives. We have here none of the feverish ecstasy that lifts Prometheus and Hellas far above the ordinary range of philosophical or political poetry. But Shelley's encouragement, probably his guidance and supervision, have raised his wife's inspiration to a place considerably higher than that of Frankenstein or Valperga. With all their faults these pages reflect some of that irradiation which Shelley cast around his own life—the irradiation of a dream beauteous and generous, beauteous in its theology (or its substitute for theology) and generous even in its satire of human weaknesses.

Footnotes

1. Essay on the Study of Literature, § 56.
2. Blake, Poetical Sketches, 1783.
3. Modern Painters, iii. 317
4. Sonnet 'The world is too much with us'; cf. The Excursion, iv. 851-57.
5. The Piccolomini, II, iv.
6. At least as far as England is concerned. For France, cf. Canat, a renaissance de la Grèce antique, Hachette, Paris, 1911.
7. J. A, Symonds, Studies of the Greek Poets, ii, p. 258.
8. As pointed out by Brunetière, Évolution de la Poésie lyrique, ii, p. 147.
9. Edinb. Rev., July 1808.
10. Cf. our Shelley's Prose in the Bodleian MSS., 1910, p. 124.
11. From the 'Boscombe' MSS. Unpublished.
12. Josh. iv. 8.—These notes are *not* Shelley's.
13. Theogn. 5 foll.; Homer's Hymn to Apollo, i. 25.
14. Probably Xenophon, Cyrop. VIII. vii. 2.
15. Gen. vi.
16. Iliad, xxiv.
17. Shelley may refer to the proverbial phrase 'to kick against the pricks' (Acts xxvi. 14), which, however, is found in Pindar and Euripides as well as in Aeschylus (Prom. 323).

18 Trelawny's letter, 3 April 1870; in Mr. H. Buxton Forman's edition, 1910, p. 229.
19 I. e. ed. H. Buxton Forman, p. 253.
20 Demeter and Persephone, 1889; The Garden of Proserpine, 1866; The Appeasement of Demeter, 1888.
21 To adduce an example—in what is probably not an easily accessible book today: Proserpine, distributing her flowers, thus addresses one of her nymphs:

>   For this lily,
>   Where can it hang but at Cyane's breast!
>   And yet 'twill wither on so white a bed,
>   If flowers have sense for envy.

22 There is one by poor Christopher Smart.
23 Perhaps her somewhat wearying second act, on the effects of the gold-transmuting gift, would have been shorter, if Ovid (Metam. xi. 108-30) had not himself gone into such details on the subject.

MYTHOLOGICAL DRAMAS.

Unless otherwise pointed out—by brackets, or in the notes—the text, spelling, and punctuation of the MS. have been strictly adhered to.

PROSERPINE.
A DRAMA IN TWO ACTS.

DRAMATIS PERSONAE

Ceres.
Proserpine.
Ino, Eunoe Nymphs attendant upon Proserpine.
Iris.
Arethusa, Naiad of a Spring.
Shades from Hell, among which Ascalaphus.

Scene; the plain of Enna, in Sicily.

ACT I.

Scene; a beautiful plain, shadowed on one side by an overhanging rock, on the other a chesnut wood. Etna at a distance.

Enter Ceres, Proserpine, Ino and Eunoe.

Pros. Dear Mother, leave me not! I love to rest
Under the shadow of that hanging cave
And listen to your tales. Your Proserpine
Entreats you stay; sit on this shady bank,
And as I twine a wreathe tell once again
The combat of the Titans and the Gods;
Or how the Python fell beneath the dart
Of dread Apollo; or of Daphne's change,—
That coyest Grecian maid, whose pointed leaves
Now shade her lover's brow. And I the while
Gathering the starry flowers of this fair plain
Will weave a chaplet, Mother, for thy hair.
But without thee, the plain I think is vacant,
Its[1] blossoms fade,—its tall fresh grasses droop,
Nodding their heads like dull things half asleep;—
Go not, dear Mother, from your Proserpine.

[2]

Cer. My lovely child, it is high Jove's command:—
The golden self-moved seats surround his throne,
The nectar is poured out by Ganymede,
And the ambrosia fills the golden baskets;
They drink, for Bacchus is already there,
But none will eat till I dispense the food.
I must away—dear Proserpine, farewell!—
Eunoe can tell thee how the giants fell;
Or dark-eyed Ino sing the saddest change

Of Syrinx or of Daphne, or the doom
Of impious Prometheus, and the boy
Of fair Pandora, Mother of mankind.
This only charge I leave thee and thy nymphs,—
Depart not from each other; be thou circled
By that fair guard, and then no earth-born Power
Would tempt my wrath, and steal thee from their sight[.]
But wandering alone, by feint or force,
You might be lost, and I might never know
Thy hapless fate. Farewel, sweet daughter mine,
Remember my commands.

Pros.—Mother, farewel!
Climb the bright sky with rapid wings; and swift
As a beam shot from great Apollo's bow
Rebounds from the calm mirror of the sea
Back to his quiver in the Sun, do thou
Return again to thy loved Proserpine.

(Exit Ceres.)

[3]

And now, dear Nymphs, while the hot sun is high
Darting his influence right upon the plain,
Let us all sit beneath the narrow shade
That noontide Etna casts.—And, Ino, sweet,
Come hither; and while idling thus we rest,
Repeat in verses sweet the tale which says
How great Prometheus from Apollo's car
Stole heaven's fire—a God-like gift for Man!
Or the more pleasing tale of Aphrodite;

How she arose from the salt Ocean's foam,
And sailing in her pearly shell, arrived
On Cyprus sunny shore, where myrtles[2] bloomed
And sweetest flowers, to welcome Beauty's Queen;
And ready harnessed on the golden sands
Stood milk-white doves linked to a sea-shell car,
With which she scaled the heavens, and took her seat
Among the admiring Gods.

Eun. Proserpine's tale
Is sweeter far than Ino's sweetest aong.

Pros. Ino, you knew erewhile a River-God,
Who loved you well and did you oft entice
To his transparent waves and flower-strewn banks.
He loved high poesy and wove sweet sounds,
And would sing to you as you sat reclined
On the fresh grass beside his shady cave,
From which clear waters bubbled, dancing forth,

[4]

And spreading freshness in the noontide air.
When you returned you would enchant our ears
With tales and songs which did entice the fauns,[3]
With Pan their King from their green haunts, to hear.
Tell me one now, for like the God himself,
Tender they were and fanciful, and wrapt
The hearer in sweet dreams of shady groves,
Blue skies, and clearest, pebble-paved streams.
Ino. I will repeat the tale which most I loved;
Which tells how lily-crowned Arethusa,

Your favourite Nymph, quitted her native Greece,
Flying the liquid God Alpheus, who followed,
Cleaving the desarts of the pathless deep,
And rose in Sicily, where now she flows
The clearest spring of Enna's gifted plain.

(By Shelley)[4]

    Arethusa arose
    From her couch of snows,
In the Acroceraunian mountains,—
    From cloud, and from crag,
    With many a jag,
Shepherding her bright fountains.
    She leapt down the rocks
    With her rainbow locks,
Streaming among the streams,—

[5]

    Her steps paved with green
    The downward ravine,
Which slopes to the Western gleams:—
    And gliding and springing,
    She went, ever singing
In murmurs as soft as sleep;
    The Earth seemed to love her
    And Heaven smiled above her,
As she lingered towards the deep.

    Then Alpheus bold
    On his glacier cold,

With his trident the mountains strook;
    And opened a chasm
    In the rocks;—with the spasm
All Erymanthus shook.
    And the black south wind
    It unsealed behind
The urns of the silent snow,
    And earthquake and thunder
    Did rend in sunder
The bars of the springs below:—
    And the beard and the hair
    Of the river God were
Seen through the torrent's sweep

[6]

    As he followed the light
    Of the fleet nymph's flight
To the brink of the Dorian deep.
    Oh, save me! oh, guide me!
    And bid the deep hide me,
For he grasps me now by the hair!
    The loud ocean heard,
    To its blue depth stirred,
And divided at her prayer[,]
    And under the water
    The Earth's white daughter
Fled like a sunny beam,
    Behind her descended
    Her billows unblended
With the brackish Dorian stream:—
    Like a gloomy stain

On the Emerald main
Alpheus rushed behind,
   As an eagle pursueing
   A dove to its ruin,
Down the streams of the cloudy wind.

[7]

   Under the bowers
   Where the Ocean Powers
Sit on their pearled thrones,
   Through the coral woods
   Of the weltering floods,
Over heaps of unvalued stones;
   Through the dim beams,
   Which amid the streams
Weave a network of coloured light,
   And under the caves,
   Where the shadowy waves
Are as green as the forest's[5] night:—
   Outspeeding the shark,
   And the sword fish dark,
Under the Ocean foam,[6]
   And up through the rifts
   Of the mountain clifts,
They passed to their Dorian Home.

   And now from their fountains
   In Enna's mountains,
Down one vale where the morning basks,
   Like friends once parted,

  Grown single hearted
They ply their watery tasks.

[8]

  At sunrise they leap
  From their cradles steep
In the cave of the shelving hill[,—]
  At noontide they flow
  Through the woods below
And the meadows of asphodel,—
  And at night they sleep
  In the rocking deep
Beneath the Ortygian shore;—
  Like spirits that lie
  In the azure sky,
When they love, but live no more.

Pros. Thanks, Ino dear, you have beguiled an hour
With poesy that might make pause to list
The nightingale in her sweet evening song.
But now no more of ease and idleness,
The sun stoops to the west, and Enna's plain
Is overshadowed by the growing form
Of giant Etna:—Nymphs, let us arise,
And cull the sweetest flowers of the field,
And with swift fingers twine a blooming wreathe
For my dear Mother's rich and waving hair.

Eunoe. Violets blue and white anemonies

[9]

Bloom on the plain,—but I will climb the brow
Of that o'erhanging hill, to gather thence
That loveliest rose, it will adorn thy crown;
Ino, guard Proserpine till my return.

(Exit.)

Ino. How lovely is this plain!—Nor Grecian vale,
Nor bright Ausonia's ilex bearing shores,
The myrtle bowers of Aphrodite's sweet isle,
Or Naxos burthened with the luscious vine,
Can boast such fertile or such verdant fields
As these, which young Spring sprinkles with her stars;—
Nor Crete which boasts fair Amalthea's horn
Can be compared with the bright golden[7] fields
Of Ceres, Queen of plenteous Sicily.

Pros. Sweet Ino, well I know the love you bear
My dearest Mother prompts your partial voice,
And that love makes you doubly dear to me.
But you are idling,—look[,] my lap is full
Of sweetest flowers;—haste to gather more,
That before sunset we may make our crown.
Last night as we strayed through that glade, methought
The wind that swept my cheek bore on its wings
The scent of fragrant violets, hid
Beneath the straggling underwood; Haste, sweet,
To gather them; fear not—I will not stray.

Ino. Nor fear that I shall loiter in my task.

(Exit.)

[10]

(By Shelley.)

Pros. (sings as she gathers her flowers.)
   Sacred Goddess, Mother Earth,
      Thou from whose immortal bosom
   Gods, and men, and beasts have birth,
      Leaf, and blade, and bud, and blossom,
Breathe thine influence most divine
On thine own child Proserpine.

   If with mists of evening dew
      Thou dost nourish these young flowers
   Till they grow in scent and hue
      Fairest children of the hours[,]
Breathe thine influence most divine
On thine own child Proserpine.

(she looks around.)

My nymphs have left me, neglecting the commands
Of my dear Mother. Where can they have strayed?
Her caution makes me fear to be alone;—
I'll pass that yawning cave and seek the spring
Of Arethuse, where water-lilies bloom
Perhaps the nymph now wakes tending her waves,
She loves me well and oft desires my stay,—

[11]

The lilies shall adorn my mother's crown.

(Exit.)

(After a pause enter Eunoe.)

Eun. I've won my prize! look at this fragrant rose!
But where is Proserpine? Ino has strayed
Too far I fear, and she will be fatigued,
As I am now, by my long toilsome search.

Enter Ino.

Oh! you here, Wanderer! Where is Proserpine?

Ino. My lap's heaped up with sweets; dear Proserpine,
You will not chide me now for idleness;—
Look here are all the treasures of the field,—
First these fresh violets, which crouched beneath
A mossy rock, playing at hide and seek
With both the sight and sense through the high fern;
Star-eyed narcissi & the drooping bells
Of hyacinths; and purple polianthus,
Delightful flowers are these; but where is she,
The loveliest of them all, our Mistress dear?

Eun. I know not, even now I left her here,
Guarded by you, oh Ino, while I climbed
Up yonder steep for this most worthless rose:—

Know you not where she is? Did you forget
Ceres' behest, and thus forsake her child?

Ino. Chide not, unkind Eunoe, I but went

[12⁸]

Down that dark glade, where underneath the shade
Of those high trees the sweetest violets grow,—
I went at her command. Alas! Alas!
My heart sinks down; I dread she may be lost;—
Eunoe, climb the hill, search that ravine,
Whose close, dark sides may hide her from our view:—
Oh, dearest, haste! Is that her snow-white robe?

Eun. No;—'tis a faun[9] beside its sleeping Mother,
Browsing the grass;—what will thy Mother say,
Dear Proserpine, what will bright Ceres feel,
If her return be welcomed not by thee?

Ino. These are wild thoughts,—& we are wrong to fear
That any ill can touch the child of heaven;
She is not lost,—trust me, she has but strayed
Up some steep mountain path, or in yon dell,
Or to the rock where yellow wall-flowers grow,
Scaling with venturous step the narrow path
Which the goats fear to tread;—she will return
And mock our fears.

Eun. The sun now dips his beams
In the bright sea; Ceres descends at eve
From Jove's high conclave; if her much-loved child

Should meet her not in yonder golden field,
Where to the evening wind the ripe grain waves

[13]

Its yellow head, how will her heart misgive.
Let us adjure the Naiad of yon brook[,]
She may perchance have seen our Proserpine,
And tell us to what distant field she's strayed:—
Wait thou, dear Ino, here, while I repair
To the tree-shaded source of her swift stream.

(Exit Eunoe.)

Ino. Why does my heart misgive? & scalding tears,
That should but mourn, now prophecy her loss?
Oh, Proserpine! Where'er your luckless fate
Has hurried you,—to wastes of desart sand,
Or black Cymmerian cave, or dread Hell,
Yet Ino still will follow! Look where Eunoe
Comes, with down cast eyes and faltering steps,
I fear the worst;—

Re-enter Eunoe.

Has she not then been seen?

Eun. Alas, all hope is vanished! Hymera says
She slept the livelong day while the hot beams
Of Phoebus drank her waves;—nor did she wake
Until her reed-crowned head was wet with dew;—
If she had passed her grot she slept the while.

Ino. Alas! Alas! I see the golden car,
And hear the flapping of the dragons wings,
Ceres descends to Earth. I dare not stay,
I dare not meet the sorrow of her look[,]

[14]

The angry glance of her severest eyes.

Eun. Quick up the mountain! I will search the dell,
She must return, or I will never more.

(Exit.)

Ino. And yet I will not fly, though I fear much
Her angry frown and just reproach, yet shame
Shall quell this childish fear, all hope of safety
For her lost child rests but in her high power,
And yet I tremble as I see her come.

Enter Ceres.

Cer. Where is my daughter? have I aught to dread?
Where does she stray? Ino, you answer not;—
She was aye wont to meet me in yon field,—
Your looks bode ill;—I fear my child is lost.

Ino. Eunoe now seeks her track among the woods;
Fear not, great Ceres, she has only strayed.

Cer. Alas! My boding heart,—I dread the worst.
Oh, careless nymphs! oh, heedless Proserpine!

And did you leave her wandering by herself?
She is immortal,—yet unusual fear
Runs through my veins. Let all the woods be sought,
Let every dryad, every gamesome faun[10]
Tell where they last beheld her snowy feet
Tread the soft, mossy paths of the wild wood.
But that I see the base of Etna firm
I well might fear that she had fallen a prey

[15]

To Earth-born Typheus, who might have arisen
And seized her as the fairest child of heaven,
That in his dreary caverns she lies bound;
It is not so: all is as safe and calm
As when I left my child. Oh, fatal day!
Eunoe does not return: in vain she seeks
Through the black woods and down the darksome glades,
And night is hiding all things from our view.
I will away, and on the highest top
Of snowy Etna, kindle two clear flames.
Night shall not hide her from my anxious search,
No moment will I rest, or sleep, or pause
Till she returns, until I clasp again
My only loved one, my lost Proserpine.

END OF ACT FIRST.

Footnotes

1. There is an apostrophe *on* the s.
2. MS. *mytles*.
3. MS. *fawns*
4. Inserted in a later hand, here as p. 18.
5. The intended place of the apostrophe is not clear.
6. MS. *Ocean' foam* as if a genitive was meant; but cf. *Ocean foam* in the Song of Apollo (Midas).
7. MS. *the bright gold fields*.
8. MS. pages numbered 11, 12, &c., to the end instead of 12, 13, &c.
9. MS. *fawn*.
10. MS. *fawn*.

ACT II

Scene.
The Plain of Enna as before.
Enter Ino & Eunoe.

Eun. How weary am I! and the hot sun flushes
My cheeks that else were white with fear and grief[.]
E'er since that fatal day, dear sister nymph,
On which we lost our lovely Proserpine,
I have but wept and watched the livelong night
And all the day have wandered through the woods[.]

Ino. How all is changed since that unhappy eve!
Ceres forever weeps, seeking her child,
And in her rage has struck the land with blight;
Trinacria mourns with her;—its fertile fields
Are dry and barren, and all little brooks
Struggling scarce creep within their altered banks;
The flowers that erst were wont with bended heads,
To gaze within the clear and glassy wave,
Have died, unwatered by the failing stream.—
And yet their hue but mocks the deeper grief
Which is the fountain of these bitter tears.
But who is this, that with such eager looks

[17]

Hastens this way?—

Eun. 'Tis fairest Arethuse,
A stranger naiad, yet you know her well.

Ino. My eyes were blind with tears.

Enter Arethusa.

Dear Arethuse,
Methinks I read glad tidings in your eyes,
Your smiles are the swift messengers that bear
A tale of coming joy, which we, alas!
Can answer but with tears, unless you bring
To our grief solace, Hope to our Despair.
Have you found Proserpine? or know you where
The loved nymph wanders, hidden from our search?

Areth. Where is corn-crowned Ceres? I have hastened
To ease her anxious heart.

Eun. Oh! dearest Naiad,
Herald of joy! Now will great Ceres bless
Thy welcome coming & more welcome tale.

Ino. Since that unhappy day when Ceres lost
Her much-loved child, she wanders through the isle;
Dark blight is showered from her looks of sorrow;—
And where tall corn and all seed-bearing grass
Rose from beneath her step, they wither now

[18]

Fading under the frown of her bent brows:
The springs decrease;—the fields whose delicate green
Was late her chief delight, now please alone,
Because they, withered, seem to share her grief.

Areth. Unhappy Goddess! how I pity thee!

Ino. At night upon high Etna's topmost peak
She lights two flames, that shining through the isle
Leave dark no wood, or cave, or mountain path,
Their sunlike splendour makes the moon-beams dim,
And the bright stars are lost within their day.
She's in yon field,—she comes towards this plain,
Her loosened hair has fallen on her neck,
Uncircled by the coronal of grain:—
Her cheeks are wan,—her step is faint & slow.

Enter Ceres.

Cer. I faint with weariness: a dreadful thirst
Possesses me! Must I give up the search?
Oh! never, dearest Proserpine, until
I once more clasp thee in my vacant arms!
Help me, dear Arethuse! fill some deep shell
With the clear waters of thine ice-cold spring,
And bring it me;—I faint with heat and thirst.

Areth. My words are better than my freshest waves[:]

[19]

I saw your Proserpine—

Cer. Arethusa, where?
Tell me! my heart beats quick, & hope and fear
Cause my weak limbs to fail me.—

Areth. Sit, Goddess,
Upon this mossy bank, beneath the shade
Of this tall rock, and I will tell my tale.
The day you lost your child, I left my source.
With my Alpheus I had wandered down
The sloping shore into the sunbright sea;
And at the coast we paused, watching the waves
Of our mixed waters dance into the main:—
When suddenly I heard the thundering tread
Of iron hoofed steeds trampling the ground,
And a faint shriek that made my blood run cold.
I saw the King of Hell in his black car,
And in his arms he bore your fairest child,
Fair as the moon encircled by the night,—
But that she strove, and cast her arms aloft,
And cried, "My Mother!"—When she saw me near
She would have sprung from his detested arms,
And with a tone of deepest grief, she cried,
"Oh, Arethuse!" I hastened at her call—
But Pluto when he saw that aid was nigh,
Struck furiously the green earth with his spear,

[20]

Which yawned,—and down the deep Tartarian gulph
His black car rolled—the green earth closed above.

Cer. (*starting up*)
Is this thy doom, great Jove? & shall Hell's king
Quitting dark Tartarus, spread grief and tears
Among the dwellers of your bright abodes?
Then let him seize the earth itself, the stars,—
And all your wide dominion be his prey!—
Your sister calls upon your love, great King!
As you are God I do demand your help!—
Restore my child, or let all heaven sink,
And the fair world be chaos once again!

Ino. Look[!] in the East that loveliest bow is formed[;]
Heaven's single-arched bridge, it touches now
The Earth, and 'mid the pathless wastes of heaven
It paves a way for Jove's fair Messenger;—
Iris descends, and towards this field she comes.

Areth. Sovereign of Harvests, 'tis the Messenger
That will bring joy to thee. Thine eyes light up
With sparkling hope, thy cheeks are pale with dread.

Enter Iris.

Cer. Speak, heavenly Iris! let thy words be poured
Into my drooping soul, like dews of eve
On a too long parched field.—Where is my Proserpine?

[21]

Iris. Sister of Heaven, as by Joves throne I stood
The voice of thy deep prayer arose,—it filled
The heavenly courts with sorrow and dismay:
The Thunderer frowned, & heaven shook with dread
I bear his will to thee, 'tis fixed by fate,
Nor prayer nor murmur e'er can alter it.
If Proserpine while she has lived in hell
Has not polluted by Tartarian food
Her heavenly essence, then she may return,
And wander without fear on Enna's plain,
Or take her seat among the Gods above.
If she has touched the fruits of Erebus,
She never may return to upper air,
But doomed to dwell amidst the shades of death,
The wife of Pluto and the Queen of Hell.

Cer. Joy treads upon the sluggish heels of care!
The child of heaven disdains Tartarian food.
Pluto[,] give up thy prey! restore my child!

Iris. Soon she will see again the sun of Heaven,
By gloomy shapes, inhabitants of Hell,
Attended, and again behold the field
Of Enna, the fair flowers & the streams,
Her late delight,—& more than all, her Mother.

Ino. Our much-loved, long-lost Mistress, do you come?

[22]

And shall once more your nymphs attend your steps?
Will you again irradiate this isle—
That drooped when you were lost?[1] & once again
Trinacria smile beneath your Mother's eye?

(Ceres and her companions are ranged on one side in eager
expectation; from, the cave on the other, enter Proserpine,
attended by various dark & gloomy shapes bearing
torches; among which Ascalaphus. Ceres & Proserpine
embrace;—her nymphs surround her.)

Cer. Welcome, dear Proserpine! Welcome to light,
To this green earth and to your Mother's arms.
You are too beautiful for Pluto's Queen;
In the dark Stygian air your blooming cheeks
Have lost their roseate tint, and your bright form
Has faded in that night unfit for thee.

Pros. Then I again behold thee, Mother dear:—
Again I tread the flowery plain of Enna,
And clasp thee, Arethuse, & you, my nymphs;
I have escaped from hateful Tartarus,
The abode of furies and all loathed shapes
That thronged around me, making hell more black.
Oh! I could worship thee, light giving Sun,
Who spreadest warmth and radiance o'er the world.
Look at[2] the branches of those chesnut trees,
That wave to the soft breezes, while their stems

[23]

Are tinged with red by the sun's slanting rays.
And the soft clouds that float 'twixt earth and sky.
How sweet are all these sights! There all is night!
No God like that (*pointing to the sun*)
smiles on the Elysian plains,
The air [is] windless, and all shapes are still.

Iris. And must I interpose in this deep joy,
And sternly cloud your hopes? Oh! answer me,
Art thou still, Proserpine, a child of light?
Or hast thou dimmed thy attributes of Heaven
By such Tartarian food as must for ever
Condemn thee to be Queen of Hell & Night?

Pros. No, Iris, no,—I still am pure as thee:
Offspring of light and air, I have no stain
Of Hell. I am for ever thine, oh, Mother!

Cer. (*to the shades from Hell*)
Begone, foul visitants to upper air!
Back to your dens! nor stain the sunny earth
By shadows thrown from forms so foul—Crouch in!
Proserpine, child of light, is not your Queen!

(to the nymphs)

Quick bring my car,—we will ascend to heaven,
Deserting Earth, till by decree of Jove,
Eternal laws shall bind the King of Hell
To leave in peace the offspring of the sky.

Ascal. Stay, Ceres! By the dread decree of Jove

[24]

Your child is doomed to be eternal Queen
Of Tartarus,—nor may she dare ascend
The sunbright regions of Olympian Jove,
Or tread the green Earth 'mid attendant nymphs.
Proserpine, call to mind your walk last eve,
When as you wandered in Elysian groves,
Through bowers for ever green, and mossy walks,
Where flowers never die, nor wind disturbs
The sacred calm, whose silence soothes the dead,
Nor interposing clouds, with dun wings, dim
Its mild and silver light, you plucked its fruit,
You ate of a pomegranate's seeds—

Cer. Be silent,
Prophet of evil, hateful to the Gods!
Sweet Proserpine, my child, look upon me.
You shrink; your trembling form & pallid cheeks
Would make his words seem true which are most false[.]
Thou didst not taste the food of Erebus;—
Offspring of Gods art thou,—nor Hell, nor Jove
Shall tear thee from thy Mother's clasping arms.

Pros. If fate decrees, can we resist? farewel!
Oh! Mother, dearer to your child than light,

[25]

Than all the forms of this sweet earth & sky,
Though dear are these, and dear are my poor nymphs,
Whom I must leave;—oh! can immortals weep?
And can a Goddess die as mortals do,
Or live & reign where it is death to be?
Ino, dear Arethuse, again you lose
Your hapless Proserpine, lost to herself
When she quits you for gloomy Tartarus.

Cer. Is there no help, great Jove? If she depart
I will descend with her—the Earth shall lose
Its proud fertility, and Erebus
Shall bear my gifts throughout th' unchanging year.
Valued till now by thee, tyrant of Gods!
My harvests ripening by Tartarian fires
Shall feed the dead with Heaven's ambrosial food.
Wilt thou not then repent, brother unkind,
Viewing the barren earth with vain regret,
Thou didst not shew more mercy to my child?

Ino. We will all leave the light and go with thee,
In Hell thou shalt be girt by Heaven-born nymphs,
Elysium shall be Enna,—thou'lt not mourn
Thy natal plain, which will have lost its worth
Having lost thee, its nursling and its Queen.

Areth. I will sink down with thee;—my lily crown

[26]

Shall bloom in Erebus, portentous loss
To Earth, which by degrees will fade & fall
In envy of our happier lot in Hell;—
And the bright sun and the fresh winds of heaven
Shall light its depths and fan its stagnant air.

(They cling round Proserpine; the Shades of Hell seperate
and stand between them.)

Ascal. Depart! She is our Queen! Ye may not come!
Hark to Jove's thunder! shrink away in fear
From unknown forms, whose tyranny ye'll feel
In groans and tears if ye insult their power.

Iris. Behold Jove's balance hung in upper sky;
There are ye weighed,—to that ye must submit.

Cer. Oh! Jove, have mercy on a Mother's prayer!
Shall it be nought to be akin to thee?
And shall thy sister, Queen of fertile Earth,
Derided be by these foul shapes of Hell?
Look at the scales, they're poized with equal weights!
What can this mean? Leave me not[,] Proserpine[,]
Cling to thy Mother's side! He shall not dare
Divide the sucker from the parent stem.

(embraces her)

[27]

Ascal. He is almighty! who shall set the bounds
To his high will? let him decide our plea!
Fate is with us, & Proserpine is ours!

(He endeavours to part Ceres & Proserpine, the nymphs prevent him.)

Cer. Peace, ominous bird of Hell & Night! Depart!
Nor with thy skriech disturb a Mother's grief,
Avaunt! It is to Jove we pray, not thee.

Iris. Thy fate, sweet Proserpine, is sealed by Jove,
When Enna is starred by flowers, and the sun
Shoots his hot rays strait on the gladsome land,
When Summer reigns, then thou shalt live on Earth,
And tread these plains, or sporting with your nymphs,
Or at your Mother's side, in peaceful joy.
But when hard frost congeals the bare, black ground,
The trees have lost their leaves, & painted birds
Wailing for food sail through the piercing air;
Then you descend to deepest night and reign
Great Queen of Tartarus, 'mid[3] shadows dire,
Offspring of Hell,—or in the silent groves
Of, fair Elysium through which Lethe runs,
The sleepy river; where the windless air
Is never struck by flight or song of bird,—

[28]

But all is calm and clear, bestowing rest,
After the toil of life, to wretched men,
Whom thus the Gods reward for sufferings
Gods cannot know; a throng of empty shades!
The endless circle of the year will bring
Joy in its turn, and seperation sad;
Six months to light and Earth,—six months to Hell.

Pros. Dear Mother, let me kiss that tear which steals
Down your pale cheek altered by care and grief.
This is not misery; 'tis but a slight change
Prom our late happy lot. Six months with thee,
Each moment freighted with an age of love:
And the six short months in saddest Tartarus
Shall pass in dreams of swift returning joy.
Six months together we shall dwell on earth,
Six months in dreams we shall companions be,
Jove's doom is void; we are forever joined.

Cer. Oh, fairest child! sweet summer visitor!
Thy looks cheer me, so shall they cheer this land
Which I will fly, thou gone. Nor seed of grass,
Or corn shall grow, thou absent from the earth;
But all shall lie beneath in hateful night

[29]

Until at thy return, the fresh green springs,
The fields are covered o'er with summer plants.
And when thou goest the heavy grain will droop

And die under my frown, scattering the seeds,
That will not reappear till your return.
Farewel, sweet child, Queen of the nether world,
There shine as chaste Diana's silver car
Islanded in the deep circumfluous night.
Giver of fruits! for such thou shalt be styled,
Sweet Prophetess of Summer, coming forth
From the slant shadow of the wintry earth,
In thy car drawn by snowy-breasted swallows!
Another kiss, & then again farewel!
Winter in losing thee has lost its all,
And will be doubly bare, & hoar, & drear,
Its bleak winds whistling o'er the cold pinched ground
Which neither flower or grass will decorate.
And as my tears fall first, so shall the trees
Shed their changed leaves upon your six months tomb:
The clouded air will hide from Phoebus' eye
The dreadful change your absence operates.
Thus has black Pluto changed the reign of Jove,
He seizes half the Earth when he takes thee.

THE END

Footnotes

1   MS. *this isle?—That drooped when you were lost*
2   MS. Look at—the branches.
3   MS. *mid*

MIDAS.

A DRAMA IN TWO ACTS.

DRAMATIS PERSONAE

Immortals.
    Apollo.
    Bacchus.
    Pan.
    Silenus.
    Tmolus, God of a Hill.
    Fauns, &c.

Mortals.
    Midas, King of Phrygia.
    Zopyrion, his Prime-Minister.
    Asphalion, Lacon, Courtiers.
    Courtiers, Attendants, Priests, &c.

Scene, Phrygia.

ACT I.

Scene; a rural spot; on one side, a bare Hill, on the other an Ilex wood; a stream with reeds on its banks.

The Curtain rises and discovers Tmolus seated on a throne of turf, on his right hand Apollo with his lyre, attended by the Muses; on the left, Pan, fauns, &c.

Enter Midas and Zopyrion.

Midas. The Hours have oped the palace of the dawn
And through the Eastern gates of Heaven, Aurora
Comes charioted on light, her wind-swift steeds,
Winged with roseate clouds, strain up the steep.
She loosely holds the reins, her golden hair,
Its strings outspread by the sweet morning breeze[,]
Blinds the pale stars. Our rural tasks begin;
The young lambs bleat pent up within the fold,
The herds low in their stalls, & the blithe cock
Halloos most loudly to his distant mates.
But who are these we see? these are not men,
Divine of form & sple[n]didly arrayed,

[36]

They sit in solemn conclave. Is that Pan,
Our Country God, surrounded by his Fauns?
And who is he whose crown of gold & harp
Are attributes of high Apollo?

Zopyr. Best
Your majesty retire; we may offend.

Midas. Aye, and at the base thought the coward blood
Deserts your trembling lips; but follow me.
Oh Gods! for such your bearing is, & sure

No mortal ever yet possessed the gold
That glitters on your silken robes; may one,
Who, though a king, can boast of no descent
More noble than Deucalion's stone-formed men[,]
May I demand the cause for which you deign
To print upon this worthless Phrygian earth
The vestige of your gold-inwoven sandals,
Or why that old white-headed man sits there
Upon that grassy throne, & looks as he
Were stationed umpire to some weighty cause[?]

Tmolus. God Pan with his blithe pipe which the Fauns love
Has challenged Phoebus of the golden lyre[,]
Saying his Syrinx can give sweeter notes
Than the stringed instrument Apollo boasts.
I judge between the parties. Welcome, King,

[37]

I am old Tmolus, God of that bare Hill,
You may remain and hear th' Immortals sing.

Mid. [*aside*] My judgement is made up before I hear;
Pan is my guardian God, old-horned Pan,
The Phrygian's God who watches o'er our flocks;
No harmony can equal his blithe pipe.

(Shelley.)

Apollo (sings).

The sleepless Hours who watch me as I lie,
    Curtained with star-enwoven tapestries,
From the broad moonlight of the sky,
    Fanning the busy dreams from my dim eyes
Waken me when their Mother, the grey Dawn,
Tells them that dreams & that the moon is gone.

Then I arise, and climbing Heaven's blue dome,
    I walk over the mountains & the waves,
Leaving my robe upon the Ocean foam,—
    My footsteps pave the clouds with fire; the caves
Are filled with my bright presence & the air
Leaves the green Earth to my embraces bare.

The sunbeams are my shafts with which I kill
    Deceit, that loves the night & fears the day;
All men who do, or even imagine ill
    Fly me, and from the glory of my ray
Good minds and open actions take new might
Until diminished by the reign of night.

[38]

I feed the clouds, the rainbows & the flowers
    With their etherial colours; the moon's globe
And the pure stars in their eternal bowers
    Are cinctured with my power as with a robe;
Whatever lamps on Earth or Heaven may shine
Are portions of one power, which is mine.

I stand at noon upon the peak of heaven,
    Then with unwilling steps I wander down

Into the clouds of the Atlantic even—
    For grief that I depart they weep & frown [;]
What look is more delightful than the smile
With which I soothe them from the western isle [?]

I am the eye with which the Universe
    Beholds itself & knows it is divine.
All harmony of instrument or verse,
    All prophecy, all medecine is mine;
All light of art or nature;—to my song
Victory and praise, in its own right, belong.

(Shelley.)

Pan (sings).

From the forests and highlands
    We come, we come;
From the river-girt islands
    W[h]ere loud waves are dumb,
        Listening my sweet pipings;

[39]

The wind in the reeds & the rushes,
    The bees on the bells of thyme,
The birds on the myrtle bushes[,]
    The cicale above in the lime[,]
And the lizards below in the grass,
Were as silent as ever old Tmolus was
        Listening my sweet pipings.

Liquid Peneus was flowing,
   And all dark Tempe lay
In Pelion's shadow, outgrowing
    The light of the dying day
       Speeded by my sweet pipings.
The Sileni, & Sylvans, & Fauns
   And the nymphs of the woods & the waves
To the edge of the moist river-lawns,
   And the brink of the dewy caves[,]
And all that did then attend & follow
Were silent with love, as you now, Apollo!
     With envy of my sweet pipings.

I sang of the dancing stars,
   I sang of the daedal Earth—
And of heaven—& the giant wars—
     And Love, & death, [&] birth,

[40]

     And then I changed my pipings,
Singing how down the vale of Menalus,
   I pursued a maiden & clasped a reed,
Gods and men, we are all deluded thus!
   It breaks in our bosom & then we bleed!
All wept, as I think both ye now would
If envy or age had not frozen your blood,
     At the sorrow of my sweet pipings.

Tmol. Phoebus, the palm is thine. The Fauns may dance
To the blithe tune of ever merry Pan;
But wisdom, beauty, & the power divine

Of highest poesy lives within thy strain.
Named by the Gods the King of melody,
Receive from my weak hands a second crown.

Pan. Old Grey-beard, you say false! you think by this
To win Apollo with his sultry beams
To thaw your snowy head, & to renew
The worn out soil of your bare, ugly hill.
I do appeal to Phrygian Midas here;
Let him decide, he is no partial judge.

Mid. Immortal Pan, to my poor, mortal ears
Your sprightly song in melody outweighs
His drowsy tune; he put me fast asleep,
As my prime minister, Zopyrion, knows;

[41]

But your gay notes awoke me, & to you,
If I were Tmolus, would I give the prize.

Apol. And who art thou who dar'st among the Gods
Mingle thy mortal voice? Insensate fool!
Does not the doom of Marsyas fill with dread
Thy impious soul? or would'st thou also be
Another victim to my justest wrath?
But fear no more;—thy punishment shall be
But as a symbol of thy blunted sense.
Have asses' ears! and thus to the whole world
Wear thou the marks of what thou art,
Let Pan himself blush at such a judge.[1]

(Exeunt all except Midas & Zopyrion.)

Mid. What said he? is it true, Zopyrion?
Yet if it be; you must not look on me,
But shut your eyes, nor dare behold my shame.
Ah! here they are! two long, smooth asses['] ears!
They stick upright! Ah, I am sick with shame!

Zopyr. I cannot tell your Majesty my grief,
Or how my soul's oppressed with the sad change
That has, alas! befallen your royal ears.

Mid. A truce to your fine speeches now, Zopyrion;
To you it appertains to find some mode
Of hiding my sad chance, if not you die.

Zopyr. Great King, alas! my thoughts are dull & slow[;]

[42]

Pardon my folly, might they not be cut,
Rounded off handsomely, like human ears [?]

Mid. (*feeling his ears*)
They're long & thick; I fear 'twould give me pain;
And then if vengeful Phoebus should command
Another pair to grow—that will not do.

Zopyr. You wear a little crown of carved gold,
Which just appears to tell you are a king;
If that were large and had a cowl of silk,

Studded with gems, which none would dare gainsay,
Then might you—

Mid. Now you have it! friend,
I will reward you with some princely gift.
But, hark! Zopyrion, not a word of this;
If to a single soul you tell my shame
You die. I'll to the palace the back way
And manufacture my new diadem,
The which all other kings shall imitate
As if they also had my asses['] ears.

(Exit.)

Zopyr. (*watching Midas off*)
He cannot hear me now, and I may laugh!
I should have burst had he staid longer here.
Two long, smooth asses' ears that stick upright;
Oh, that Apollo had but made him bray!
I'll to the palace; there I'll laugh my fill

[43]

With—hold! What were the last words that Midas said?
I may not speak—not to my friends disclose
The strangest tale? ha! ha! and when I laugh
I must not tell the cause? none know the truth?
None know King Midas has—but who comes here?
It is Asphalion: he knows not this change;
I must look grave & sad; for now a smile
If Midas knows it may prove capital.

Yet when I think of those—oh! I shall die,
In either way, by silence or by speech.

Enter Asphalion.

Asphal. Know you, Zopyrion?—

Zopyr. What[!] you know it too?
Then I may laugh;—oh, what relief is this!
How does he look, the courtiers gathering round?
Does he hang down his head, & his ears too?
Oh, I shall die! (*laughs.*)

Asph. He is a queer old dog,
Yet not so laughable. 'Tis true, he's drunk,
And sings and reels under the broad, green leaves,
And hanging clusters of his crown of grapes.—

Zopyr. A crown of grapes! but can that hide his ears[?]

Asph. His ears!—Oh, no! they stick upright between.
When Midas saw him—

Zopyr. Whom then do you mean?

[44]

Did you not say—

Asph. I spoke of old Silenus;
Who having missed his way in these wild woods,
And lost his tipsey company—was found

Sucking the juicy clusters of the vines
That sprung where'er he trod:—and reeling on
Some shepherds found him in yon ilex wood.
They brought him to the king, who honouring him
For Bacchus' sake, has gladly welcomed him,
And will conduct him with solemnity
To the disconsolate Fauns from whom he's strayed.
But have you seen the new-fashioned diadem[2]
That Midas wears?—

Zopyr. Ha! he has got it on!—
Know you the secret cause why with such care
He hides his royal head? you have not seen—

Asph. Seen what?

Zopyr. Ah! then, no matter:—*(turns away agitated.)*
I dare not sneak or stay[;]
If I remain I shall discover all.

Asp. I see the king has trusted to your care
Some great state secret which you fain would hide.
I am your friend, trust my fidelity,

[45]

If you're in doubt I'll be your counsellor.

Zopyr. *(with great importance.)*
Secret, Asphalion! How came you to know?
If my great master (which I do not say)
Should think me a fit friend in whom to pour

The weighty secrets of his royal heart,
Shall I betray his trust? It is not so;—
I am a poor despised slave.—No more!
Join we the festal band which will conduct
Silenus to his woods again?

Asph. My friend,
Wherefore mistrust a faithful heart? Confide
The whole to me;—I will be still as death.

Zopyr. As death! you know not what you say; farewell[!]
A little will I commune with my soul,
And then I'll join you at the palace-gate.

Asph. Will you then tell me?—

Zopyr. Cease to vex, my friend,
Your soul and mine with false suspicion, (*aside*) Oh!
I am choked! I'd give full ten years of my life
To tell, to laugh—& yet I dare not speak.

[46]

Asph. Zopyrion, remember that you hurt
The trusting bosom of a faithful friend
By your unjust concealment.

(Exit.)

Zopyr. Oh, he's gone!
To him I dare not speak, nor yet to Lacon;
No human ears may hear what must be told.

I cannot keep it in, assuredly;
I shall some night discuss it in my sleep.
It will not keep! Oh! greenest reeds that sway
And nod your feathered heads beneath the sun,
Be you depositaries of my soul,
Be you my friends in this extremity[:]
I shall not risk my head when I tell you
The fatal truth, the heart oppressing fact,

(stooping down & whispering)

(Enter Midas, Silenus & others, who fall back during the scene; Midas is always anxious about his crown, & Zopyrion gets behind him & tries to smother his laughter.)

Silen. (*very drunk*) Again I find you, Bacchus, runaway!
Welcome, my glorious boy! Another time
Stray not; or leave your poor old foster-father
In the wild mazes of a wood, in which
I might have wandered many hundred years,
Had not some merry fellows helped me out,
And had not this king kindly welcomed me,
I might have fared more ill than you erewhile
In Pentheus' prisons, that death fated rogue.

Bac. (*to Midas.*) To you I owe great thanks & will reward
Your hospitality. Tell me your name
And what this country is.

Midas. My name is Midas—

The Reeds (*nodding their heads*).

[49]

Midas, the king, has the ears of an ass.

Midas. (*turning round & seizing Zopyrion*).
Villain, you lie! he dies who shall repeat
Those traitrous words. Seize on Zopyrion!

The Reeds. Midas, the king, has the ears of an ass.

Mid. Search through the crowd; it is a woman's voice
That dares belie her king, & makes her life
A forfeit to his fury.

Asph. There is no woman here.

Bac. Calm yourself, Midas; none believe the tale,
Some impious man or gamesome faun dares feign
In vile contempt of your most royal ears.
Off with your crown, & shew the world the lie!

Mid. (*holding his crown tight*)
Never! What[!] shall a vile calumnious slave
Dictate the actions of a crowned king?
Zopyrion, this lie springs from you—you perish!

Zopy. I, say that Midas has got asses' ears?
May great Apollo strike me with his shaft
If to a single soul I ever told
So false, so foul a calumny!

[50]

Bac. Midas!

The Reeds. Midas, the king, has the ears of an ass.

Bac. Silence! or by my Godhead I strike dead
Who shall again insult the noble king.
Midas, you are my friend, for you have saved
And hospitably welcomed my old faun;
Choose your reward, for here I swear your wish,
Whatever it may be, shall be fulfilled.

Zopyr. (*aside*) Sure he will wish his asses' ears in Styx.

Midas. What[!] may I choose from out the deep, rich mine
Of human fancy, & the wildest thoughts
That passed till now unheeded through my brain,
A wish, a hope, to be fulfilled by you?
Nature shall bend her laws at my command,
And I possess as my reward one thing
That I have longed for with unceasing care.

Bac. Pause, noble king, ere you express this wish[.]
Let not an error or rash folly spoil
My benefaction; pause and then declare,
For what you ask shall be, as I have sworn.

Mid. Let all I touch be gold, most glorious gold!

[51]

Let me be rich! and where I stretch my hands,
(That like Orion I could touch the stars!)
Be radiant gold! God Bacchus, you have sworn,
I claim your word,—my ears are quite forgot!

The Reeds. Midas, the king, has the ears of an ass.

Mid. You lie, & yet I care not—

Zopyr. (*aside to Midas*) Yet might I
But have advised your Majesty, I would
Have made one God undo the other's work—

Midas. (*aside to Zopyr*).
Advise yourself, my friend, or you may grow
Shorter by a head ere night.—I am blessed,
Happier than ever earthly man could boast.
Do you fulfil your words?

Bac. Yes, thoughtless man!
And much I fear if you have not the ears
You have the judgement of an ass. Farewell!
I found you rich & happy; & I leave you,
Though you know it not, miserably poor.
Your boon is granted,—touch! make gold! Some here
Help carry old Silenus off, who sleeps
The divine sleep of heavy wine. Farewell!

Mid. Bacchus, divine, how shall I pay my thanks[?]

(Exeunt.)

END OF FIRST ACT.

Footnotes

1 A syllable here, a whole foot in the previous line, appear to be missing.
2 Another halting line. Cf. again, p. [47], 1. 3; p. [55], 1. 11; p. [59], 1.1; p. [61], 1. 1; p. [64], 1. 14.]

ACT II

Scene; a splendid apartment in the Palace of Midas.

Enter Midas
(with a golden rose in his hand).

Mid. Gold! glorious gold! I am made up of gold!
I pluck a rose, a silly, fading rose,
Its soft, pink petals change to yellow gold;
Its stem, its leaves are gold—and what before
Was fit for a poor peasant's festal dress
May now adorn a Queen. I lift a stone,
A heavy, useless mass, a slave would spurn,
What is more valueless? 'Tis solid gold!
A king might war on me to win the same.
And as I pass my hand thus through the air,
A little shower of sightless dust falls down
A shower of gold. O, now I am a king!
I've spread my hands against my palace walls,
I've set high ladders up, that I may touch
Each crevice and each cornice with my hands,
And it will all be gold:—a golden palace,
Surrounded by a wood of golden trees,
Which will bear golden fruits.—The very ground
My naked foot treads on is yellow gold,

[53]

Invaluable gold! my dress is gold!
Now I am great! Innumerable armies
Wait till my gold collects them round my throne;
I see my standard made of woven gold.
Waving o'er Asia's utmost Citadels,
Guarded by myriads invincible.
Or if the toil of war grows wearisome,
I can buy Empires:—India shall be mine,
Its blooming beauties, gold-encrusted baths,
Its aromatic groves and palaces,
All will be mine! Oh, Midas, ass-eared king!
I love thee more than any words can tell,
That thus thy touch, thou man akin to Gods,
Can change all earth to heaven,—Olympian gold!
For what makes heaven different from earth!
Look how my courtiers come! Magnificent!
None shall dare wait on me but those who bear
An empire on their backs in sheets of gold.
Oh, what a slave I was! my flocks & kine,
My vineyards & my corn were all my wealth
And men esteemed me rich; but now Great Jove
Transcends me but by lightning, and who knows
If my gold win not the Cyclopean Powers,
And Vulcan, who must hate his father's rule,

[54]

To forge me bolts?—and then—but hush! they come.

Enter Zopyrion, Asphalion, & Lacon.

Lac. Pardon us, mighty king—

Mid. What would ye, slaves?
Oh! I could buy you all with one slight touch
Of my gold-making hand!

Asph. Royal Midas,
We humbly would petition for relief.

Mid. Relief I Bring me your copper coin, your brass,
Or what ye will—ye'll speedily be rich.

Zopyr. 'Tis not for gold, but to be rid of gold,
That we intrude upon your Majesty.
I fear that you will suffer by this gift,
As we do now. Look at our backs bent down
With the huge weight of the great cloaks of gold.
Permit us to put on our shabby dress,
Our poor despised garments of light wool:—
We walk as porters underneath a load.
Pity, great king, our human weaknesses,
Nor force us to expire—

Mid. Begone, ye slaves!
Go clothe your wretched limbs in ragged skins!
Take an old carpet to wrap round your legs,

[55]

A broad leaf for your feet—ye shall not wear
That dress—those golden sandals—monarch like.

Asph. If you would have us walk a mile a day
We cannot thus—already we are tired
With the huge weight of soles of solid gold.

Mid. Pitiful wretches! Earth-born, groveling dolts!
Begone! nor dare reply to my just wrath!
Never behold me more! or if you stay
Let not a sigh, a shrug, a stoop betray
What poor, weak, miserable men you are.
Not as I—I am a God! Look, dunce!
I tread or leap beneath this load of gold!

(Jumps & stops suddenly.)

I've hurt my back:—this cloak is wondrous hard!
No more of this! my appetite would say
The hour is come for my noon-day repast.

Lac. It comes borne in by twenty lusty slaves,
Who scarce can lift the mass of solid gold,
That lately was a table of light wood.
Here is the heavy golden ewer & bowl,
In which, before you eat, you wash your hands.

Mid. (*lifting up the ewer*)
This is to be a king! to touch pure gold!

[56]

Would that by touching thee, Zopyrion,
I could transmute thee to a golden man;
A crowd of golden slaves to wait on me!

(Pours the water on his hands.)

But how is this? the water that I touch
Falls down a stream of yellow liquid gold,
And hardens as it falls. I cannot wash—
Pray Bacchus, I may drink! and the soft towel
With which I'd wipe my hands transmutes itself
Into a sheet of heavy gold.—No more!
I'll sit and eat:—I have not tasted food
For many hours, I have been so wrapt
In golden dreams of all that I possess,
I had not time to eat; now hunger calls
And makes me feel, though not remote in power
From the immortal Gods, that I need food,
The only remnant of mortality!

(In vain attempts to eat of several dishes.)

Alas! my fate! 'tis gold! this peach is gold!
This bread, these grapes & all I touch! this meat
Which by its scent quickened my appetite
Has lost its scent, its taste,—'tis useless gold.

Zopyr. (*aside*) He'd better now have followed my advice.

[57]

He starves by gold yet keeps his asses' ears.

Mid. Asphalion, put that apple to my mouth;
If my hands touch it not perhaps I eat.
Alas! I cannot bite! as it approached

I felt its fragrance, thought it would be mine,
But by the touch of my life-killing lips
'Tis changed from a sweet fruit to tasteless gold,
Bacchus will not refresh me by his gifts,
The liquid wine congeals and flies my taste.
Go, miserable slaves! Oh, wretched king!
Away with food! Its sight now makes me sick.
Bring in my couch! I will sleep off my care,
And when I wake I'll coin some remedy.
I dare not bathe this sultry day, for fear
I be enclosed in gold. Begone!
I will to rest:—oh, miserable king!

(Exeunt all but Midas. He lies down, turns restlessly for some time & then rises.)

Oh! fool! to wish to change all things to gold!
Blind Ideot that I was! This bed is gold;
And this hard, weighty pillow, late so soft,
That of itself invited me to rest,
Is a hard lump, that if I sleep and turn

[58]

I may beat out my brains against its sides.
Oh! what a wretched thing I am! how blind!
I cannot eat, for all my food is gold;
Drink flies my parched lips, and my hard couch
Is worse than rock to my poor bruised sides.
I cannot walk; the weight of my gold soles
Pulls me to earth:—my back is broke beneath
These gorgeous garments—*(throws off his cloak)*

Lie there, golden cloak!
There on thy kindred earth, lie there and rot!
I dare not touch my forehead with my palm
For fear my very flesh should turn to gold.
Oh! let me curse thee, vilest, yellow dirt!
Here, on my knees, thy martyr lifts his voice,
A poor, starved wretch who can touch nought but thee[,]
Wilt thou refresh me in the heat of noon?
Canst thou be kindled for me when I'm cold?
May all men, & the immortal Gods,
Hate & spurn thee as wretched I do now.

(Kicks the couch, & tries to throw down the pillow but cannot lift it.)

I'd dash, thee to the earth, but that thy weight

[59]

Preserves thee, abhorred, Tartarian Gold!
Bacchus, O pity, pardon, and restore me!
Who waits?

Enter Lacon.

Go bid the priests that they prepare
Most solemn song and richest sacrifise;—
Which I may not dare touch, lest it should turn
To most unholy gold.

Lacon. Pardon me, oh King,
But perhaps the God may give that you may eat,
And yet your touch be magic.

Mid. No more, thou slave!
Gold is my fear, my bane, my death! I hate
Its yellow glare, its aspect hard and cold.
I would be rid of all.—Go bid them haste.

(Exit Lacon.)

Oh, Bacchus I be propitious to their prayer!
Make me a hind, clothe me in ragged skins—
And let my food be bread, unsavoury roots,
But take from me the frightful curse of gold.
Am I not poor? Alas! how I am changed!
Poorer than meanest slaves, my piles of wealth
Cannot buy for me one poor, wretched dish:—
In summer heat I cannot bathe, nor wear
A linen dress; the heavy, dull, hard metal
Clings to me till I pray for poverty.

[60]

Enter Zopyrion, Asphalion & Lacon.

Zopyr. The sacrifice is made, & the great God,
Pitying your ills, oh King, accepted it,
Whilst his great oracle gave forth these words.
"Let poor king Midas bathe in the clear stream
"Of swift Pactolus, & to those waves tran[s]fer
"The gold-transmuting power, which he repents."

Mid. Oh joy! Oh Bacchus, thanks for this to thee
Will I each year offer three sucking lambs—
Games will I institute—nor Pan himself
Shall have more honour than thy deity.
Haste to the stream,—I long to feel the cool
And liquid touch of its divinest waves.

(Exeunt all except Zopyrion and Asphalion.)

Asph. Off with our golden sandals and our cloaks!
Oh, I shall ever hate the sight of gold!
Poor, wealthy Midas runs as if from death
To rid him quick of this meta[l]lic curse.

Zopyr. (*aside*) I wonder if his asses['] ears are gold;
What would I give to let the secret out?
Gold! that is trash, we have too much of it,—
But I would give ten new born lambs to tell
This most portentous truth—but I must choke.

Asph. Now we shall tend our flocks and reap our corn
As we were wont, and not be killed by gold.

[61]

Golden fleeces threatened our poor sheep,
The very showers as they fell from heaven
Could not refresh the earth; the wind blew gold,
And as we walked[1] the thick sharp-pointed atoms
Wounded our faces—the navies would have sunk—

Zopyr. All strangers would have fled our gold-cursed shore,
Till we had bound our wealthy king, that he
Might leave the green and fertile earth unchanged;—
Then in deep misery he would have shook
His golden chains & starved.

Enter Lacon.

Lacon. Sluggards, how now I
Have you not been to gaze upon the sight?
To see the noble king cast off the gift
Which he erewhile so earnestly did crave[?]

Asph. I am so tired with the weight of gold
I bore to-day I could not budge a foot
To see the finest sight Jove could display.
But tell us, Lacon, what he did and said.

Lac. Although he'd fain have run[,] his golden dress
And heavy sandals made the poor king limp
As leaning upon mine and the high priest's arm,
He hastened to Pactolus. When he saw
The stream—"Thanks to the Gods!" he cried aloud
In joy; then having cast aside his robes
He leaped into the waves, and with his palm

[62]

Throwing the waters high—"This is not gold,"
He cried, "I'm free, I have got rid of gold."
And then he drank, and seizing with delight

A little leaf that floated down the stream,
"Thou art not gold," he said—

Zopyr. But all this time—
Did you behold?—Did he take off his crown?—

Lacon. No:—It was strange to see him as he plunged
Hold tight his crown with his left hand the while.

Zopyr. (*aside*) Alas, my fate! I thought they had been seen.

Lac. He ordered garments to the river side
Of coarsest texture;—those that erst he wore
He would not touch, for they were trimmed with gold.

Zopyr. And yet he did not throw away his crown?

Lac. He ever held it tight as if he thought
Some charm attached to its remaining there.
Perhaps he is right;—know you, Zopyrion,
If that strange voice this morning spoke the truth?

Zopyr. Nay guess;—think of what passed & you can judge.
I dare not—I know nothing of his ears.

Lac. I am resolved some night when he sleeps sound
To get a peep.—No more,'tis he that comes.
He has now lost the boon that Bacchus gave,
Having bestowed it on the limpid waves.

[63]

Now over golden sands Pactolus runs,
And as it flows creates a mine of wealth.

Enter Midas, (with grapes in his hand).

Mid. I see again the trees and smell the flowers
With colours lovelier than the rainbow's self;
I see the gifts of rich-haired Ceres piled
And eat. (*holding up the grapes*)
This is not yellow, dirty gold,
But blooms with precious tints, purple and green.
I hate this palace and its golden floor,
Its cornices and rafters all of gold:—
I'll build a little bower of freshest green,
Canopied o'er with leaves & floored with moss:—
I'll dress in skins;—I'll drink from wooden cups
And eat on wooden platters—sleep on flock;
None but poor men shall dare attend on me.
All that is gold I'll banish from my court,
Gilding shall be high treason to my state,
The very name of gold shall be crime capital[.]

Zopyr. May we not keep our coin?

Mid. No, Zopyrion,
None but the meanest peasants shall have gold.
It is a sordid, base and dirty thing:—
Look at the grass, the sky, the trees, the flowers,

[64]

These are Joves treasures & they are not gold:—
Now they are mine, I am no longer cursed.—
The hapless river hates its golden sands,
As it rolls over them, having my gift;—
Poor harmless shores! they now are dirty gold.
How I detest it! Do not the Gods hate gold?
Nature displays the treasures that she loves,
She hides gold deep in the earth & piles above
Mountains & rocks to keep the monster down.

Asph. They say Apollo's sunny car is gold.

Mid. Aye, so it is for Gold belongs to him:—
But Phoebus is my bitterest enemy,
And what pertains to him he makes my bane.

Zopyr. What [!] will your Majesty tell the world?—

Mid. Peace, vile gossip! Asphalion, come you here.
Look at those golden columns; those inlaid walls;
The ground, the trees, the flowers & precious food
That in my madness I did turn to gold:—
Pull it all down, I hate its sight and touch;
Heap up my cars & waggons with the load
And yoke my kine to drag it to the sea:
Then crowned with flowers, ivy & Bacchic vine,
And singing hymns to the immortal Gods,

[65]

We will ascend ships freighted with the gold,
And where no plummet's line can sound the depth
Of greedy Ocean, we will throw it in,
All, all this frightful heap of yellow dirt.
Down through the dark, blue waters it will sink,
Frightening the green-haired Nereids from their sport
And the strange Tritons—the waves will close above
And I, thank Bacchus, ne'er shall see it more!
And we will make all echoing heaven ring
With our loud hymns of thanks, & joyous pour
Libations in the deep, and reach the land,
Rich, happy, free & great, that we have lost
Man's curse, heart-bartering, soul-enchaining gold.

FINIS.

Footnotes

1   MS. *as he walked.*

CPSIA information can be obtained
at www.ICGtesting.com
Printed in the USA
BVHW061211130620
581303BV00002B/29